# THE WORST IS OVER
## What to Say When Every Moment Counts

by

## JUDITH K. ACOSTA, LISW, CCH

## JUDITH SIMON PRAGER, PhD

*Verbal First Aid* ™
*to Calm,*
*Relieve Pain,*
*Promote Healing*
*and Save Lives.*

*Hailed as "The 'Bible' of Crisis Communication"*

NEW UPDATED EDITION

ISBN: 1494376539
ISBN 13: 9781494376536

First printing, March 2002
Second Edition, updated 2014

# Acclaim for *The Worst Is Over*

*The Worst Is Over* will be known as the seminal work for teaching compassionate crisis intervention communication to anyone who works with medical and emotional emergencies. All future books by others will reference this source as the "bible" for crisis communication.

*Patti White, Ph.D., Editor, International Journal of Emergency Mental Health.* Vol. 4, No. 2, Spring 2002.

*The Worst Is Over* is like an answer to a prayer. It gives everyone, from parent to firefighter, the knowledge and courage to say exactly the right thing at the right time in a way that is healing, uplifting, and also life-saving.

*Christiane Northrup, M.D.* Author,
*Women's Bodies, Women's Wisdom (Bantam, 1998)*
and *The Wisdom of Menopause* (Bantam, March 2001)

I've just had the pleasure of reading your manuscript, Verbal First Aid. I found it well written and very informative. I agree that what one says in the first few moments of a physical or psychological crisis can have a lasting effect on the person in crisis. Your book is the best example of a practical, common-sense approach to providing psychological support yet written for the lay public.

*George S. Everly, Jr.*
*Chairman of the Board, Emeritus,*
*International Critical Incident Stress Foundation, Inc.*

It's finally becoming apparent that what we say during a medical emergency is often as important as the treatment we provide.

*Alan Mistler, Associate Professor and Program Director,*
*Center for Prehospital Education Department of Emergency Medicine,*
*University of Cincinnati Medical Center*

After reading the book *The Worst Is Over - What to Say When Every Moment Counts* I became a believer in Verbal First Aid. I run the first aid training unit for our department and have incorporated it into our program. As Police Officers, we talk to people in a variety of situations, and unfortunately some of these conversations are not pleasant ones. Verbal First Aid is a valuable "tool" we can use with the public that we serve. The feedback thus far from the field has been great.

*F/Lt Mike Harvitt, Michigan State Police*

Look for the latest in Verbal First Aid,

*Verbal First Aid: Help Your Kids Heal From Fear and Pain—*

*And Come Out Strong (Berkley Books, 2010).*

If you work with or care for children, this book will give you the

words to turn a hurt into a healing, a scare into a calm,

and a potential trauma into a memory of

rescue and courage.

"Remember not only to say the right thing in the
right place, but far more difficult still,
to leave unsaid the wrong thing at the tempting moment."
*Benjamin Franklin*

"During periods of great stress, words that seem immaterial
or are uttered in jest might become fixed in the patient's
mind and cause untold harm."
*Emergency Care and Transportation of the Sick and Injured,*
*American Academy of Orthopaedic Surgeons*

This book was dedicated in its first edition to my dear friend and mentor, the late Ann Tully Ruderman. Neither the long line of time nor the distance of death has changed the impact she has had on my work and my ability to see the possibilities instead of the problems we face. Tully, this is still for you.

— *Judith Acosta*

I dedicate this book to Captain Patrick Brown of the New York Fire Department, lost, as were so many of his brothers, in the World Trade Center tragedy. He died as he had lived, boldly, generously, gallantly. One of the most decorated members of the fire department, a Vietnam hero, swashbuckling yet gentle, beloved by the men he led, he was the best of a rare breed and the world is less colorful, less glorious, and less safe for his loss. I'm proud to have called him a friend.

*…And flights of angels sing thee to thy rest!*

— *Judith Simon Prager*

# CONTENTS

# PREFACE TO THIS REVISED EDITION

*Since The Worst is Over was published in 2002, we have received so many wonderful testimonials and stories from people who have used the principles of Verbal First Aid in the field.*

*We felt it was time not only to update the text to reflect some of the newer science that lies behind Verbal First Aid, but to add a chapter inspired by you, our readers, about how it's worked in the world.*

*We also wanted to make The Worst is Over available in both print and e-book formats. Much from the first edition remains as it was. We hope and trust that it provides you with the tools you can make your own whenever and wherever you find them needed.*

*Warmly,*
*Judith and Judith*

# ACKNOWLEDGMENTS

*Judith Acosta*

In the get-it-done-yesterday, no-time-to-think-straight world of publishing, revised editions are an interesting phenomenon, a peculiar and special second chance to review and introspect that which has worked, what has not, what has been a blessing and where yet more Grace is needed.

In reviewing **The Worst Is Over** for republication, I saw it this time with the eyes of a reader, not an author and I was deeply moved by how seminal and important this work still is. I still feel blessed to have been a part of it in its birth and delighted to be able to present it anew to a broader audience.

When I thought about all that has transpired since it was first published right after the events of 9/11, I could not help but think of all the people who have received it and unfortunately how necessary it has become on a global scale. I thought of all the military, first response, and medical personnel who learned the protocol, used it in practice to save lives, give comfort to the wounded, and bring peace to the panicked at such a critical moment in our country's history.

When I thought of all the work and thought and time that went into making it a reality, I have a long list of thanks to give:

First of all of these is to my mother, Mollie, who died this year. She was an endless source of inspiration, encouragement and love. Having a mother like her was the Lord's Grace.

Secondly to my brother, Bill, who died in 2008. As he lay in hospital, in quite a bit of discomfort, he beckoned me over to the bed and asked me to "do that talking thing you do." So, I did. I talked about seasons and how winter gives way to spring every year. I talked about plants and how things that are full of life can be right under the surface. I talked about healing things, hopeful things, sleepy and soothing things.

At one point as he lay quietly, his eyes still closed, the monitors beeped. I looked up and noticed that the blood oxygen level had dropped. His pulse had also dropped. It wasn't precipitous, but it was enough. I told him, "Bill, while you're resting here with me, you can take a good, slow breath and bring your oxygen level back to 96, right where it was when you felt quiet and comfortable." I waited. "And while you're doing that, you can also just feel your pulse rate responding the same way…just bringing it back to where it needs to be." The results were instantaneous. And with his levels steady, he was able to sleep. We did this together several times before he passed, each time bringing him just a bit of relief. But I believe it was a gift to us both.

To my family and friends who listened with patience, who read till your heads hurt, and who stayed steadfast through my long absences with this project—

To all the men and women of the New York City Police Department, particularly those affiliated with POPPA at the time of Verbal First Aid's introduction—Bill Genet, Hal Tannenbaum, Dr. Richard Levenson, Jr., and especially Gene Moynihan, Clinical Director at the time, all of whom truly understood the value of this work from the beginning and made sure it was presented to all the POPPA volunteers even before the book came out—

To the Tuckahoe Police Department, the Sleepy Hollow Volunteer Fire and Ambulance Corps, New Rochelle Fire Chiefs Association, Montefiore Medical Center and Westchester County Medical Center for their support when Verbal First Aid was just starting so many years ago—

To George Thompson, author of *Verbal Judo,* for his kind permission to reprint the story in the chapter on suicide—

To Marcy Kniffin for her excitement about Verbal First Aid and for providing me with the opportunities to present the concept to county organizations, school districts and corporations long before they even knew how much they would need it—

To Retired Officers Dr. Mike Popp and Del LeFevre, for introducing me to the people at NYPD and being part of an ever-growing chain of strength and goodness—

To Kathleen Loddo, CSW, for showing what true, heartfelt pacing can do—

To the New York Society for Ericksonian Psychotherapy and Hypnosis and all the amazing, demanding teachers there, especially Jane Parsons Fein, CSW, Dorothy Larkin, R.N., and Dr. Sidney Rosen–

To Dan Gallagher for the NLP training that started it all back at Daytop—

To Winnie Maggiore, NREMT-P, and Dave Johnson, MD, who have been the staunchest supporters of Verbal First Aid, understanding its value in the field from first-hand experience—

To Patrick Tyrrell, Director, NASW-NM, and Angie Wagner, Operations Director, as well as John Wilkinson, Director, NASW-MT, who have brought the concept of therapeutic communication to hundreds of social workers, and through them made a difference to thousands for generations to come—

To the whole team at the Journal of Emergency Medical Services (both online and print media) for their understanding of the importance of Verbal First Aid and their editorial support in providing a forum for disseminating it at the International JEMS Convention—

To George Everly, Jr. and the International Critical Incident Stress Foundation for seeing the value and necessity in Verbal First Aid—

To Harris Straytner, PhD., CASAC, Director, Addiction Recovery Services; Associate Professor, Department of Psychiatry, Weill Medical

College of Cornell, who presented Verbal First Aid on WFAS-AM numerous times—

To the National Center for Missing and Exploited Children for teaching the protocol to their crisis volunteers in Rochester—

To Ingrid Parry and everyone at the American Burn Association: a more dedicated group of professionals I have rarely met—

To all the clients, friends, and colleagues who lovingly shared their stories of struggle and survival with us—

To the love that sustains me through everything, Dave—

Finally to all the rescue workers, police officers, firefighters, EMTs and paramedics and the millions of non-uniformed men and women who risk their lives and limbs to help save others, and most of all, to God—I re-dedicate this volume with a gratitude and love that has finally left me speechless.

Thank you. Thank you. Thank you. I now understand the meaning of being "filled with His blessings." My heart flows over and words are insufficient. May this take us all from strength to strength.

My late father, Al Simon, used to say, "Don't even think about the balance sheet of giving and receiving. Just put more good in the world, and there will be more good to go around." Those words to live by inspired a book about words to heal by.

There are so many people who should be acknowledged here for having "put more good" in the world.

First, last, and always, to my husband, Harry Youtt, who brought poetry, music, love, and magic into my life, one word: Everything.

Professionally, particular thanks must go to Donald Trent Jacobs, Ph.D., psychologist, author, teacher, emergency medical technician, for his generous spirit in leading the way in words in critical care response and to all those dedicated heroes who blazed this emergency rescue trail.

Deep thanks, as well, to those innovative pioneers in the Cardio-Thoracic Surgery Unit at Cedars-Sinai Medical Center, including Dr. Gregory P. Fontana and Dr. Alberto Trento, for their early willingness to trust me in proving the value of words in critical surgery. Thanks, too, to Pediatricians Sharon Young, M.D. and Debra Lotstein, M.D. and to Kitty Wack, Kathy Wanderer, R.N., and Marcus Hong for their support at Cedars-Sinai Medical Center.

It is with pleasure that I acknowledge the help of Timothy Trujillo, CHT, founder First Medicines and the Hypnosis AIDS Project, for his inspired wisdom in this field.

Love and thanks to Mala Spotted Eagle and Sky Pope for their stories and their support.

I would like to acknowledge some of my teachers, including Bruce Lipton, PhD, friend and inspiration, Larry Dossey, MD, whose kind support of this work has been invaluable, as well as that of Candace Pert, PhD (who, sadly, passed this year), Rick Hanson, Ronald Wong Jue, Ph.D., former President of the Association for Transpersonal Psychology; the late Gil Boyne, Executive Director, American Council of

Hypnotist Examiners, and David Quigley, founder of the Alchemy Institute for Healing Arts.

Thank you to Dr. Helena Guo, MD, who brought me to China in 2008 to train crisis counselors in Verbal First Aid after the devastating earthquake in Sichuan killed 80,000 people in a matter of moments. Her faith in this work has been so important to me.

Thank you to Susan Clark, MD, Ruby Roy, MD, and Kathleen Archibald Simon, RN, among many others in the medical profession whose belief in Verbal First Aid translated into a world of support.

Thank you to Professor Renzo Molinari for connecting me with the European School of Osteopathy and to Corinne Jones there for helping me introduce Verbal First Aid to Great Britain. Your open-armed reception has been both generous and inspirational.

Thank you to Dr. Jules Morel and Ruth Moore, RN, for opportunities to share Verbal First Aid with the Kingdom of Brunei.

Thank you to the Association of Pre and Perinatal Psychology and Health (APPPAH), especially to Marcy Axness, Maureen Woolf, and Wendy Ann McCarty, for welcoming me as a keynote speaker and embracing me in their incredibly wonderful mission of bringing awareness to the consciousness of beings even before birth. Thanks to Lisa Garr and Nita Valens, hosts on KPFK Los Angeles, for helping me bring early recognition to Verbal First Aid.

Thank you to Sandy Salway-Beers, EMD-I Quality Improvement Coordinator and others at the Rochester/Monroe County Emergency Communications whose invitation to train the 9-1-1 telecommunicators contributed a valuable perspective to my work and teaching.

Thanks to the psychiatric nurses at New York University Hospital, especially Lisa Hasnosi, for inviting me to share Verbal First Aid with them after the events of September 11th, and to Dr. Leo Shea, Clinical Assistant Professor of Rehabilitation Medicine, NYU School of Medicine and Clinical Neuropsychologist NYU-Rusk Institute of Rehabilitation Medicine for his wonderful work and for sharing his important insights on trauma.

My heart goes out to the valiant fire fighters of New York City. Thanks especially to Lieutenant Steve Browne and John Gates of Ladder Company 3, who lost their Captain, Patrick Brown, and half of their brothers in the September 11th disaster, and to Sal D'Agostino, Bill Butler, Mike Meldrum, and Tommy Falco of Ladder Company 6 for generously sharing their time and stories with me.

Thank you to Westwood Publishing for permission to use the quotes of Dr. David Cheek, Captain Frank Neer, and Dr. Jerrald Kaplan from Don Jacob's video, *Hypnosis for Medical Emergencies.*

Thanks, too, to Barry Kibrick for his beautiful support on his PBS program Between the Lines.

Personally, I want to thank my late parents, Al and Pauline Simon, ever present. To my many wonderful children—Danielle Prager, Jennifer and George Hatzmann (and grandchildren Jack, Tanner, Madeleine, and Isadora), Jonathan Youtt, and Brad Prager—thank you for being the exceptional people you've turned out to be. You have filled my life with pride and joy. Thanks to cousin Marilyn, goddaughter Sarah, Inger Lanese, and my sisters and brothers in life and in law for just being there and caring.

To friends, teachers, clients, and colleagues, blessedly too numerous to mention by name, thank you, thank you, thank you.

Thanks to the UCLA Extension Writers Program and Linda Venis, Ph.D. for giving us a home where Harry and I can spread our wings and share our love of creativity.

May this book and the thoughts behind it "put more good in the world." Once we know the effects of our words and thoughts on each other, we can do no less than fill the way we speak to one another and the way we care for one another with kindness…kindness blossoming forth on every occasion. May we each become a blessing to all we encounter, that we may move together, hearts joined, into a kinder, more loving future.

# THE POWER OF WORDS

*"Words are, of course, the most powerful drug used by mankind."*
*–Rudyard Kipling*

One day, maybe sooner, maybe later, someone you love will experience a medical emergency. Perhaps a friend or co-worker will collapse in a meeting, or a car ahead of you on the road will veer off and crash into a tree, or something less dramatic could happen—a cut, a bruise, or a broken bone. One day, without doubt, someone you know will be diagnosed with a serious chronic disease. One day, someone you care about—an elderly parent, a spouse, a child—will experience mental or emotional pain, or a panic attack or a bout of depression.

After you've done everything you can, including calling 9-1-1 in a medical emergency, what do you *say? Hang in there, Joe,* doesn't seem quite adequate, and *Don't die on me, damn it,* may work in the movies, but it's less effective in real life.

There **are** words, and ways of saying them, that are not only helpful, but can turn a medical situation around. They can positively affect Joe's heart rate, temperature, breathing, in fact his entire cardiovascular, limbic, endocrine, circulatory and respiratory systems. The effect of specific words is so powerful that, in certain circumstances just saying, *Stop bleeding and save your blood!* can help an accident victim do exactly that. The right words can help you calm a person in the throes of a panic attack or soothe a chronically ill person into a sound and restful sleep.

*Not* knowing the techniques that we present in this book can also have serious implications. In everyday emergencies, the wrong words can amplify the problem, despite the best of intentions, making the situation worse. Lily, a little girl of three or four years old (could she be your daughter?) slips on a throw rug and falls against a coffee table. Her teeth tear through her lower lip and split it in two. When her parents find her she is crying and bleeding profusely. Years later she looks back on the moment.

"When my parents saw my lip, they lost control. As they drove to the hospital I vividly remember hearing *Oh, my God,* and *Oh God what are we gonna do? She's gonna need stitches. Oh my poor baby! Do we have to give her stitches? Isn't there anything else we can do?* My lip still hurts sometimes when I think of it. My mother was so upset she got my father worried, which terrified me. When I finally got to the hospital, the doctors rushed me into surgery and kept saying, "*Someone hold her down!*" There was very little that enabled me to find a comfort zone. There was no calm center anywhere to support me, which made the whole experience much worse than it had to be."

Lily's parents probably did everything right concerning physical first aid. They probably applied compresses to reduce the bleeding and an ice pack to reduce swelling. And the Emergency Room doctors, we may assume, did everything necessary and proper to clean, stitch, and dress the wound. The only problem was that nobody knew what to *say* to the little girl, and saying the wrong things only made things worse. Perhaps it literally generated a cascade of chemicals in her body that impeded the healing. And those wrong words also kept that minor wound alive and festering emotionally for years.

The same human and emotional effects of the trauma suffered by Lily apply to far more serious emergency physical traumas—to motor vehicle and industrial accidents, to serious burns, and to respiratory and heart attacks, as well as to people facing surgery and suffering from physical, chronic and emotional illness.

The good news is this: saying the right words can physiologically and emotionally alter the outcome of serious situations, can ease what

St. John of the Cross called *the dark night of the soul,* both in the present and in the *future.* When we use Verbal First Aid in a trauma, we are changing the way it is processed and mitigating its impact down the line.

What we will show you in this book can reduce anxiety, diminish pain, promote healing, and save lives. The program presented here is based on techniques used by professionals trained to deal with the first hour of trauma, including firefighters, nurses, EMS personnel and police officers. Studies of these methods show they allow patients to arrive in the Emergency Room in significantly better-than-expected condition.

All this is possible because when people are in an accident, when they are blindsided by trauma, they enter ***an altered state of consciousness*** in which they are unusually open to influences on the autonomic system that facilitate healing. We call this "the healing zone." People with basic training in what we call "Verbal First Aid" can empower patients or accident victims to begin their own natural healing within moments. We will show you our step-by-step protocols for communication in the healing zone: how to establish and utilize rapport and how to give therapeutic suggestions to set the course for healing. Stories and examples will illustrate how to connect with the parts of a person's mind that actually regulate the healing functions.

Sometimes the altered state becomes shock; sometimes people slip into unconsciousness. But even under those extreme circumstances it is still possible to use Verbal First Aid to facilitate relaxation, pain relief, anxiety reduction and progress toward recovery.

Although this protocol was developed for medical emergencies, it is also valid for people with chronic conditions. The impact of an illness can be heightened by the trauma of a frightening diagnosis. When people receive a dire diagnosis—for instance, of lymphoma or AIDS— they often report having had the sensation of seeing the doctor's lips move but not hearing a thing. Timothy Trujillo, founder of the non-profit organization First Medicines, created to reduce suffering and enhance health worldwide, has found that all that people receiving such a diagnosis can hear are the words in their head, "I am going to die!" and that they are feeling "as if the rug were being pulled out from under me." In some ways, Trujillo says, "the mindset of a person hearing a terrifying prognosis is not unlike that of a person lying on the ground bleeding."

Because of the on-going sense of crisis that a frightening diagnosis brings, people suffering physical illnesses, like people in medical emergencies, are looking for something solid to hang onto. Trujillo believes that literally or figuratively taking their hand and letting them know authoritatively that you can help, reassuring them and redirecting their thoughts can break the spell of the original negative experience. When you speak with authority, through your words and presence you can provide vital assistance. He likens this process to throwing a rope to a falling person and tying the other end around a tree. The rope is a new idea, thought, or belief.

This is the first book of its kind written with everyone in mind. It details the methodology designed for talking to the autonomic nervous system to evoke a desired change. It provides the means for people to help each other through medical emergencies, as well as through emotional and chronic illness and pain, using the one skill we all share, no matter what level of medical training we have—the ability to communicate.

Parts One and Two of this book give you the background and the protocols for using these important, perhaps even life-saving, techniques and teach you how to recognize when people are in the "healing zone." Part Three provides specific words and scenarios for use in medical emergencies and other care-giving situations. Part Four addresses the rescuer, the person who has helped in a medical emergency or with chronic illness, who feels either exhausted or discouraged in the aftermath. Here we discuss language you can use on yourself and how, with awareness, your perception of the situation could shift.

In the end we offer you "The Last Laugh." In Chapter 15 you'll see why doctors recommend laughter, the ultimate life-affirming technique when all seems bleak. And it is followed by testimonials from people in the work of rescue and people just living their lives who have found in Verbal First Aid a gift to share in a moment when it made all the difference.

We believe that between the covers of this book you will find wonderful ways to learn and use Verbal First Aid and make it your own to help change the course of medical situations for your family, friends and anyone who needs you.

We have seen the power of words first-hand, in our practices and in our trainings, in our offices, and on the streets. We have seen children stop bleeding, the chronically ill develop a remarkable tolerance for pain, and elderly patients in respiratory distress return to easy, healthy breathing. We want you to see the power of words as we have. We want to introduce you to the practice of Verbal First Aid so you can see its benefits at work in your own life as we have in ours. When you hear the stories, examine the evidence, and learn the skills, you will be preparing yourself for whatever comes your way. No matter what your level of medical skill may be, by choosing your words with care you can make a positive difference in someone's life.

In Barbara Kingsolver's best-selling novel, *The Bean Trees*, the narrator tries to have a conversation with a silent, sad woman whose child is missing in Guatemala. "This conversation would have been hard enough even with two people talking. No matter what I said, it was sure to be the exact wrong thing to say to someone who recently swallowed a bottle of baby aspirin. But what would have been right? Was there some book in the library where you could look up such things?"

Yes. Now there is. You're holding it in your hands.

**Words, Words, Words**

In the United States of America, where free speech is a cornerstone of our way of life, no one is allowed to shout "Fire!" in a crowded theater. Why? Because the image that word creates can cause panic and a stampede among otherwise calm and reasonable adults, even if there is no fire, and no smoke. The power of words is phenomenal. Other countries know it; they put their dissenting poets in archipelagos, or throw them in jail. Advertisers know it. They say, "Coke is it!" and we get the message literally and subliminally until we finally pick up the bright red cans or bottles in the supermarket. In a courtroom, the lawyer with the right words ("If it doesn't fit, you must acquit") has the edge. A mere slogan ("Remember the Maine," "Remember the Alamo," "The Mother of All Battles,") can turn a peaceful nation into a fighting machine.

What happens when words are used to help people in dire situations, to help them recover, to bring them back from the edge?

In the late '80s, at a drug rehabilitation center in New York, a man stepped out onto the roof of the building. A passer-by noticed, came into the building, and called 9-1-1. Within minutes, the patients, the counselors, the director, EMS personnel and police (not to mention the shoppers from across the street) were all outside looking up at this agitated young man shouting incoherently. Numerous attempts had been made to communicate with him and get him quieted, or to distract him long enough to allow rescue workers to climb up on the roof and get him down. Nothing was working. Two hours passed and even the rescue workers were becoming edgy, their nerves frayed. The director of the center called in the resident clinical social worker. When she arrived what she saw was frustration and lack of communication.

She was introduced to the potential jumper by one of the firefighters. She took a deep breath, paused to get centered, and simply asked him, "Can you tell me what hurts?" The potential jumper looked at her, paced a bit, sat down, and started talking.

The right words at the right time. The fact that the world turns on words may not be news. But most people, even institutional medical personnel, are not aware of the full power of a mental image to change the course of an emergency or an illness.

Ironically, in a culture that seems to be preoccupied with safety, the number one cause of death in people under 45 years old is accidents and adverse effects. Heart disease ranks number 1 in the population over 65 years of age. Cancer and other chronic diseases are reaching epidemic proportions. These are situations that affect everyone at some point, all of us—children, parents, friends and neighbors. One day you will find yourself sitting beside someone in an emergency situation, and you will want to know how to make a difference. Using the words you have learned here, you will be able to provide comfort and relief to an aging parent, a spouse, a friend, or a stranger who needs rescue or help.

Verbal First Aid does not replace the medical help on which we all rely and for which we are at times deeply grateful. It gives you, the person at the scene, or the one standing helplessly at the bedside, a valuable gift to pass along—the magic of healing words.

Although all this may be news to many of us who are just beginning to recognize the power of words and thoughts on the outcome of events, other cultures have understood their impact all along. "When we plant a seed," our friend Sky Pope, a Tlingit Native woman says, "we pray over it. When we water it, we talk to it. When we harvest and cook it, we sing to it. And before we eat it, we pray over it and sing to it again. And then," she said, as if it were too obvious for words, "and then, it's medicine."

In so many words, **every** interaction is an opportunity for healing, emotional and physical. And by knowing that, and treating all we encounter with care, you can move through life like an angel. Words, song, prayer—their effects can be myriad, profound, even, as you shall see, life-saving.

PART ONE

# Verbal First Aid™

# CHAPTER ONE

# VERBAL FIRST AID: HOW IT WORKS WHEN EVERY MOMENT COUNTS

*"I've learned that people will forget what you said, people will forget what you did, but people will never forget how you made them feel."*
-Maya Angelou

*"One word frees us of all the weight and pain of life; that word is love."*
-Sophocles-

You're driving along a country road. The motorcycle ahead of you takes a bad turn, spins off the road and disappears off the shoulder in a cloud of smoke. You pull your car over to the side and jump out to find a badly injured rider, his leg twisted and bleeding, moaning and writhing in pain.

In that kind of crisis, most of us would spend at least a few seconds thinking, *oh my God!* and trying to think clearly first about what we can **do**. (In emergencies this means calling 9-1-1, and then possibly applying bandages and splints, when and where indicated.) *Doing* something in an emergency or crisis is often essential, but that's only one of the healing tools available to us. In our haste to find the right thing to do, few of us think, *What can I say?* Often, we rush to do something simply to cover up the fact that we can't even think of anything to say. Indeed, why should we think that words could have any effect? Certainly

11

there is nothing in our upbringing or medical culture to suggest that. We are a country of doers and our cultural stoicism is often worn as a badge of honor. Nonetheless, it has been demonstrated in the medical literature that every word, every thought, even every intention causes a measurable bodily reaction.

There is another way of approaching that accident with the biker. You see him go down, you stop the car. You make your 9-1-1 call. Then you get out of your car and take a deep breath to calm and center yourself. You walk over to the rider and kneel down beside him. You determine whether any essential first aid must be administered and then you say:

*"My name is Timothy and I'm going to help you. The worst is over. I've called 9-1-1 and they're on the way. I can see that your leg needs attention. Why don't you just scan the rest of your body for me now to see that everything else is all right? How's your other leg? How do your arms feel? (Pause)*

*"Because the ambulance is on its way, you can relax a little now and let your body do what needs to be done to protect your life and begin healing. (Pause)*

*"I'm sure there's some place you'd rather be right now. Where is that? The beach? Okay, while your body is tending to the healing, you can allow your mind to go to your favorite beach, to that place you really love to be, and you can begin to feel comfortable being in that place right now…"*

That event, that gruesome motorcycle spill, actually happened right before the eyes of Timothy Trujillo as he drove along a country road one lazy Sunday afternoon. Trained in Verbal First Aid, he knew what to do and what to say. He identified himself and established rapport with the injured man. Then he began to provide suggestions for pain relief and healing.

"It took an interminable 45 minutes for the ambulance to come," Trujillo said, during which time the man, whose corkscrew fracture had broken his leg in seven places, writhed in agony and fear. "I had him visualize swimming in a pool," Trujillo said. "Floating stimulates endorphin production, and the feeling of suspension offers pain relief and comfort." Throughout the long wait, whenever the pain surged up again, Trujillo would remind the man of the pool, having him "do the backstroke, which drew attention away from his legs."

Then Trujillo taught the man the "control room technique" to help manage his pain, showing him how to dial it down to a more comfortable level. (See Chapter 8 on pain management for more information.) Three days later, when he visited the man in the hospital, the patient reported that he no longer needed his pain medication because "it's on zero," meaning he had used the control dial to turn down the pain himself.

After several months, Trujillo received a letter from the man's wife, thanking him and telling him that his intervention *had set the course for her husband's recovery.* And all Trujillo had at his disposal on that country road were words. There was no way he could have set that leg out there by himself, even if he knew how. But his words and demeanor helped to ease the biker's fear and pain, so he could begin the healing process.

Verbal First Aid is a program born out of the needs of crisis and rescue personnel. The idea is both simple and scientific. What you say to a person in an emergency situation can have a profound physical and emotional effect; it can shape the course of healing and its outcome.

Verbal First Aid is not designed to take the place of a doctor or paramedic, or any medical treatment. It is designed to complement it. Standard first aid practices still apply, and you can learn them from one of the many first aid books on the market—how to help restore breathing, control bleeding, help a victim keep warm. And all the warnings apply too: do not move an accident victim, do not remove a foreign object that's deeply embedded in a wound, do not play doctor or therapist, unless of course you are one. Verbal First Aid is about using language to help the body initiate its own inner healing.

You may recall a time yourself when you were ill or injured, perhaps in an emergency room at a hospital, when you seemed to see everything as if through a tunnel. Or perhaps time moved very slowly, as if you were under water. Perhaps you had trouble focusing. In a crisis, body and mind slow down to protect us and keep us from further injury. To accomplish this, the mind dissociates us a bit from our environment. People who are chronically ill or in emotional crisis are in a similar altered state.

Fear, pain, and distress can trigger a shift from ordinary waking consciousness to this vastly more receptive and suggestible state. This is nature's way of contributing to our survival. In an emergency, we don't have time to consider complicated scenarios: we are programmed to respond to authority, to follow a leader to safety. This is a vestige of ancient herd behavior. Most social animals function like this, including primates, lions, wolves, antelopes—and human beings are no exception. A threat requires instinctive action, not analysis. (This is also the basis for military training.) Due to this hardwiring, genetic programming, a person who knows Verbal First Aid can readily assume the role of authority in an emergency and provide the victim with mind/body tools that stimulate the healing process.

In an emergency, or any time people are in an altered state of consciousness, extraordinary things are possible. The part of the mind that governs automatic responses can be spoken to directly. With the right words, you can have impact on a host of bodily functions.

Here is just a partial list of some of the functions we can influence with Verbal First Aid:

Pain
Heart rate
Respiration
Blood pressure

Bleeding
Inflammatory response
Itching
Contractions
Bowel motility
Smooth muscle tension
Sweating
Allergic responses
Asthma
Rate of healing
Dermatitis
Dryness of mouth
Immune response
Glandular secretions
Emotional reactions

Medical research shows that even when people are unconscious they still hear or experience everything that is going on around them. It is not uncommon, for example, for people to remember what has been said in the operating room while they were under general anesthesia. Knowing this, trained medical caregivers will encourage family members to talk to patients in a coma or after surgery when they are not quite conscious.

Donald Trent Jacobs, Ph.D., reported a vivid example of the positive effect words can have in his book, *Patient Communication*. It took place in an Oakland, California hospital emergency room, where Jacobs had trained first responders with methods similar to those described in this book. One of Dr. Jacob's paramedic students brought in a patient suffering a heart attack. He had performed CPR in the ambulance and had used the patient communication techniques he had learned from Jacobs. As the E.R. physician began working on the patient, he turned to the paramedic and said, "It looks like this fellow is going to be all right, doesn't it..." The paramedic responded, "It looks like he's going to be fine." At just that moment, the EKG that had been irregular jumped into a normal rhythm.

One of our clients, Gary, required surgery to remove calcium accumulations on his spine—a dangerous and painful procedure. The doctors told him that as a result of the surgery, he might never walk again. (While information required for informed consent is legally necessary, it is not necessarily good Verbal First Aid. The doctor might have offered Gary statistics that show how so many people recover completely, might even have put him together with a former patient who had had a brilliant recovery so that Gary had a picture in his mind that not only comforted him but granted him a trajectory of recovery that his body might pattern.) During the operation, the surgeon became frustrated. Upset and worried, he walked out of the Operating Room, muttering "I can't do this!" and "It isn't going to work." He soon calmed down, returning several moments later with renewed confidence. The surgery was successful, and the patient was able to walk.

However, Gary left the hospital suffering from unexpected depression, all the more mysterious given the success of the operation. Under hypnosis it emerged that his unconscious mind had registered the moment in the operation when the doctor gave up and left the room. For this patient, healing involved shifting his unconscious mind from the memory that "it isn't going to work" to an awareness of the ultimate success of the operation.

The point is clear: words affect healing–even when we do not seem to be aware of them.

Noted psychologist and psychiatrist M. Erik Wright conducted a pioneer study with paramedics at a municipal hospital in Kansas. He trained three groups with a simple protocol for emergencies. Whenever they picked up a patient or attended to someone in the field, these three experimental groups were asked to follow these simple procedures:

1. Remove the patient from his or her environment as soon as possible to minimize external distractions.

2. Memorize and recite a simple paragraph designed to calm the patient and help the patient to begin his/her own healing. They were to do this speaking softly into the patient's ear, whether or not the patient was conscious.

3. No other unrelated conversation between the paramedics that could possibly be construed as negative would take place.

4. These rules were to be used as an adjunct to standard medical procedures.

This is the paragraph they recited:

*"The worst is over. We are taking you to the hospital. Everything is being made ready. Let your body concentrate on repairing itself and feeling secure. Let your heart, your blood vessels, everything, bring themselves into a state of preserving your life. Bleed just enough so as to cleanse the wound, and let the blood vessels close down so that your life is preserved. Your body weight, your body heat, everything, is being maintained. Things are being made ready in the hospital for you. We're getting there as quickly and safely as possible. You are now in a safe position. The worst is over."*

Control groups were not trained in this protocol and continued to practice emergency medical care as usual. This experiment lasted six months while the hospital collected data on patient recovery rates and treatment outcomes. Wright reported that there was so much enthusiasm among the paramedics using this method that it was hard to keep them from sharing it with the control group and "spoiling the experiment."

The results were significant. The patients who were attended to by the paramedics trained in this protocol proved to be more likely to survive the trip to the hospital, have shorter hospital stays and experience quicker recovery rates. Unfortunately, although medical science has repeatedly documented the powerful effects of words and images on the body and mind, rescue and medical personnel are still only sporadically being trained in these protocols.

Verbal First Aid can not only give *you* a sense of control in seriously out-of-control or demoralizing situations, it can return a sense of control to the person you are aiding and it can help to begin the healing process from within. If you are concerned about using Verbal First Aid, feeling you might be overstepping your bounds because you are not a doctor or therapist, consider this. A person attending another person in crisis has three verbal options. We can:

1) Say nothing.
2) Say something harmful.
3) Say something helpful that promotes healing.

Verbal First Aid is safe and simple. It is not meant to take the place of good medicine, but rather to make good medicine better. You can benefit by learning these basic steps toward effective healing communication: how to **generate rapport** that begins the communication; how to **give suggestions** for pain relief that actually stimulate the body to produce chemicals that support healing, and how to **create an atmosphere** that helps to turn fear into hope and panic into calm.

The techniques will be explained in the upcoming chapters, so you will learn how to apply them on your own, but here are some experiences from those in the field who already practice a form of Verbal First Aid.

Even before he was lost so tragically in the World Trade Center disaster, the late Patrick Brown was a legend and a hero in New York City. A captain in the New York City Fire Department, he was a Vietnam veteran with a special radar for pulling the weakest among us—babies and animals—from blazing buildings. Known for his daring rescues, he was quoted in a *TIME* Magazine (September 6, 1999) cover story on taking risks. He explained that fire fighters do not take "stupid risks... We don't do this for sport or for thrills or money. You're risking your life to save somebody. That's what makes this job special. We take risks for the greater good." He was one of the most decorated men in the history of the department, but for all his heroics, he leaned into his spiritual side, studying yoga and earning a black belt in karate. In his spare time, he taught self-defense to the blind. Some who knew him well called him "an enlightened being." He was a friend whose way in the world was in itself healing.

Pat Brown was a master in the Verbal First Aid technique of gaining rapport—building the bridge of trust with the victim. In his parlance, there were "rescuers" and "civilians." He noted the importance of tone of voice and of maintaining a calm, centered presence. "Sometimes the rescuers are more nervous than the victims," he told us, "and they can overdo some of the enthusiasm, or get harsh or shrill. I try not to do that. I keep my voice calm, direct, and reassuring. If your voice is nervous, it makes the civilian nervous and that can get in the way."

Ironically, this hero of heroes, this man of action, found that one of the ways he stayed calm was by spending a moment with the victim in silent meditation. Sometimes it took only a few seconds, other times a little longer. "It depends on the situation," he explained. "With some victims, I will put my hands on them and do a little meditation, breathe into it, think into the universe and into God. I try to connect with their spiritual natures, even if they're dying. It helps to keep me calm as much as I hope it helps them."

As spiritual as this may sound Pat Brown was actually quite focused on reality and he always believed in acknowledging the difficulty of the situation, of which the victim is already fully aware. "Sometimes the person is so hurt or so upset they can't talk. So, I reassure them. I let them know what I'm going to do for them. I empathize with them and support what they're feeling. When you talk to a victim this way they're relieved. At some level, they know you're not BS-ing them. When I say, 'In two minutes, the emergency rescue team will be here, it's like having a whole hospital operating room here, and in two minutes they're going to get you out,' the victim is reassured."

It is reported that the last words he said outside the World Trade Center, the last building he entered, were in response to someone's calling out, "Don't go in there, Paddy!" His answer was "There are people in there!" We can only imagine that whoever was with him in that hellish inferno at the end was also treated to a glimpse of heaven through his calming, courageous, and loving presence.

When we connect in the profound way that Patrick Brown described with the people whom we desire to help, we can move beyond bandages and splints to rescues that invite in what is sometimes called grace.

Timothy Trujillo tells us about a time he was called to a hospital to help a patient dying of liver cancer. The condition of Tom's liver ruled out strong medications, and he was suffering from terrible pain and depression. Tom's wife and daughter were in great distress, so Trujillo was called in to consult for pain management. Tom had not slept in days, had great difficulty moving and was unable to speak because he had a tube in his throat. There seemed to be no way to comfort him.

Trujillo spoke with Tom's daughter who filled him in on the situation and he walked into the room to find Tom staring fixedly at the ceiling. "Tom," he said. "I am here to help you be more comfortable. Blink your eyes if you can hear me."

Tom blinked. Trujillo went on: "Did you know that your body knows how to provide chemicals that can make you more comfortable?" He paused to let Tom consider what that could mean to him. "Let me show you how this works. Close your eyes and remember some place you love to be, where you feel fine and relaxed and happy."

Tom closed his eyes. Then tears began to roll down his cheeks. He reached up and took Trujillo's hand as his daughter watched, amazed. "Any time you want to be comfortable, just close your eyes and go to this place." Tom's face visibly relaxed. Then he fell asleep. Elated, Tom's daughter rushed from the room to tell her mother what had happened. The two women thanked Trujillo profusely when he emerged. Their faces were completely transformed. "When you work with a person, you work with a community of individuals," Trujillo says. "Providing comfort for Tom provided comfort for his entire family."

In some medical emergencies, these techniques can be as elegantly simple as they are effective. Two weeks after one of our training sessions with paramedics, a student called, all excited. "It worked," he said.

"You sound surprised," we responded.

"I guess, but really, I was surprised at how simple it was. We picked up a little girl with the ambulance and her breathing was really shallow. She was gasping for breath. Her mother was panicked. So, I had one of the guys follow your recommendation, you know, get the mother busy with something else, then I started pacing and leading the girl's breathing, starting where she was, matching her breath for breath, and then slowing down."

"So, what happened?"

"Well, by the time we got to the hospital, she was breathing just fine."

Verbal First Aid helps people experiencing emotional distress as well. A young woman, Lisa, was severely allergic to bees. While visiting her friend Jody for a weekend in the country, Lisa noticed a bee at the window. When she realized it was on the inside of the screen, she was consumed by terror. She reached for her purse, looked for her anti-allergen EpiPenTM and realized she'd left it at home. Although the bee had not moved, Lisa's throat began to tighten, her breathing became rapid and shallow, and her hands clammy. Jody took charge of the situation immediately. She closed the window and led Lisa into another room. Sitting down next to her she began to match Lisa's breathing, then slowed it down. She said, "I'm right here and the bee is trapped far away from you in the next room. The danger is over and you're safe. As you sit with me on the couch, you can begin to feel the comfort and safety relaxing your chest…" She continued to talk and use pacing breathing until Lisa's panic subsided.

A colleague Janet recalls an incident with her niece, Elza, during a visit to Elza's grandparents' house that nicely demonstrates a wide range of Verbal First Aid techniques. "While I'd gone out to run an errand, Elza had been playing in the kiddie pool with her sisters and one of them fell. Somehow her younger sister's foot wound up in Elza's mouth and Elza started bleeding profusely. Her grandparents panicked when they saw that her front tooth was hanging loose. Though terribly upset, they finally managed to get some ice and compresses on the wound. When I got back, I took a moment to size up the situation and took Elza aside, where her grandparents' well-meaning concern and confusion couldn't affect her as much. I whispered, 'Looks like we're the only sane ones here.' She laughed. And that was my opening. I said to her quietly, clearly, and very firmly, 'I'm gonna tell you a story now and you're gonna stay with my voice, no matter what else goes on... okay? And while I tell you the story, *you can stop the bleeding.*' She nodded. Then I said, 'I knew a girl, 10 years old, who lost a big chunk of her front tooth, knocked it against a big old metal bus seat. She cried, but then she stopped crying because she knew the worst was over and that the healing could start *right now.* And guess what?' Elza said, 'What?' And I smiled at her, pointed at my front tooth and said, 'That little girl was me, and everything turned out just fine. And after you get better you can tell this story to some other little girl who needs your help.' She relaxed after that. And it turned out just fine for her, too."

As important as Verbal First Aid information is, it is easy to learn. In the pages that follow you will learn specific techniques and find scripts you can use to help change the outcome in medical emergencies, to calm those in emotional distress, and to provide pain relief and comfort to those who are physically ill. This practice involves both the mind and the heart.

Out of the tragedy of September 11th came a story that reveals the secret magic of doing this work, the circle effect that means that, in helping others, we can never really tell who is giving and who is receiving.

As the NYFD firefighters of Ladder Company 6 told us (a story that they also shared as an NBC *Dateline* report on September 29, 2001 as "The Miracle of Ladder Company 6"), they entered the building at

Number One World Trade Center after the first plane had mortally wounded it. They were helping in the evacuation, carrying more than 100 pounds of equipment per man, when, somewhere between the 12th and 15th floor, the police handed over to them 60-year-old book-keeper, Josephine Harris, whose descent from the 72nd floor in the smoke and heat had completely exhausted her.

Bill Butler said, "The only one way to keep Josephine moving was to keep rapport." The words they used to calm and encourage her were the right words. ("Josephine, we're going to get you out of here today," and, as their sense of urgency grew, "Josephine, your kids and your grandkids want you home today. We gotta keep moving.") But by the fourth floor, she could walk no more.

Because the men of Ladder Company 6 refused to even consider leaving Josephine, they tried again to encourage her to move on, but her legs could no longer support her. Suddenly, there came an un-earthly hurricane of sound that meant the building was collapsing, and all of the firefighters prepared to die, then and there.

But there were other plans in store for them. The staircase and floor at which Josephine had insisted they stop miraculously withstood the destructive weight of 105 floors crashing down on top of it. It was one of the only fragments of the structure not turned to dust.

When the building fell they were not killed, but seemed to be bur-ied alive. Tommy Falco held Josephine's hand when she said she was scared and gave her his coat when she said she was cold, but, the fire-fighters later told us, she never complained. "She was a trooper," Sal D'Agostino said, with admiration. They were trapped together in the rubble for four hours. Finally, they were discovered by Ladder Com-pany 43. The men told us they didn't want to leave Josephine, didn't want to pass her on to other firefighters, but special equipment was needed to get her out.

The firefighter who came to their rescue was "pumped up," they said, excited at having found them alive. He began to help Josephine, saying, 'We'll take care of you, doll, we got you."

But there had been a shift in understanding in that dark tomb in which they had been buried together, and D'Agostino grabbed the rescuer's arm. "Listen, her name isn't doll. Her name is Josephine." He later explained, "I wanted him to get personal with her the way I had gotten personal, the way we all had." The other firefighter, quickly understanding, said 'Josephine, right. Sorry, Josephine, we'll take good care of you.'"

Ultimately they were rescued. And they all believed, to a man, that Josephine was their guardian angel, sent there to hold them in that sacred space so that they could survive. "You saved our lives," they said to her. "You saved mine," she responded. It was all true, and it's a wonderful metaphor for the way it really works. Rescue is only partially about digging or pulling people out of a disaster scene, only indirectly about materiel and "the jaws of life." It is also about rising above the debris on wings of faith and love in such a way that we are rescued in every moment from fear and harm.

Verbal First Aid is more than the words themselves. It embodies an attitude, a statement both literal and spiritual. It is a process we can witness in ourselves and a position we lovingly assume with the people around us. The words are the tools, but their power derives from awareness and love. It is born from a decision we make to participate in our wellness and in the well being of others.

### Verbal First Aid Key – Chapter 1
### How it Works

- Words affect the course of healing: anything you say in the presence of a sick or injured person has the potential to help or to harm.
- Verbal First Aid is an adjunct to medical treatment, not a substitute.
- A person in a medical or emotional crisis is in a more suggestible state, which we call a "Healing Zone."
- Our words can affect all sorts of autonomic nervous system physical processes: Pain, heart rate, blood pressure, respiration, and inflammatory response, to name a few.
- Even in the unconscious state a person can hear and respond to the images your words generate.
- M. Erik Wright's study showed that patients attended by paramedics trained in a special protocol designed to verbally promote healing were more likely to survive emergency transport, have shorter hospital stays and enjoy quicker recovery rates.

CHAPTER TWO

# THE MIND/BODY CONNECTION:
# THE EVIDENCE

*"Miracles happen, not in opposition to Nature, but
in opposition to what we know of Nature."*
–St. Augustine

This chapter provides the science behind the notion that mind and body are not separate, but are part of an integrated whole, and that thoughts, therefore, have a dramatic physiological effect on bodily functions. To many of the people we have worked with and trained, Verbal First Aid seems like magic. Although these techniques can be extremely effective in an emergency, there is no magic involved. The reasons are very concrete. The documentation we present now is just the tip of a monumental and ever-growing iceberg of evidence, research, and clinical experience that support and explore the fascinating potential of the human being, in which body, mind, and spirit all play a critical role in medical outcomes.

For some people it doesn't matter **why** Verbal First Aid works, just **that** it works. If you are one of those people, you could skip ahead to the chapters on Verbal First Aid technique. If, however, you are the kind of person who feels more convinced and satisfied when a proposition is supported by evidence, please read on.

The unity of mind and body is an old idea, one that has been accepted for thousands of years by the great wisdom traditions. It was a keystone of the Vedic teachings of India, where it was developed into a sophisticated mind/body medical system called Ayurveda. Travelers carried this knowledge to China, where it was modified and became the source of ancient China's system of medicine. Native Americans also believed firmly in the healing power of the mind. The late Corbin Harney, a Western Shoshone Nation Spiritual Leader, was world renowned for his activism in defense of the future of the Mother Earth. Asked about mind/body wisdom, he explained that simply using an herb or a pharmaceutical part of an herb is not nearly as effective as using the herbs backed with a belief system. "If you're going to use something like this [chaparral for cancer, which is very effective among the Native people], your minds have got to be connected with it, with whatever you're using. You can't have your doubts," he wrote in his book, *The Way It Is.* "A miracle thing can happen, but in order for it to happen you are the one who is going to have to allow it—in your mind. We are the ones, ourselves, who work with the Spirit. Somebody else can't do it for you."

The separation of mind and body, while it can be traced back to the ancient Greeks, is most often laid at the doorstep of the 17th century philosopher Rene Descartes. Since the Roman Catholic Church claimed *man* as its domain, Descartes and the church struck a deal: *science* became anatomy, the mechanical functions of the body, divorced from any involvement with spirit; and the realm of the church became the mind and soul of man. It was tacitly agreed that the mind controlled the thoughts, reason, and emotion, leaving the spiritless body a distinct and separate scientific entity that could be studied without traipsing on moral, spiritual issues. In this way Descartes was able to pursue his interests despite the power of the church, and an artificial dualism was born. This philosophical position may have served Descartes well, but when it evolved into a medical approach that cut mind and spirit out of the health equation, it did the rest of us a great disservice. By focusing solely on external causes of disease, such as bacteria and viruses, science dissuaded us from exploring the reasons why one person exposed to a virus might *not* get sick. When it dismissed the evidence that a person having a heart transplant might be more likely to survive if his emotions were taken into account, it ignored common sense.

While there were those who spoke out in favor of a more holistic approach to healing, such as the father of Homeopathy, Dr. Samuel Hahnemann, their voices were barely heard by the vast majority in the western world (although they continue to be well-respected in countries such as Great Britain and India). In 1974, however, a serendipitous finding in a lab at the Rochester School of Medicine and Dentistry changed that forever.

Robert Ader and his associates were conditioning rats to experience nausea with an intake of saccharine water and a drug called cyclophosphamide. What they found was that the rats' immune systems became conditioned, so that even when given only the saccharine, the rats took ill. This was an enormous breakthrough, for it suggested that the immune system could *learn*. Adler continued his research with Dr. Nicholas Cohen, a respected immunologist and the field of pscyhoneuroimmunology was born. The interplay between thought, emotion, belief, imagery and biochemical process had been revealed. The doors of discussion had been opened and they would not be closed again.

In the last twenty years, Mind/Body Medicine has earned its place in the pantheon of modern scientific thought in the United States (thanks to the efforts of Candace Pert at the National Institutes of Health, Carl and Stephanie Matthews Simonton in the field of guided imagery, and the persistence of innumerable researchers with both creative talent and the data to match, complemented by such articulate popular thinkers as Deepak Chopra, Larry Dossey, Andrew Weil and others). Once greeted with ridicule, mind/body medicine has now gained the acceptance and piqued the curiosity of those with the funding for continued research and schooling.

The world has opened up to this concept as well. At the University of Heidelberg, Germany, Yugoslav psychologist Ronald Grossarth-Maticek conducted a ten-year study on 1,300 Yugoslavs with no previous medical diagnosis. Based entirely on what he knew of their personalities and emotions, Grossarh-Maticek was able to predict their deaths from cancer (for those with repressed emotions and hopelessness) or heart disease (for those with hostility and aggression) with statistically significant accuracy.

In fact, the power of the mind to intervene outside the body has been demonstrated in studies of what is known as non-local healing. In his best-selling books (*Healing Words, Prayer Is Good Medicine, Reinventing Medicine*, and the latest *One Mind: How Our Individual Mind is Part of a Greater Consciousness and Why it Matters*, an among many others) Larry Dossey, M.D., provides a detailed review of the studies in the power of words and thought in the healing process and discusses experiments with notable outcomes involving prayer for AIDS patients as well as patients with advanced heart disease.

Many insurance and health plans have begun to promote affiliations with and reimbursement for the services of "holistic practitioners," knowing that people are seeking solutions in alternative treatments and are finding them there in increasing numbers. It has also not escaped their attention that enlisting the mind early in the process can save money and reduce their customers' suffering. In the *American Journal of Health Promotion*, Dr. Wallerstein (1992) makes the case that a sense of powerlessness or "the lack of control over one's destiny emerges as a broad-based risk factor for disease." And it has become common knowledge that the "type A" personality, which is not much more than a composite of personality traits—beliefs, thoughts, and emotions as expressed behaviorally—has a much higher propensity for serious medical illness. When researchers Lawler and Schmied at the University of Tennessee studied a group of female secretaries, they found that the Type A woman had a higher blood pressure, heart rate, and frontalis EMG as she engaged in a series of work-related tasks. Overall reactivity was not related to Type A behavior so much as it was related to stress levels and powerlessness.

In his article in the *Journal of the American Medication Association,* "Why Patients Use Alternative Medicine," John A. Astin of the Stanford University School of Medicine expresses the belief that it is the transformational aspect of alternative health care that appeals to most who choose it. "They find in [alternative therapies] an acknowledgement of the importance of treating illness within a larger context of spirituality and life meaning," he writes.

By not making the illness something the body just randomly "got," and therefore something to be excised or dismissed with a pill, but rather a message about who we are and how we might live differently, we step up to the plate and our lives are restored to us.

Consider your own experience. How do you know you're angry? How do you know you're sad? Do you see an image in your mind? Do you feel, as most people do, a sensation somewhere in your body first? Some people experience anger as a kick somewhere in the solar plexus (an activation, probably, of the adrenals). Others feel it as a tightening throat or a flushed face or a revved-up heartbeat. However you experience them, emotions are not just mental constructs—they are physical in the fullest sense of the word. Candace Pert, PhD, former Chief of the Section on Brain Biochemistry of the Clinical Neuroscience Branch of the National Institute of Mental Health (NIMH) explained the reason that you feel your feelings in your body this way: "Your body is your subconscious mind."

Our responses to the world around us—electrochemically, physically, and emotionally—are based on a complex and intimate interrelationship of internal and external stimuli. An internal stimulus could be a memory, a fear, a thought, or a sensory response, and an external stimulus could be environmental, cultural, or situational.

In mind/body medicine, your interpretation of an event may be as important to your well being as the event itself. In his book, *Unconditional Life,* Dr. Deepak Chopra cites the example of two people riding on the same roller coaster. The rider who is terrified creates stress hormones, which over time will cause his immune system to weaken. The rider who is exhilarated by the roller coaster ride produces a flood of chemicals, among them interferon and interleukin, that strengthen his immune system. In each case the ride was the same; it was only the interpretation that differed. And it was that *perception*—that the ride was a life-threatening or a thrilling experience—that triggered the production of chemicals that could compromise or promote health.

There are many consequences of this realization, but they are particularly significant for people suffering from acute or chronic trauma, physical, life-threatening or chronic illness, and emotional distress. If how we react to an event is at least as important as that event itself, when people are in an accident or a crisis or when they are emotionally upset, their inner response will stimulate—or fight—their own self-healing mechanism. What's more, as Joan Borysenko, Ph.D., notes, the "body cannot tell the difference between the events that are actual threats to survival and events that are present in thought alone." The memory of being mugged produces the same racing heartbeat, sweaty palms, the same shower of adrenaline, as the event itself.

Mind/body medicine, which includes psychoneuroimmunology, neurolinguistics and medical hypnosis, sees the human being as a complex network of energy. In her book *The Quantum Self,* physicist and philosopher Danah Zohar writes, "The mind/body duality in man is a reflection of the wave/particle duality, which underlies all that is. In this way, human being is a microcosm of cosmic being." Mind and body are same thing, so much so that having two distinct words for them is misleading. They are inextricably interrelated. Perhaps before too long a new word will emerge that would more properly reflect our true natures.

Whether we see it as a new word or an old truth, most leaders in the field agree: we express thought and feeling not just in our minds, but in our *bodies,* and we manifest physical illness or chemical imbalance not just in our bodies, but in our *minds.* If it is true that "we are what we eat," it may be even more accurate to say that, "we are what we *believe* we're eating." The line Descartes drew between our minds and our bodies once literally cut us off at the neck. Fortunately, that line has been loosened and new boundaries have been drawn that stretch far out into horizon, leading us into knowledge and understanding we are only beginning to imagine.

**Spontaneous Remissions**

In both of our clinical practices we have seen serious, even terminal illnesses simply disappear as belief systems or thoughts changed. Spontaneous remissions are among the most fascinating phenomena in medicine. These are said to occur when a patient recovers from a serious disease with no perceivable clinical intervention. We hear about them all the time in the lunchroom, in the line at the supermarket, at family gatherings. "I knew this woman," some affable stranger will comment, "and she was just in the worst shape. She had cancer for a year and was fighting it with chemo and radiology and any alternative treatments she could find. The doctors told her that they just couldn't do any more for her and sent her home. Well she just wouldn't hear of it, she was too busy, she said to me. She had children to care for and a garden to tend and a job to do and she just had no time to die. Do you know that six months later, when she went back for a check up, the cancer was gone? Isn't that just amazing?"

Yes, it is. And medical doctors like Andrew Weil (*Spontaneous Healing*), Deepak Chopra and Larry Dossey are writing the books that change, as St. Augustine said, what we know of nature, so we can begin to see the role we play in our own healing. It is said that the two most amazing things about living beings is that they have the ability to reproduce themselves and the ability to repair themselves.

In an October 26, 2009 article in the New York *Times* entitled, *Cancers Can Vanish Without Treatment, But How?*, Dr. Barnett Kramer, associate director for disease prevention at the National Institutes of Health explains that the old idea that cancer was a linear process, destined to go in only one direction is being modified. "Cells need the cooperation of surrounding cells and even," he said, "'the whole organism, the person,' whose immune system or hormone levels, for example, can squelch or fuel a tumor." The same article reported a study in Canada of people with kidney cancer that had spread throughout their bodies. "As many as 6 percent who received a placebo had tumors that shrank or remained stable. The same thing happened in those who received the therapy, leading the researchers to conclude that the treatment did not improve outcomes." (http://www.nytimes.com/2009/10/27/health/27canc.html?_r=1&em)

The article does not answer the "why" in the headline, but others have recognized for years that in some people, diseases come and then go by themselves. One night in 1979 over dinner, Brendan O'Regan, of the Institute of Noetic Sciences, asked cancer researcher Caryle Hirshberg what he knew about spontaneous remission. Hirshberg replied that tumors in his animals frequently simply went into remission. Sparked by this dinner conversation to conduct a search of the literature on the subject, the two men discovered there was very little to be found. O'Regan had already been thinking of developing a project to examine why some people were "really healthy"—the healthy elderly, people with exceptional immune systems, people who never went to doctors—in light of the two systems of the body described by Norman Cousins: "the belief system" and "the healing system." If such a thing as "the healing system" existed, O'Regan had wondered, how did one research it? Then he realized that people who recovered without a rational, medical explanation, from life-threatening diseases—that is, people whose illnesses went into spontaneous remissions—might hold the answer.

Since that time, The Institute of Noetic Sciences, in a project led by O'Regan, has published the results of its search through more than 3,500 references, from more than 800 journals in 20 languages, assembling the largest database of medically reported cases of spontaneous remission in the world.

## The Embodied Mind

In an article in *Harvard's Mental Medicine Update (Vol. III, No.1, 1994)* it was estimated that 80 percent of office visits to physicians are stress-related. *Four patients out of every five!* We are the only known species who dies on schedule: more people die on Monday between 8 and 9 in the morning than at any other time and day of the week. Why is that? Could it have anything to do with the stress of going to work? And how do we explain the data showing how death peaks in Christians the day after Christmas and in Chinese people the day after Chinese New Year? These findings have been echoed in the research of Kroenke and Mangellsdorf, published in the *American Journal of Medicine*, who found that in less than 16 percent of the clinical cases reviewed were the problems caused solely by a biological problem. They concluded that over 70 percent of the symptoms reported were related to psychosocial factors.

The late Candace Pert, PhD was one of the major forces in the growing acceptance of mind/body medicine. A brilliant scientist, Dr. Pert was one of the discoverers of opiate receptors in the brain, as well as many other peptide receptors in the brain and elsewhere in the body. Her groundbreaking work led to a new understanding of what she calls "the biochemical correlates of emotions" and the "intercellular communication through the brain and body." When Bill Moyers, in his PBS series *Healing & The Mind*, asked Dr. Pert whether anger was physical or mental, she responded, "It's both! That's what's so interesting about emotions. They're the bridge between the mental and the physical or the physical and the mental. It's either way."

Pert's work illuminates this connection as no other research has. Where at first she focused on endorphins (our endogenous painkillers), later she reported that throughout the entire intestinal tract, perhaps throughout the whole body, certain white blood cells (monocytes) play a pivotal role in the immune system. These cells not only have receptors for various chemicals that control mood in the brain, but they also manufacture the substances that control our moods.

There is an extraordinary aspect to these discoveries. Whereas our previous ideas supported the reductionist paradigm (the chemicals of neuro-transmission are limited to the cranium, and the mind and body are literally kept apart by a blood-brain barrier), now we find these monocytes traveling all over the body. Once considered quite limited in their scope, these white blood cells have been proven to have the intelligent complexity of brain cells. The implication, according to Dr. Pert, is that, rather than being located just in the brain, the mind is "part of a communication network throughout the body."

Now we can begin to understand how the mind takes part in so many physiological decisions and outcomes. Pert explained, for example, that the AIDS virus, which uses the same receptor as a neuropeptide, can enter a cell when the receptor is available due to low neuropeptides, a situation that fluctuates with our emotions. "So our emotional state will affect whether we'll get sick from the same loading dose of a virus," she said, concluding, *"Emotional fluctuations and emotional status directly influence the probability that the organism will get sick or be well."* (Italics, ours.)

We think of "thought" or "consciousness" as being housed in the brain. But these neuropeptides, released during different emotional states, occur throughout the body, including the immune system. Emotions, previously considered isolated psychological or literary events (good for poets and analysts, but having no real bearing on medical science), are now seen as interwoven and intimately connected with specific chemical processes throughout the entire body, not just the brain.

### Belief, Placebos and The True Power of Verbal First Aid

What does this mean to us in terms of Verbal First Aid? It means that what we see affects us. What we hear affects us. What we feel affects us. And what we believe affects us–not just in our minds, but in our bodies—especially in a critical situation, when every image in our minds has an acute and immediate impact.

Nothing demonstrates this quite so simply or dramatically as the placebo effect. A placebo is a substance, like a sugar pill, that is not expected to cause a medical effect in the body. When given with by an authority figure such as a doctor, with the suggestion that it will cure something, there are often amazing results. A placebo is considered "simply" a psychological influence, but it has exquisitely real physiological effects, which can often be measured.

In his book, *Placebo-Effect Healing: The Power & Biology of Belief*, Dr. Herbert Benson, MD, explores the nature of the placebo effect and marvels at how the medical community ignores the true significance of this effect, which is *self-healing and the ability of a person to affect his or her physiological well being with just a thought*. Beyond the usually accepted 33 percent effectiveness of a placebo, Benson reports that the suggestion of healing plus a little sugar pill has been "effective in approximately 70 percent of cases of angina pectoris, bronchial asthma, herpes simplex [which is a virus], and duodenal ulcer."

Deepak Chopra, in *Creating Health*, remembers a study in which a group of patients with bleeding ulcers were given what their doctors told them was the "most potent current drug for treating ulcers." It worked beautifully in more than 70 percent of the cases. Another group, however, was told that the drug was "only experimental and therefore unknown in its efficacy." It was effective in stopping only 25 percent of the bleeding ulcers. As it turned out, both groups had taken a placebo. The variable in this study was the therapeutic suggestion. Dr. Chopra goes on to make the real point: *"If we look ahead far enough, we can see that placebos may be the best medicine of all."*

Placebos work through the release of neurotransmitters in the same way that a thought does. In essence, the placebo's active agent is not the doctor but the patient's thought process. Our ulcers go away because we believe they will. Our beliefs, our thoughts, create the cascade of chemicals necessary for healing. They can go so far as to actually change the reality of a drug's clinically proven action, as they did in one study cited by Chopra. In it, patients were relieved of nausea when given a pill they were told was a powerful anti-nausea drug. In reality, the pill was designed to *induce* nausea.

You don't need a study to see the placebo effect. It is at work around us all the time. We remember one woman who had reached for a non-narcotic sleep aid in her medicine cabinet and by accident took a couple of Echinacea capsules, not knowing what they were. Within a half-hour she was so drowsy she dropped off to sleep on the couch with the TV on and people talking around her.

One reason the placebo effect has not been studied more is because it cannot be manufactured and marketed. There's no profit in it. When you tell someone it's "just a placebo," you are reflecting the negative stance of a medical environment that has emphasized pharmacology and surgery as the primary if not exclusive treatment modalities for the last 100 years. Yet, over and over again, studies and life experiences show us that what we believe, what we think, and what we feel is manifested in our bodies.

For our purposes in Verbal First Aid, the implication is striking: **Suggestion can be a formidable healing tool.** The pill might be nothing but sugar, and the inhaler could contain nothing but saline solution, but our minds and bodies, having visualized a positive (or negative) outcome, can make that sugar or salt water a potent force. In fact, the body, believing it has taken a medication that relieves pain, can actually release its own painkillers—endorphins, according to a study at the University of Michigan published in the *Journal of Neuroscience* in 2005. As researchers using the latest imaging devices report, whether we actually look out at a scene or just visualize it with closed eyes, the same areas in the brain become active.

As we suggested earlier, these notions are not really "new" at all. They are older than Hippocrates, the father of western medicine, who said, "A patient who is mortally sick may yet recover from his belief in the goodness of his physician." Our perceptions, thoughts, and feelings were acknowledged in the healing process thousands of years ago.

## Medical Uses of Guided Imagery and Visualization

As early as the 1920's, studies were being done by Dr. Edmund Jacobson to measure muscular contractions. He had patients visualize activities such as running or swimming, and then was able to measure the heightened activity of the muscle, *simply in response to the **thought** of exercise.*

In 1971, Dr. Carl Simonton, a radiologist at the University of Texas, documented a striking example of the power of mental images. He was treating a patient with advanced, terminal throat cancer. The patient weighed 98 lbs. and his odds for survival were only 50 percent. Weak and severely ill, he still needed radiation. But Simonton knew that it was very unlikely that the patient would survive it. Desperate, Simonton and his wife Stephanie Matthews-Simonton , a psychologist, investigated biofeedback. After discussions with Drs. Joe Kamiya and Elmer Green, of the Menninger Clinic, who explained that using relaxation techniques, one could picture and imagine a desired goal to have it occur in the body, the Simontons decided to give visualization a try. They asked the patient to *see* or form a mental image of his immune system as white blood cells successfully attacking the cancer as he received the radiation. The patient saw it as snow gradually covering a black rock, until it was gone. The result was a total remission.

Dr. Dabney Ewin, the renowned surgeon and professor at Tulane University's Medical Center, has been using therapeutic suggestion at the Burn Unit for many years. He recounts one case in which a man was severely burned by an explosion and admitted to the hospital with had third degree burns. Ewin immediately gave the man suggestions that set his mind to remembering experiences of being *cool and comfortable.* By imagining packing the afflicted area with snow or ice, for example, the patient could feel numb, which kept the body from sending histamines that cause swelling. By the second day, the intern who examined the patient claimed he could only diagnose second-degree burns. The man's healing time was remarkably short, and he never developed the swelling that so often impedes progress with burns. He was out of the hospital in six weeks.

A 1994 study conducted at the Montreal Heart Institute showed that heart attack survivors suffering from major depression have three to four times the risk of dying within six months as compared to non-depressed survivors, making depression as great a mortality risk factor as degree of heart failure or history of a previous heart attack.

At Ohio University, a study on heart disease was conducted in which rabbits were fed toxic, high cholesterol diets to block their arteries. The results started to come in as expected, with all the requisite symptoms. However researchers were puzzled to discover that one of the trial groups experienced 60 percent fewer symptoms. They examined the physiology of the rabbits and found nothing. What could be the variable? They finally discovered that the student whose job it had been to feed the rabbits had a soft spot for his charges, and always stopped to pet them. That was the only significant difference. The scientists repeated the study a number of times, adding the petting as a controlled variable and found the same results. The rabbits who were petted seemed to gain enhanced immunity.

How does this work? If images have this much power, if suggestions for a cool and comfortable environment can help inhibit the unwanted autoimmune response responsible for complications and edema in burn patients, and if a caring touch can indeed help to lower a rabbit's susceptibility to high cholesterol, what is happening? What mechanism is at work?

**The Complex Mechanism**

Cellular biologist Bruce Lipton, Ph.D., is challenging the notion that our genetic inheritance is fixed at birth. Since 1953, biologists have assumed that DNA "controls" life. In multicellular animals, the organ that "controls" life is known as the brain. In a cell, if the gene were the control, the nucleus would be the equivalent of the cell's brain, they thought. In his work, Lipton discovered that cells could live for months without their nucleus continuing to behave and react to the environment. What then, if not the genes, was controlling the cell's behavior? Recognizing that genes cannot turn themselves off and on, he concluded that rather than running the show, DNA simply responds by making choices based on our *perception* of the environment. This happens, he believes, through the cell membrane. Built into the membrane are special proteins called Integral Membrane Proteins (IMPs), which come in receptors and effectors. They regulate what crosses into the cell. According to Lipton, "Research clearly reveals the regulatory influence that electromagnetic fields have on cell physiology. Pulsed electromagnetic fields have been shown to regulate virtually every cell function, including DNA synthesis, RNA synthesis, protein synthesis, cell division, cell differentiation, morphogenesis and neuroendocrine regulation."

These findings acknowledge that biological behavior can be controlled by *invisible* energy forces, which include thought. Because the structure of our bodies is defined by our proteins, and because the binding or releasing of regulatory proteins is directly controlled by environmental signals, how we perceive the world and threats to us actually shapes our biology. Cells respond to perception by activating either *growth* or *protection* behavior programs, Lipton believes. If our perceptions are accurate, the resulting behavior will be life enhancing. If we operate from "misperceptions" or fears, our behavior will be inappropriate and will jeopardize our vitality by compromising our health. "What happens," he asks, "if a cell experiences a stressful environment but does not have a gene program (behavior) to deal with the stress? It is now recognized that cells can 'rewrite' existing gene programs in an effort to overcome the stressful condition. These DNA changes are mutations." A gene cannot turn itself on, he contends.

But the environment in which it functions can signal that a change is needed: if we perceive (or even misperceive) an environment to be stressful and therefore go into "protection" mode, our bodies, down to our genes, respond to accommodate the ambient stressors.

What this means is that health is a reflection of the perception of the environment. Beliefs are translated into chemistry and chemistry is translated by the system. **Ultimately what this means is that what we think and feel literally changes our genes and our destiny.** There is, it seems, no immutable control panel. We are literally a part of the world around us. The life within is the life without. As the saying goes, "The scientists climbed the mountain and found the mystics waiting there."

Using Verbal First Aid with those who are in emergency situations, frightened, or seriously ill means understanding that what you say and do in their presence can affect that inner response directly. Knowing this, you can use your communications to create a healing or calming effect in the moment, and one that can change the outcome for the better.

**The Anatomy of Verbal First Aid**

The brain is technically considered part of the *nervous system,* which is divided into the *central nervous system* (CNS—the brain and the spinal cord) and the *peripheral nervous system* (PNS—made up of the somatic nervous system and the autonomic nervous system). The *autonomic nervous system* (ANS) conveys sensory impulses from the blood vessels, the heart and all of the organs in the chest, abdomen and pelvis through nerves to various parts of the brain (mainly the medulla, pons and hypothalamus). The term *autonomic* implies that these impulses often do not reach our consciousness, and that, in response to environmental conditions in the body and mind (e.g., changes in body temperature, injury, stress), they elicit largely automatic or reflex responses in the heart, the vascular system, and all the organs of the body. The ANS regulates heart rate, respiratory rate, digestion, hormonal production, balance and more.

The ANS that is the part of our brain that responds during an emergency is also the part that responds to visual images and vivid, emotionally-laden verbal descriptions. There are two components to the ANS: the sympathetic and the parasympathetic nervous systems, which are the keys to mind/body inter-connectivity. When the body is relaxed and peaceful, the parasympathetic system creates balance, harmony, and healing. This includes moderating the heart and respiratory rate and regulating blood pressure. When we feel threatened, the sympathetic system takes over and orders adrenaline to be dispersed, initiating fight or flight readiness, accelerating the heartbeat, increasing respiration, and dilating the pupils. Many stress researchers claim that over-activation of this system taxes the body and works to lower immunity, thereby facilitating disease. Although our *fight-or-flight* response was part of an excellent design—to give us a surge of energy to escape threats such as saber tooth tigers in the wild—without the *all clear* signal, the tiger never goes away. Today we're faced with constant traffic, bills to pay, crime, the economy, the threat of terrorism, not to mention natural disasters. The stress this produces costs us dearly in vital energy.

The cerebral cortex is responsible for the functions of thought, voluntary movement, language, reasoning and perception and it is often divided into what we commonly call the right and left brains— the left for linear, logical thinking (and, some say, for dealing with the *outside world*), the right for images and non-verbal thought (and the *inner world*). The right brain is also connected with the limbic system (our emotional life), the hypothalamus (which regulates the immune system and body chemistry) and the pituitary gland (which handles metabolic process).

So, roughly speaking, perceptions come either from the outer or inner world. In either case, neurons fire in the cerebral cortex and images form in the brain, causing reactions through the limbic system, the hypothalamus, and the pituitary gland. Whether the parasympathetic or sympathetic nervous system is activated depends on whether the interpretation is peaceful or upsetting. Whatever our interpretation, the adrenal glands will respond accordingly. The resulting nervous system and endocrine changes will affect every single cell in the body.

## Choosing the Healing Response

When people have been burned in a fire, when they are having a heart attack, suffering from a fall or serious abrasion, when something in the inner or outer world goes terribly wrong, often their first reaction is no reaction. Odd as this may seem to you, it is very common. Like a deer at the water's edge frozen by the scent of lion and waiting for an indication from the herd leader as to where to run, we initially hesitate in our reaction to a threat, waiting for direction. Dr. Donald Trent Jacobs, author of *Patient Communication For First Responders and EMS Personnel: The First Hour Of Trauma* calls this natural protective mechanism a "primitive survival function" and says, "It makes sense that it is initiated in the limbic system, the oldest part of the brain." For perhaps as long as an hour, we suspend judgment in a catastrophe and try to figure out what to do on the basis of our understanding of the situation. If a strong voice comes along and says "duck!!!" or "run!" or "lie down," generally we do. If no one comes along to tell us what to do, or explain what is going on, we resort to our memories, real or imagined–as seen in a movie or read in a book. We dredge up emotions appropriate to the real or imagined magnitude of the event and our bodies are flooded with fight-or-flight chemicals.

Many people in Los Angeles reacted in just this way to the Earthquake of 1987. They had been exposed to so much hype about "The Big One," that when the earth finally did quake, even though they were unhurt, they had measurable physiological reactions to the event, generated by imagination, fear, and confusion. Within four hours of the event, blood taken from people who experienced the quake showed an increase in killer cells, implicating the involvement of the immune system. Moreover, the earthquake never rocked the ground under several people it killed—they literally died of fright, their fears having led to fatal heart attacks.

The point in Verbal First Aid is to help manage just that sort of response so that it facilitates healing. Researchers have found that after the adrenal glands have been mobilized to release epinephrine/norepinephrine and stimulate the fight or flight response, once the threat has been nullified the adrenals send out cortisol to silence the alarm and give the "All's well." In traumatic stress, mobilization persists and cortisol is not released in sufficient quantities to halt the adrenal response. Studies have shown that individuals with post-traumatic stress disorder have reduced cortisol levels. The limbic system seems to be responsible for assessing the situation. If it perceives a reasonable escape, it stimulates the flight response. If it assesses that there is no way to run, but a good chance to defend oneself, it will initiate the fight response. However, if there is no hope of either one, or if we have no automatic program to deal with this situation and fall back on, it will choose a third option: freeze.

In the terrible hours in the Twin Towers on September 11, 2001, many people inadvertently found themselves choosing that option. They stayed in place, frozen and leaderless. As Amanda Ripley wrote of the psychology of people in crises (How to Get Out Alive in TIME Magazine, April 25, 2005), "People in peril experience remarkably similar stages. And the first one–even in the face of clear and urgent danger–is almost always a period of intense disbelief. ... In the case of the Twin Towers, at least 135 people who theoretically had access to open stairwells–and enough time to use them–never made it out... Most of us become incredibly docile."

In the freeze response, time is slowed down, fear is diminished and pain is dulled. It is an acute and vivid altered state, which may, according to Babette Rothschild, author of *The Body Remembers*, increase chances for survival, especially if the stress is an attack by a predator. Those who have survived bear attacks have reported this feeling of being "out of body," as do survivors of serious car accidents or critical incidents.

Once the trauma has passed, even if all we can do physically is wait for the ambulance or sit with the person in the waiting room, there is a great deal we can say to help the parasympathetic aspect of the autonomic nervous system kick in so the person can begin the healing process. As we discussed earlier with regard to placebos, a simple suggestion ("this pill stops asthma attacks") can have profound physical consequences.

Therapeutic suggestion, visualizing, and belief can all contribute to that feeling of *calm* so necessary for healing to begin. Sometimes simply allowing frightened accident victims to feel they are cared for and then helping them to visualize a place they'd *rather be*, can generate that carpet of calm in which neuropeptides can communicate healing rather than fear.

Thoughts can heal and thoughts can harm. No matter what the circumstances of our environment may be, what we believe can positively or negatively affect our health and well being.

**Power to Reach the Unconscious**

In *Love, Medicine & Miracles*, Bernie S. Siegel, M.D. writes about his experiences using words in the operating room and their effect on people who are under anesthesia. Operating on a young man who had experienced much trepidation before the procedure, Dr. Siegel surprised his colleagues by telling his patient to bring his pulse to 83. During the next few minutes, without any other medications, the patient's pulse came right down to 83 and remained there.

On another occasion, when the heart of one of his patients, a very obese young man, stopped, and the anesthesiologist had given up, Siegel said out loud, "Harry it's not your time. Come on back." The cardiogram at once began to show electrical activity and the young man eventually made a full recovery. Siegel believes it was this verbal message that made the difference between life and death for Harry. Dr. Siegel's experiences are a reminder that what we say can have a profound impact, whether the victim or patient is conscious or not. They also serve to underscore the point that during a period of crisis (which includes operations and accidents and the on-going trauma of serious physical and emotional illness) the autonomic nervous system is particularly open to suggestion. In the next chapter on the "Healing Zone," we explain how to recognize and work with this altered state so that you can help make small *miracles* happen where—and when—they are needed most.

**Verbal First Aid Key – Chapter 2**
**The Evidence**

- We are greater than the sum of our parts: The mind and body are in fact one.

- The effect of imagery and thought on our health is documented by the National Institutes on Health.

- Candace Pert's discovery of neuropeptides on monocytes (white blood cells) demonstrates the importance and potency of thought and feeling in physical wellness.

- Placebo =effect healing is really self-healing with just a thought. Studies show that the body may produce its own chemicals in the belief that they've been administered.

- An Ohio University study links caring touch with lower cholesterol.

CHAPTER THREE

# THE HEALING ZONE: RECOGNIZING AND FACILITATING ALTERED STATES

*"What lies behind us and lies before us are small matters compared to what lies within us."*
– *Ralph Waldo Emerson*

There are at least two times every day that we all enter into *altered* states: when we slide into that early sleep we call twilight, and when we awaken in that soft, heavy time just before our first morning stretch. These are what many people refer to as "delicious" moments: a not-here, not-there, heavy-yet-light, safe-and-simultaneously-open feeling. Perhaps you have had the experience of being so totally absorbed in a novel or a creative project that you lose all track of time, and the world around you seems to disappear. Perhaps one Sunday you're driving on the highway when you start to mull over a conversation you had with your date the night before. Suddenly, you focus on the road only to find yourself halfway to work. "What am I doing?" you wonder, shaking your head as you make a u-turn.

Milton Erickson, M.D., frequently wrote about the "common everyday trance" that naturally occurs to everyone, all throughout the day. These trances are so commonplace that we move in and out of these altered states and barely pay them any mind. Indeed, much of the time we enjoy them. You are driving to work and you hear a song that reminds you of someone you knew twenty years ago. Suddenly the two of you are driving down a country road, smelling that signature cologne or perfume, laughing at the corny jokes that used to make you laugh. You smile. You're still driving to work, but you're living twenty years in the past.

**Real Toads in Imaginary Gardens**

Most of us relish our "altered" moments, and consciously or not we see them as our special safe times, our "beach-feelings," our creative reservoirs. The writer John Gardner called this state—when we are lost in our own creativity, when we conjurer up poet Marianne Moore's "real toad in an imaginary garden"—the "fictive dream." In that state, like mystics, we lose touch with ordinary time and space. We can read about the scent of blackberry in a teacup and the rain tapping on the roof and be transported forty years back. Once awakened by the dream, we long for the grace of it, and though we seek it, we value it most when it surprises us.

Writers eager to bring the dream alive again do strange things to evoke the muse. In *A Natural History of The Senses* Diane Ackerman reports that the great poet, T.S. Eliot, "preferred writing when he had a head cold. The rustling of his head, as if full of petticoats, shattered the usual logical links between things and allowed his mind to roam." She also tells us that Benjamin Franklin brought the bathtub to America in the 1780's primarily because he found inspiration for his writing by soaking in it. Ackerman discloses that she herself lays a pine plank across the sides of her tub and writes in a bubble bath for hours. She enjoys the lightness and freedom she feels when both her body temperature and the water temperature are "one."

**The Altered State as a Portal To Healing**

These alterations of consciousness, what clinicians call *altered states* and what artists call the *fictive dream*, can serve as portals to what we call the *healing zone.* In those moments in which time flies or we're lost in reverie, our attention is so finely tuned, so focused and narrow, that we are able to perceive both inner and outer realities differently.

The altered state, in and of itself, is a blank slate. While what we have been describing is the pleasant side of this condition, it also occurs spontaneously in moments of stress, shock, confusion, trauma, fear—whenever the ordinary course of events and expectations are suddenly tossed upside down—and we lose our psychological footing. At those times, we literally go into neutral, awaiting input. If we do not receive it from outside, we provide it from within. Often, by default, we call upon earlier experience, old fears and unhealed traumas, and that response, leading us farther and farther away from healing, is not in our best interests.

Hans Selye's research in 1974 bore this out when he showed what happens to our neurochemistry in moments of great stress and how our interpretation of the events affects our performance. He was able to measure the differences in the chemicals our bodies made, depending on whether we saw events as challenging and stepped up to the task, or felt overwhelmed by stress.

For most people, a medical emergency or an emotional crisis is experienced as a tremendous stress, sometimes as a threat to our very survival. As a result, stress hormones are released. The question becomes, then, what can do to help ourselves through it and begin the process of healing.

David Cheek, M.D., an international lecturer on the importance of hypnotic communication in medical emergencies, studied cases of severe stress for over 25 years. He concluded, as have many other clinicians and researchers, that **severe stress invariably causes an altered state**. When we are afraid, in pain, or shocked by grief, we revert to earlier moments of great stress, both in our minds and *in our bodies*. If our only guide through the experience is the trembling voice of our oldest fears and injuries, we are left with poor company.

Some people, particularly those who have been trained to think their ways through stressful situations (the "stress-hardy"—police, military, EMS, firefighters), go into a state called "auto-pilot" in which thinking is all they do and feelings are put all the way on the back burner. "I'm fine," is a typical autopilot response to a tragedy. Meanwhile they're frantically cleaning or can't stop working, terrified of the stillness that comes with down time. Other people go into shock and panic right away. Verbal First Aid is the balancing beam that turns a frightening, isolated, confusing moment into a moment of reassurance, comfort, and clarity so that healing may begin.

## The Choice: Traumatic Stress or Healing Zone

An altered state is like fertile soil. We can either plant healthy seeds that grow into fruit-producing plants, we can let the weeds overrun it, or we can let erosion wash it away in the storm. We can either say or do nothing, use our words and our presence to heal, or use our words to harm. We think the choice is clear. So does Lt. Colonel Dave Grossman, a former West Point Psychology Professor and Army Ranger.

As Lt. Col. Grossman describes it, when we are terribly frightened, we stop thinking with our forebrain (the part of us that analyzes, processes, communicates with language, and knows how to wait) and start operating with the midbrain, which is, after millions of years, still the same as the midbrain of a crocodile. The midbrain's primary function is to ensure survival, for which it relies on only several levels of experience: fear, aggression, avoidance of pain, sexuality, and hunger.

In extreme situations, particularly those generated by human conflict, the Lt. Col. says the "midbrain reaches up and takes hold of the forebrain. Afterwards there appears to be an immediate, neural 'shortcut' to the midbrain, which mobilizes the body for survival in response to any 'cue' associated with the traumatic incident. Increased heart rate, respiration, perspiration and a host of other physiological responses will occur for even the slightest of reasons, and sometimes for no discernible reason whatsoever."

There is no greater stimulus to learning than a trauma. What we learn from it, of course, depends to a great extent on what cues are given. Verbal First Aid becomes, then, critical—not only to facilitate healing in the present moment, but to give the cues that will record over the negative cues of the past and facilitate wellness in the future.

Among their patients, many therapists have seen the effects of what Lt. Col. Grossman calls *one-trial learning*, sometimes years after than the event itself, when a patient comes in with nightmares, flashbacks, a disrupted marriage, alcoholism. A recent study by C.A. Morgan III reports that symptoms of dissociation were prevalent in healthy subjects exposed to high stress, with up to 96% reporting symptoms. In another study on trauma and dissociation, authors Koopman and Spiegel report that "Stress associated with experiencing or witnessing physical trauma can cause abrupt and marked alterations in mental state." They explain that "people who experience a series of traumatic events may be especially vulnerable to a variety of dissociate states."

Apparently, when the midbrain takes hold of the forebrain, people are not only feeling the initial rush of terror, but the sense of losing control. Lt. Col. Grossman calls it a hijacking and claims that it can result in erratic, uncontrollable physiological reactivity. Our fear and our physiology become enmeshed in a cycle that sometimes becomes Post-Traumatic Stress Disorder (PTSD).

But Grossman contends that it doesn't have to be this way. "If, at the very beginning, we can teach the subject to control their autonomic, physiological arousal, then they can nip this whole process in the bud, stopping the vicious cycle of fear and anxiety before it consumes them." He suggests that, although autonomic responses are often automatic, "the bridge between the somatic and autonomic nervous system is breathing, and an increasing body of research and law enforcement experience indicates that if we teach the victim to control their breathing, then they can control their physiological arousal."

Imagine yourself behind a glass barrier. You are surrounded by it. You don't know how to get out. You are scared and alone. People move around you, but you can't reach them. The worst thoughts are racing through your mind. You don't know what to do. There seems to be no way out. Your heart is pounding. Your breathing is rapid, uneven, shallow. Then, gently and surely, a hand reaches through the glass and a calm voice says: "The worst is over. I'm going to help you. Take my hand and follow me."

Anxiety is truly the major culprit in trauma. How we fare both during and after a traumatic event—whether medical or emotional— depends in large degree on how we deal with our anxiety. Having something concrete to do, to say, to focus on, and having an authority to lead us to safety (whether physical or psychological) can turn the tide.

**Verbal First Aid: Choosing the Healing Zone**

Another recent piece of research demonstrated that patients who were in acute stress had higher levels of hypnotizability. Hypnosis itself is actually a range of altered states, and among its major components is suggestibility. As we slip into an altered state, especially one connected with stress, we are more receptive to suggestion—good or bad; we are more attuned to inner realities—good or bad; we are more visual and responsive to imagery—again, good or bad. What we hear we interpret literally. Although we move into and out of one kind of altered state or another all day, there are certain processes that spontaneously occur that let us know we have access to a healing zone. There are both physical and psychological characteristics that can serve as clues or guideposts. Because altered states provide a healing zone portal through which you can help a person in crisis or pain, they are invaluable in Verbal First Aid. The next sections are designed to show you how to recognize and how to facilitate that healing state.

## How to Recognize the Healing Zone

*Physical Signs of The Healing Zone*

1. *Unfocused, rambling speech.* The connection between thoughts and words has been disrupted. A person may speak unusually slowly or rapidly, or not at all; words and phrases may be repeated, yet seem empty of content.

2. *Tears and fluttering eyelids with eyes closed or partially closed.* Tears may form at the corners of the eyes. You may notice pupil dilation, as well. As people begin to shift their awareness, their eyelids may flutter. In addition, rapid eye movements under the eyelids may be seen.

3. *Breath changes.* A person's breathing may speed up, or slow down to a smooth, shallow rhythm.

4. *Pulse rate changes.* This can be seen most easily in the carotid artery in the neck, or if one has permission to touch the other person, it can be felt in the wrist.

5. *Muscle relaxation.* All muscle groups—especially in the face– may relax, sometimes accompanied by muscle twitching.

6. *Profound stillness.* Clinicians call this state "catalepsy." It is stillness resulting from deep absorption, commonly seen in fishermen, artists, musicians, writers, carpenters, accountants—indeed, in anyone who gets completely engrossed in some task.

*Psychological Symptoms of the Healing Zone*

1. *Time distortion.* Time slows down or speeds up dramatically. People in chronic pain, for example, may spend a great deal of time

feeling that time itself has betrayed them by slowing down. "When will this ever end?" may be a sign of time distortion. People in a medical emergency may experience the collapse of time, as if everything were happening at once, or feel time stretched out like a rubber band, as if they were moving in slow motion. We can use this time distortion to bring comfort and help with healing. "This medicine is so wonderful, it makes every hour seem like five minutes and we can be done before you even know it." Or "Count backwards from 10 to 1 and the closer you get to 1 the quicker you are starting to feel better."

2. *Selective awareness–seeing what we want to see.* Selective awareness—which happens all the time when we tune out the loud drone of the refrigerator but hear the tiniest floorboard creak in a room that should be empty—is another aspect of an altered state. Sometimes elderly or chronically ill people will insist you haven't done something that you have, in reality, done. "You never bring me juice when I ask for it," they will say, although you do so frequently. They may be suffering from selective awareness, remembering or registering only those things on which they are focused, in this case, perhaps, thirst (or a "thirst" for attention).

For another example let's go to a small town baseball green where a little league game is in progress. Fifteen seven-year-olds are playing for the Tiger Tails. It is the first game of the season and little Sean is at bat. He is so excited to have gotten his turn that when the ball comes too close, he forgets to step back and the ball slams into his hand, breaking his finger. Suddenly, for Sean, the only thing in the world is his agonizing pinkie. His mother, who knows Verbal First Aid, runs up when she hears his cry and holds him. "I'm here, Sean. Mommy's here to help. Let me see your hand." Sean howls. "Oh, I can see what's happening here. How about your other hand, Sean. How is that?" Sean is a little confused, but looks at his other hand, trying to see if it has been hurt. The moment he takes his attention away from the pained pinkie, he gets some pain relief. "Your foot," Mom continues. "Did the ball bounce off your foot? Are your feet okay?" At this point, Sean has sent his mind through his body on a mission of assessment. As he checks out other regions, he keeps his mind off his finger and continues to alleviate some distress.

We can only be conscious of so many things at a time. If you are focused on your foot, you cannot think of your broken finger. The same is true for emotional pain. How many times have you heard, "I can't think about that now, I'm too busy worrying about paying the bills."

3. *Age regression.* When people get that dreamy look and begin to reminisce, it is almost as if they were transported to another space and time. We recognize this in others, because we see it in ourselves. People often experience age regression in the presence of their parents: "I feel like I'm 10 years old every time I go back home for Thanksgiving." "I'm 45 years old, but when I feel sick, I want my mommy." Conversely, when we're young, we can feel positively ancient. Theresa, a 19-year-old with a long history of trauma, looked at her therapist with profound sadness, "I feel like I've lived two lifetimes already. I'm as weary as a 90-year-old."

Reminding people of times in which they were happier, stronger, more loving can bring those times into the present and, with them, some of the qualities they may have forgotten they had. When you encounter someone suffering emotional or physical distress, and you can facilitate a positive age regression, you can begin to use Verbal First Aid in remarkable ways.

4. *Sensory distortion.* In the healing zone we hear, see, feel, taste, and smell things differently, which can be particularly helpful with the alleviation of pain, whether acute or chronic. Clinicians experienced with this resource regularly assist their patients in developing anesthesia or altering the perceptions of particular parts of the body. This can be exceedingly important in a truly traumatic situation, when this ability can protect us from focusing on information that would impact us so negatively that it could further compromise recovery.

5. *Negative Hallucination.* Have you ever, in a panic, looked for something frantically, emptied your purse or pockets twenty-seven times and never seen the thing you were searching for, although it was there all the time? Clinically, this is called a *negative hallucination*, not seeing something that is actually there. Sometimes it is a very good thing not to see or hear things that could harm you.

Leslie was a passenger in a serious car accident in which the car rolled over several times and crashed into a pole. The driver was so shaken and stunned she could not even give the paramedics her name. Leslie, also in the front seat, knew that her head had hit the windshield and felt that her scalp and face were wet. She reached up and pressed her hand to her forehead. Then she withdrew her hand and looked at it. It looked fine, so she helped the emergency personnel, answering their questions, and got through the crisis. It was only later that she saw all the blood, received the stitches and realized the magnitude of her injuries. "I don't know," she says. "When I looked at my hand, I just didn't see *red*." She shakes her head. "If I had, I would have been horrified. I would have panicked. But for some reason, I just didn't see it."

6. *Dissociation.* This symptom of the healing zone can be seen in a young girl daydreaming in class during the last week of school. Although to the teacher the girl is seated firmly in her chair, the young girl is already smelling the fresh cut grass and pounding her new baseball mitt on her left hand, relishing the cheers as she catches the fly ball that signals the winning of the game. She is on the field *and* in the chair, enjoying what Dr. Michael Yapko calls a *parallel awareness* of both states. You know the state intimately if you have ever been forced to attend a long meeting, or if you've taken a long train ride and let your mind drift away as the train wheels clack rhythmically across hundreds of miles of endless, monotone plains of wheat. You are there and not there, able to respond to your physical environment should you need to, yet enjoying a respite somewhere far away.

This inborn capacity can be developed and utilized to access the healing zone. When people are dissociated, what we say to them may not register consciously or even be acknowledged, but we know it is being received.

7. *Literal or concrete interpretation.* What we hear when we are in an altered state comes through very literally, much the way a child might hear it. Our colleague Timothy Trujillo tells a funny story about going to dinner with a ten-year-old boy who had a headache. He whipped out a five-dollar bill and said, "I'll tell you what. I'll buy your headache for five dollars." The boy thought about it for a while and then grabbed the money. Then he considered the proposition saying, "Do you really want my headache?" "Well, not now," Trujillo said, "but I may want it sometime. But, anyway, it's mine now. You can't have it anymore." Within a few minutes, the boy looked up in surprise and said, "Hey, my headache's gone!" The words Trujillo had used were, "You can't have it any more." We say we *have* a headache, the boy had sold his, and so he literally could not *have* it anymore.

8. *Trance-logic.* As people move through those states of consciousness that lead them to the healing zone, they may be more likely to *suspend disbelief* much the way we do when we go to the movies and watch a person fly faster than a speeding bullet. We are able to accept as *true* that which may seem *illogical* in another, more analytic state.

This allows us to use visualization, as we will explain later, to change the body's responses or to provide pain relief. As you saw in the story in which Timothy Trujillo had the man with the broken leg imagine "doing the back stroke," that image provided pain relief because "water is buoyant," even though the man was lying on the shoulder of a dusty dirt road.

**How to Facilitate the Healing Zone**

In medical emergencies and trauma, it is exceedingly common for us to go into a suggestible altered state. In chronic illness, however, because of its ongoing nature, the traumatic state associated with it fluctuates, and as a result so do the opportunities to utilize the healing zone. We'd like to suggest some means by which you can encourage people into this state so that you, in turn, can make the suggestions that could improve their condition.

*Imagery*

From the time we are children we are encouraged to use our imaginations to *see* and *feel*—to experience—different places in our minds. This ability to use our imaginations or dream of another reality can be used to help transport people to the healing zone, as well.

Evidence that imagery has the effect of moving people into altered states has been demonstrated by the Mind Mirror, a piece of equipment designed in England by Dr. Maxwell Cade for the purpose of measuring the wavelengths of our various mental activities. Dr. Cade discovered that the depth of the relaxation response in both hypnotized and guided imagery subjects was a function of characteristics of the imagery itself and how the imagery was communicated. After receiving a brief word picture of 150-200 words, a majority of subjects were able to experience faster and deeper relaxation than subjects given traditional hypnotic inductions.

This indicates that helping people *go* somewhere in their minds, simply painting a scene for them that *takes them* somewhere they can feel relaxed and calm, can put them in the healing zone. The more rich the detail, the more you involve the senses, the more readily a person will follow you to the place you describe. "Wouldn't it be great to be back in Hawaii, right now? Those breezes, the way you could see them and hear them swaying through the trees. The whole place smells like flowers and perfumes…and those birds of every color—who even *knew* there were orange birds and purple birds and even fuchsias? And the fish, too, in those crystal clear waters, swimming between your feet in reds and yellows and stripes…."

*Story Telling*

This is a variation of the imagery transport process discussed above. As you will see in Chapter 9 on Physical Illnesses, this is a technique used often and brilliantly by Dr. Milton Erickson, a psychiatrist whose use of metaphor and story is legendary among psychotherapists.

Since the days when cavemen sat around a campfire and one of the men rose to tell of his hunt, or to boast of his courage in fending off a ferocious beast, we have been spellbound by story.

Judith Simon Prager and her husband, Harry Youtt, teach in the Writer's Program at UCLA Extension and always marvel at the effect that reading myths has on grown men and women. Tapping into archetypes, settling down into long ago's and far away's, the adults seem to almost visibly regress to childhood.

Something happens to all of us when a story is told, no matter how old or young we are. As the yarn is woven, the listener is captivated, as if led by curiosity and instinct to answer the question: "Does this story have something to do with my present predicament? Is it telling me something? How do I fit in here?" And if the story has a point or *moral*, even if it is unspoken, the unconscious mind *gets it*. There is a problem and a solution presented in every good story and our unconscious minds, ever in search of solutions for ourselves, listen to see how we can identify. We insert ourselves into that story. We *become* the boy on the back of the dragon, exhilarated as we fly through the air. We *suffer* as the hero making our way through the tortures of Hades. We *feel* the frustration of unrequited love and the *longing* of Dr. Zhivago. Imagine the benefits of this sort of mind-travel to those in need of medical treatment, especially when the story is laden with metaphors of healing, comfort, and love.

Sometimes the most healing thing we can do is let people know that they belong, that we appreciate them, that simply because they feel different, they are not alone and outcast. Barbara Brennan, the energy healer and former research scientist for NASA who wrote the book *Hands of Light*, says unequivocally that, "All suffering is caused by the illusion of separateness, which generates fear and self-hatred, which eventually causes illness."

When our clients express the feeling that they don't belong any-where, that they are outsiders and they believe themselves to be unwant-ed, we tell them the classic story of the Ugly Duckling. You remember…

A mother duck sits on her eggs and hatches a brood of cute little yellow ducks, all except for one. That one is gray and gawky. All the little ducklings laugh at him. As he sees his own reflection in the water and understands how different he is, he feels ashamed. As the others grow up, they honk neat little duck honks, but our hero makes a very strange, long, loud "Hooooonk." Again, they laugh at him.

Then, one day, as he is swimming alone, having given up on trying to fit in any longer, he comes upon the most beautiful birds he has ever seen, and they greet him and invite him to join them. He looks at his reflection in the water, then back at their babies and he understands. He's not an ugly duckling at all. He's a beautiful swan. What was wrong was that he just wasn't where he belonged, where he could be recog-nized for what he truly was.

Who hasn't dived into that story as a child and taken comfort from its suggestion that we are all beautiful and special when we are in our right place, where we belong.

Stories lead to the healing zone in the simple act of telling. The messages or suggestions embedded in them lead us further down the road to comfort or calm.

Memories, too, are a form of storytelling:

"Remember when grandma made those apple pies and left them to cool on the window ledge and grandpa took them and hid them for himself and told her he thought he'd seen a thief and she called the sheriff and…"

"Oh, for goodness sake, yes, I do. And the sheriff was in on it with grandpa the whole time. Oh, lord, do you remember how angry she was?"

Storytelling is easy to drop into ordinary conversation. "Once upon a time," and "a long time ago" were always great trigger phrases for us as children. As adults we're just as susceptible to "I know a man who…" or "Do you remember…" or "Did I ever tell you about the time…"

When telling a story, there are ways to hold the listener's attention and to help him or her stay in the healing.

1. *Using tone and phrasing.* It is important to keep our tone measured and clear, yet dramatic. When we get into the story, our tone and phrasing will naturally communicate it so that others feel it as well. Try to keep your voice low-pitched, as if telling them an important secret, though not too soft. It is perfectly all right if people have to strain just slightly to hear you. It forces them to focus.

2. *Pacing the person you are with.* We always have to be aware of what listeners are doing and to stay with them as well. This is the same principle we explain in more detail in later chapters on Rapport and Therapeutic Suggestion. Watch for cues of distraction or boredom, as well as signs that you're in the healing zone.

3. *Using descriptive detail.* Try to evoke all the senses—touch, smell, sight, hearing, taste. You could describe your experience at an elegant restaurant by saying, "Oh, wow, it was great!" But is this enough? Have you truly shared the experience? Or is it better to describe the way the linen napkins were laid across your lap with a flourish, the scent of fresh rosemary and basil that was growing in planters near your table, and the velvet caress of the wine on your tongue.

4. *Keeping the end of the story in sight.* What are you trying to convey to the person listening to you? There's nothing less interesting than a rambling tale with no focus and no relevance.

One woman we know found herself in a state of physical panic whenever she considered saying what she felt to the man in her life. She thought more about how he would react than about what she might say. She thought if she brought up her needs, she would rock the boat and he would leave. She literally lost herself in her fear. We painted the following word picture for her about how words spoken— as our Native American friends say, "in a good way"— reverberate in the world.

"Imagine a lake, still as glass, quiet and deep, filled with the reflections of the sky, the snow-capped mountains surrounding it, and an occasional bird, skimming its blue-green surface. Imagine dropping a penny into the lake along with a wish, watching it break the surface and sinking deeper, deeper past the fish and the dark tendrils of grass into the sand at the lake bottom. Notice the concentric circles that carry that intention, that wish out across the still lake, making a pattern in the world that changes everything for a time. Maybe the ripples *rock the boat* a little as they make their way across the lake's surface. Maybe they change the course of the boat with their flow. The circles emanate endlessly, carrying the wish that created them. Things will be calm again, but different, for the wish… the wish has a life of its own now."

This woman had been afraid of *hurting* someone with her words, afraid that her words would create the only ripples in an otherwise smooth lake. There were many ripples, as it turned out. She began to understand, unconsciously, that she could not and did not have to control every outcome or every ripple. To speak the truth with love was all she could do. It was, in essence, a serenity prayer in images. In a subtle way, these images drew a picture for her unconscious of its being all right if what she says or wishes "rocks" somebody else's "boat." That it may even "change the course of that boat." Finally, what remains is calm. In her altered state, these pictures suggested that she would not lose herself if she spoke her truth as if it were a penny cast into a lake. Later, she told us, something inside of her shifted. She was able to speak from her heart differently after that.

The repercussions of the words of the heart are both real and unfathomable.  Mother Theresa put it very well:

*"Kind words can be short or long to speak,*
*but their echoes are truly endless. "*

**Verbal First Aid Key – Chapter 3**
**The Healing Zone**

- Every day we enter an "altered state" at least twice: when we get up and when we go to sleep.

- Altered states are normal, ordinary events that lead us to the healing zone.

- Recognizing the Zone:

    o Physical Signs—unfocused speech, tears, fluttering eyelids, breath changes, pulse rate changes, muscle relaxation, and stillness.

    o Psychological Signs—time distortion, seeing what we want to see, age regression, sensory distortion, dissociation, increased responsiveness, literal or concrete interpretation, trans-logic.

    o Facilitating the Zone: Imagery, storytelling, tone and phrasing, selective attention.

PART TWO

# Heart To Heart Communication

# CHAPTER FOUR

# RAPPORT: THE FOUNDATION FOR HEALING COMMUNICATION

*"So when you are listening to somebody, completely, attentively,
then you are listening not only to the words, but also to the
feeling of what is being conveyed, to the whole of it, not part of it."*
–Jiddu Krishnamurti

Without *rapport*, effective communication is simply not possible. In simplest terms, rapport is a state in which a relationship of trust, compliance, and healthy expectation can be developed. It is understanding and a feeling of being understood. Just as you would never think of building a house without first putting in a foundation, you would not expect people to follow your suggestion without first having or establishing rapport. Healing communication takes place within the context of a relationship—even if it is an exceedingly brief one.

In this chapter we demonstrate the three steps for gaining rapport: getting centered, establishing alliance, and getting a contract. But before we show you how to gain rapport, let's explore how rapport works and why it is so crucial to any program that hopes to help those in need.

Rapport is empathy taken a step farther—you might say it's empathy in practice. Rapport builds a bridge to the victim from anyone who is trying to help, whether that person is the paramedic, or first responder to an accident scene, or a relative standing by the bedside of a chronically ill individual. Rapport opens a line to carry healing messages. Rapport is the foundation for effective Verbal First Aid.

When we present this training to professionals, we often start by asking them to close their eyes for a minute. Then we ask them the following questions. When was the last time you were hurt, angry, or wounded and terribly afraid? Where were you? Who else was there? What did they do? What helped? What made it worse? Although the situations vary wildly, many say what helped most was that the other person stayed calm and helped them focus on getting better and staying positive.

One survivor of the Oklahoma City bombing lay trapped under concrete and metal for many hours and suffered severe injuries, not to mention the mind-numbing sense of aloneness and fear she endured in the dark. When finally extricated from those hellish conditions, she explained to reporters that she wouldn't have made it had one particular rescue worker not stayed with her and held her hand, the only part he could reach or see, throughout. It was his presence, his soothing voice, the way he earned her trust—and most of all, the gentle, firm touch of his hand—from which she borrowed strength.

In relation to that "borrowed strength," James Coan, assistant professor of psychology and the neuroscience graduate program at the University of Virginia, conducted a study in which, "We found that holding the hand of really anyone, it made your brain work a little less hard in coping," adding that any sort of hand-holding relaxes the body. (*http://www.nytimes.com/2006/10/05/fashion/05hands.html?pagewanted=all*)

And hands are generally a safe and non-intrusive place to touch.

Almost invariably, trauma victims say that the worst thing someone can do is tell them, "Just relax," or "Hang on" without really listening to them. In one episode of the television series "Trauma One," one of the proliferating ER shows, a doctor could be overheard yelling "Chill, chill!" to a patient with six gunshot wounds. Needless to say, the patient did not "chill." He became increasingly agitated and the doctor became increasingly frustrated.

Remember Lily, the little girl whose parents unwittingly heightened her fear as they tried to help? ("Do we have to give her stitches? Oh, damn, not *stitches*!!") Both the way the adults related to the child and the suggestions they unintentionally provided undermined Lily's ability to remain calm. In contrast, the life-saving experience of the woman in the Oklahoma City bombing was attributable to the healing connection we know as rapport.

By now you've seen how what we communicate to each other (verbally and non-verbally), even in benign circumstances, has a profound effect. A smile, a gentle squeeze of the hand, an offer to help a stranger who, up until that very moment, has been having a miserable day, can change not only how we think and feel in a conscious way, but it can also have a marked influence on our limbic, nervous, endocrine, and cardiovascular systems. In addition, a foundation—an alliance—must be established for Verbal First Aid to be effective. Without rapport, suggestions for healing are not accepted as readily, possibly not at all. The greater the rapport, the more likely your suggestions will be internalized.

Once we establish rapport, we can go right ahead and say, "You can relax now," and people can comfortably comply. If there is no rapport, that suggestion can be annoying and counterproductive, and can even generate exactly the opposite response. You can probably recall numerous moments when someone told you, "Why don't you just relax," and you replied, "Why don't *you*!" *No* one relaxed.

What was missing in that interaction? Rapport. The person may not have had the authority, nor demonstrated the appropriate understanding or empathy. That person's "relax" meant, "I dismiss your feelings. I don't want to be bothered. Now go away."

Under all communication lies a subtext. Rarely do we communicate directly, even when we think we're saying what we mean. Words are the map, not the territory. As a result, what we say, what we think we said, and what the other person heard may be worlds apart.

For example, a simple, ordinary phrase, such as "Excuse me," may have dozens of subtexts:

"Pardon me, I need to get past you."
"Get out of my way. I'm coming through."
"May I interrupt?"
"What, are you kidding?"
"Who do you think you are?"
"I didn't hear you."
"How dare you?"
"Did I hear you say what I thought you said?"
"I know it's not my place, but..."
And the obvious:
"I'm sorry."

With the vast continuum of possibilities open to interpretation, when every word counts, rapport can create the subtext that says, "I am here for you and when you do as I say, we are working together to help you heal." In his bestseller, *Love, Medicine & Miracles,* Bernie S. Siegel, M.D., recognized the value of empathy in regard to his *exceptional patients,* those who seemed to heal themselves, by imagining the fear and pain his patients felt and then realizing that what he had to offer them was more than medical expertise and technical procedures. His partner, surgeon Dick Selzer, described what the empathetic physician brings to the healing by saying that it gathers like "the cry of certain solitary birds until it is a calling, a *resonance* between doctor and patient building to the moment when there may spring that profound courtesy that the religious call Love."

When we connect with others in that way, it makes room for miracles to happen.

In fact, having a "heart-to-heart" may be a more accurate description than the poets had imagined. The integrated research of Dr. Allan Schore "shows how areas related to social-emotional functioning in the right hemisphere of an emotionally healthy therapist's brain unconsciously induce healing structure and functional influences in the right hemisphere of the client's brain. The heart's electromagnetic field may be one of the ways these changes are induced since there are unmediated connections between the human heart and the right hemisphere." (http://insideoutfreedom.wordpress.com/2010/10/16/in-response-to-becoming-the-change-the-practice-of-liberation/)

And it is certainly more common than most of us realize. We naturally resonate with others whether or not we are conscious of it. Using it to facilitate healing in another person is where rapport comes in.

For instance, if Joan falls off a horse and Jim dismounts and runs to her side, he may feel empathy because he himself has fallen before, he remembers how embarrassing and painful it was for him, and he can see similar feelings play across Joan's features as she lies on the ground and holds her ankle. However, Jim may not be able to express all this to her. If all he can manage to say is, "What'd you do? I'll go get help," he hasn't used that empathy at all and he certainly hasn't developed any rapport with Joan. It is like the difference between having romantic feelings and courting that person. Romantic is the feeling, courting is the demonstration of that feeling. As Shimon M. Glick, M.D. said, "Sobbing uncontrollably along with a distressed patient may represent the ultimate in empathy. But the patient needs effective empathy." We call effective empathy *rapport*.

So, what should Jim do differently, assuming, of course, that he really wants to help Joan while they're waiting for the paramedics? How can he take that empathy and translate it into a healing rapport?

## Steps to Gaining Rapport

We have identified three steps that are necessary for establishing rapport in emergency situations:
1. Get centered
2. Establish alliance
3. Get a contract (if you can)

1. *Center Yourself*

Initially, this may seem like an obvious step. However, because it is so easy to overlook or forget in a time of crisis, we felt it was important to underscore its importance. Leo J. Shea III, Ph.D., who trained mental health trauma response teams at New York University Medical Center says, "No matter how well educated you may be, no matter how many of these experiences you have been part of, when you sit down with someone who has been traumatized, know that you are entering a hallowed space. Revere it. Remove from your thoughts any assumptions or preconceived notions about the dialogue that may occur. Know that you are being invited into a person's private sanctuary. Embrace that space with reverence."

When someone is hurt, particularly if it is someone we care about, our first instinct is to rush into action. However, as we've seen, it is distinctly possible to do more harm than good unless we're thinking clearly and moving deliberately.

In almost every emergency situation you can take one or two seconds to close your eyes and take a deep breath. Use that moment, as brief as it may be, to let that breath calm you and strengthen you.

Taking a breath also brings you into present time, rather than allowing you to be flooded with doubts from the past or worry for the future. Moreover, it brings oxygenated blood to the prefrontal cortex, the part of the brain that thinks rationally, so that you are in the clearest position to be truly helpful.

If you meditate in your daily life, meditate as you begin to establish rapport.

If you pray, pray for guidance, clarity, and fortitude. Pray for the well being of the person to whom you will be attending.

If you use affirmations, tell yourself that you can handle whatever comes up in a helpful, healing way.

In suggesting that you center yourself spiritually, Dr. Shea advises that, if you have time, you "Sit and ask yourself what is happening with me right now? What is going on in my life that could have impact? Am

I prepared to go into someone else's world and accept whatever that offers me, or brings me?"

Once you've centered yourself, know that you will have done the very best that you can. And that is all you can do.

It is also very helpful to connect with something or someone beyond yourself in that critical moment, whether it's God or your great grandmother who always crossed herself, rolled up her sleeves, and gently saved the day. If you have a role model for calm in the face of chaos, call it to mind and feel it in your body.

### 2. *Establish Alliance*

Alliance is empathy in action. It connects you to the person suffering pain, illness or emotional distress as a fellow human being, so that you both become fully aware that you are in this together.

Here are four components to use in establishing alliance with a victim in a medical emergency or crisis:

A) Establish Authority
B) Begin Communicating Realistically
C) Solicit their Help/Provide a Distraction
D) Avoid Contra-Alliances

### A) *Establish Authority*

When someone steps in to take charge of the situation, this enables the victim/ill person to feel protected. The victim/patient can relax, if only just a little. Taking charge in the manner we suggest communicates a plan and a purpose to the victim, instilling confidence. Handled properly, taking charge also communicates that you understand the person's plight and are willing to listen.

The authority inherent in a uniform is irrefutable. When we asked the New York firefighters in Ladder Company 6 about authority, they said simply, "When people see us coming, they start to relax." One woman who was trapped in debris during the 1993 bombing of the World Trade Center said she was sure she would die there in that dark, dusky prison. Then she saw a light breaking through the inferno and felt that an angel must be coming to take her to heaven. When she realized the light was attached to a fireman's helmet, her relief was enormous.

Authority is extremely important in a crisis situation. Someone must assume control and help make injured or sick people feel that they *can* relax. Clearly, if no one is in charge, relaxing is out of the question. Someone has to step forward and say, "I'm the boss. I can handle it. I know what I'm doing. I'll help you. Just follow me." Often, though not always, a uniform or badge is sufficient to accomplish this—at least in the beginning, unless something happens to break that rapport. However, even if you wear a uniform, we suggest that, at the scene of a medical emergency, you use specific language to reinforce that rapport. For instance you might want to say, "Hi, I'm Roslyn. I'm with the fire department and I'm here to help you. Tell me what you need (or tell me what you're feeling)."

If you do not have a badge or a uniform, you can still establish an alliance and command authority just by promising to help. Let's take the example of Frank, who is driving down the road when he sees a car pulled over on the shoulder with its hood bashed in, steam gushing from the radiator, and a man and a little boy sitting in the vehicle. He pulls over. He gets out of his car and sees that they both seem to be conscious, but as he approaches them, he notices that they are bleeding and clearly in shock. He has no formal first aid training but he has a sincere desire to help them. He comes closer and kneels down beside them. He says in a calm, clear voice: "My name is Frank and I'm going to help you." If Frank's voice and demeanor match up, he doesn't need a uniform to become the authority for that moment. At this place, in this time, he is it. Of course he calls 9-1-1, reporting both their condition as he sees it (out of their range of hearing) and the location.

*I am here to help you.* That is my purpose here—to help you feel better. Your goal matches the victim's need. We are allies because we share this objective. By making this clear you have begun to build trust. In the story Timothy Trujillo told of the man with liver cancer, he simply said, "I am here to help you." That patient, in pain and suffering, welcomed those words from Trujillo and accepted his suggestion for comfort.

Another way to establish, or build on, your authority is to give a command that can be carried out (e.g., "Take a nice, even breath now." "Take my hand." "Tell me how this feels," etc.) Each time the person complies, your authority is further confirmed. Later on, in the next chapter, you will learn how to give therapeutic suggestions and how to pace the victim's feelings as a way of leading them toward healing. In everything we say, we want to convey that we understand the other person's point of view, and that we respect them and their feelings.

### B) Communicate Realistically

When people are in a medical emergency or a crisis caused by illness or emotion, they know something terrible has happened. The good news is that the terrible thing has *already happened.* While you may lose credibility by saying "everything is going to be all right," when it clearly is *not,* there is one *magic sentence* that opens the door to rapport in acute situations: **The worst is over.**

The effect that one little sentence has on the chemical processes in the body can be profound. Instead of the panic and fear that can fill people when they're in crisis, those words create a slight but significant sense of relief. The worst is over. It is almost always true. The person has *already* been hit by a car, fallen off a ladder, been burned in a fire. Now we are going to make things better. Now the healing can begin. After identifying ourselves, and saying that we are there to help, the next best thing to say in an emergency is "the worst is over" and let the victims begin to understand that idea in every cell of their frightened bodies.

If you are not certain that the worst is, in fact, over—if, for instance, another earthquake or after-shock threatens to rumble through the building—you can still claim, "The worst is over for now," and reap the physiological benefits of that calming statement. Of course, everything that you say has to build trust in order for your healing suggestion to be accepted. Being overly positive is as easy a way to lose rapport as being overly negative. It is absolutely essential to stick to the truth and then *lead* into relief and healing from there.

It is equally important to communicate realistically to people suffering from emotional disturbance or chronic conditions. There are ways to acknowledge the gravity of the situation or even new and enlightening facts that can further build a bond so that suggestions for healing will be accepted. Here's an example of a conversation you might have with your friend who's being treated for cancer.

YOU

I can see that the chemo's been making you feel really tired.

YOUR FRIEND

It's a side effect. Like hair loss. This stuff is hard.

YOU

Seems like it. Added un-benefits! Hey, you know, I just read an article that says that exercise can actually *help* with that tired feeling from chemo. It was in, um, women with breast cancer. In Canada, I think. It was just walking, nothing fancy. People who walked 3-5 days a week reported measurable lifts in their energy over those who didn't. Interesting, huh?

YOUR FRIEND

Really? I'm pretty weak. How much walking?

YOU

Hey, we can conduct our own study. Whenever you like. We could start slow.

If you start where a person is and show her that you understand and sympathize, you can use facts to help.

Alliance and authority combined to help Susan, a 35 year-old woman who went into the emergency room of a major NY hospital with severe abdominal pain. "I'd had ovarian cysts and I figured it was another one," she explained, "but there's always a lot of mystery with abdominal problems, a bit of the unknown that makes it scary every time. It's a busy, compact part of the body where numerous organs can be affected. So, even though I knew what it probably was, I wasn't sure and was subject to some anxiety. Besides, it really hurt.

"It was a busy ER and a Saturday night in New York. For the most part I was ignored. Then, like an angel of mercy, this one doctor comes over, introduces himself, and puts my right hand in his and his free hand on my abdomen. He looks at me and says, 'It's probably already beginning to feel better, isn't it?' And don't you know it, within a few moments and a couple of deep breaths, it *did* start to feel better. At least I was out of the writhing zone. Just 30-45 seconds and look what he did."

Decisions are made quickly in an emergency. Words have to be chosen carefully. Don't say, "You're fine," if the person is not fine. Don't even say, "You're going to be fine," because that may not be entirely believable. While encouragement is wonderful when it is reality-based, if you over-inflate your observations to try and bolster someone's sense of security or self-esteem, you will only succeed in losing your own credibility.

Always focus on something that is working. One paramedic, during his examination of patients, would deliberately touch parts of the person that he knew were not injured, just as Sean's mom did when he was hurt by the baseball. The paramedic would then ask the patient how that part felt, subtly but cleverly getting them to relocate their attention away from the pain and discomfort. He never told them they were fine when he knew they weren't. He just gently shifted their attention elsewhere, where things were all right. And it helps the person remember that there *are* parts of them that are all right. Very smart.

If we are confined to the truth, how do we present a positive or healing perspective when, for example, a person is bleeding profusely. Obviously, things are not "all right." Stitches, and perhaps more complex surgery may be required. What do we say?

Let's take a common scenario between mother and child. Rosie, a 5 year-old girl, rushes into the kitchen, crying, wailing at that particular pitch that makes every mother's heart stop. Adrenaline rushing through her body, the mother turns quickly and asks (perhaps not in the calmest tone), "What's the matter? What happened?" And in between Rosie's gulps of air and sniffing and screaming, the mother begins to understand that Rosie was pushed in a game and fell down, landing on a sharp object. She's bleeding profusely from her wrist. What might the mother say while quickly assessing the damage to learn whether she would have to seek help?

One extremely effective way that Rosie's mother could handle the situation would be to begin by taking a deep breath and then looking at Rose directly, eye to eye, and saying in a calm, clear voice, "I'm here, Rosie. Mommy's going to help you. And you can be my partner today, can't you? Just like Dora and Diego. Good. Well, that is quite an impressive boo-boo. Let's see that. Look at all that healthy blood cleaning your cut already. Now, while I get a bandage, you can tell me how it happened." (Pause as Rosie speaks and her mother listens.) "I'm going to take your wrist now and put a big, soft cloth on it to make it feel better right away. And as I wrap it, you can hold the end for me. And, since your blood has done such a good job of cleaning that cut already, *you can stop the bleeding.*"

Notice what happens in this scene. Many Verbal First Aid techniques have been used. First, Mommy centers herself so she avoids panic and doesn't say something she may regret. Then she establishes an alliance (Mommy's here to help you). This is *Mommy* after all, so she already has authority; she doesn't need a badge or uniform. She then gets a contract (be my partner) and solicits Rosie's help, further confirming authority (hold the bandage). She is confident, credible and realistic (impressive boo-boo). We don't diminish for a second that it is quite difficult for the child. It's scary. Rosie is counting on her mom for more than a band-aid. She's counting on her to stay calm, validate her, and lead her to healing. And her mother does just that.

### C) *Soliciting Their Help/Providing a Distraction*

When Mommy asked Rosie to hold the bandage, she made Rosie part of the healing process. Rather than being simply a victim, Rosie became her own rescuer. This technique is excellent for children, who love being included and thought of as capable, and is also well suited to adults, for exactly the same reasons. This technique also provides *distraction,* which helps people focus on something other than their pain or injury, thereby reducing distress, increasing comfort, and creating an opportunity for building trust. If we can provide even a small measure of relief to a person in pain, we have gone a long way toward building a healing relationship. Distraction is particularly useful with children. They are such naturally good candidates for Verbal First Aid because they are so much less defensive than adults. Many pediatricians understand and utilize this principle on a regular basis. As they prepare the injection, they've gotten the child to play with a toy or focus on an item across the room.

Rosie's mother used other Verbal First Aid techniques which we'll cover in much greater detail in Chapter 6 on giving therapeutic suggestions ("Look at all that healthy blood...make it feel better right away... You can stop the bleeding"), but you can begin to see how simple, yet effective this protocol can be.

### D) Avoid Contra-Alliances

In an accident, emotional distress or chronic illness, the sense of helpless is pervasive and devastating. Words such as, "Oh, not again!" or (dismissively) "It'll be fine!" undermine the rapport necessary for any therapeutic suggestion to be accepted. This is especially true when the victim and the helper have known each other for a long time. If the history is a good and loving one, rapport is a natural extension of the relationship that already exists. When the shared history is fraught with tension a new rapport may have to be established. One way to prepare for this is to become aware of the habits of communication you have developed over the years and their subtexts. Notice, for instance, when you go on "automatic" and surprise yourself by sounding "just like my mother!" Listen to yourself and imagine if you would be saying these same things to someone you just met, or to someone you wanted to impress, or if a television camera were recording you going through your day.

What we call *contra-alliances* are those unfortunate utterances that pop out in those moments of sudden shock or anxiety that we know (a moment too late) will be counter-productive. Unless we consciously suppress them, we can blurt them out before we have a chance to think better of it. "Didn't I tell you **never** to do that?!?!?" "What the hell were you thinking?" "I knew you'd hurt yourself!" Contra-alliances have to be consciously censored because they interfere with the healing process.

Let's go back to the example of the horseback riders, Jim and Joan. Joan is on the ground. She has had a bad fall. She is conscious, but we don't know the extent of her injuries. She can't seem to move very well, but she is grasping her ankle. Her face shows she is in pain. She is flushed and may also be embarrassed, since she prides herself on her riding abilities. Jim rides over to her, dismounts, and kneels down, taking those first moments to center himself. What is the first thing he can say to her to establish an alliance?

He may be thinking, "What did you do?" or, "I told you not to jump that fence! You never listen." Those statements do *not* build rapport and set the stage for healing. Joan already feels foolish and upset with herself. The last thing she needs is a lesson about why she is responsible for the injury and how it should have been avoided.

Using Verbal First Aid Jim can center himself, bend down beside Joan, hold her hand or touch her shoulder, make solid eye contact and say to her gently, "Wow, Joan, that was quite a fall. But I'm right here. You might want to take a nice, easy breath right now. That's good. The color is coming back to your face. The way you're holding your ankle, I can see that it needs attention. I'm going to go get some help. I'll be right back. In the meantime, the worst is over and I can see that your body has already begun the healing process. So, even while I'm not here you can get busy making yourself feel more comfortable."

### 3. *Get a Contract (if you can)*

The next thing you need to do, particularly in the case of trauma, in which a person may be in further danger if action is not taken, is to make a contract. This sounds formal, but what it means is that the person you are trying to help agrees to accept your authority and work with you toward relief and healing. The words of the contract may be quite direct: "I will do this, if you will do that. Will you agree?" Or it can be more subtle, or even simply understood if it is made with someone very weak or in a coma.

You may recall the example of Frank, who was on his way to work when he saw a man and a boy on the street beside a crushed car. He has approached them, ascertained that they are in shock but conscious and has called 9-1-1, reporting both their condition as he sees it and the location.

"My name is Frank and I'm going to help you," he says. "Will you do what I say?" or "Is it all right for me to help you?"

This is a direct form of securing a contract. You ask the victim to say "okay." If the person cannot speak, suggest a nod, a blinking of eyes, or wiggle a finger to indicate "yes." It means you've got their acknowledgment and their agreement so that you can help them. Our goal is to use words to facilitate healing, but even that cannot happen without the victim's even tacit permission.

Assume for a moment that the two accident victims are unconscious. Frank calls

9-1-1 immediately. He kneels down next to them. Because he does not know whether they have been seriously injured (and it does not look like the car is on fire or about to explode), he doesn't touch or move them, in case they have spinal injuries.

Instead, Frank begins speaking directly into the grown man's left ear. (According to Dr. Dabney Ewin of Tulane University, it may be helpful to speak into the left ear to more readily access right brain involvement.) Frank says in a gentle, firm and calm voice, "My name is Frank and I'm here to help you. The worst is over. You *can* take comfort in knowing that the worst is over and the paramedics are on the way. You *can* be comfortable and use everything you've got to survive and start the healing *now.* I'm sure you will want to listen to what I say and do as much as you can to help me help you."

Where was the contract? In the word **can**. The man was given permission. The choice was his. As we've seen, people who are unconscious can still hear what is being said and done around them. We may not be aware of their response, or, in our scenario, their unconscious agreement or *acceptance* of the contract. If conscious, they may say "no, I'm not comfortable and I will not be comfortable," in which case we do not have a contract, at least in that area. But we can phrase things in ways that increase the likelihood that the injured or sick person will agree to a healing contract.

For instance, if comfort seems to be a word that is clearly not appropriate, we can alter the request for agreement to: "As I help you (bandage you, hold this compress, etc.), you can focus all your energies on healing." The more we reduce the opportunity for unconscious argument or disagreement (e.g., "I'm not comfortable," or "I'm not okay," or "I won't relax."), the greater the chances that we can solicit a contract for healing. Whether it involves acute care or chronic distress, any form of healing requires a willingness, an agreement, and participation on the part of the sufferer. "Will you take these pills, now?" solicits an agreement, as does "Would you like me to sit here next to you?"

### The 4C's: Compassion and Concern, Confidence, and Credibility

Getting a contract and establishing an alliance is easiest when you exude confidence, maximize credibility, and show and feel compassion and concern.

#### Compassion and Concern

Compassion and concern are just that—straightforward, caring and empathic: our words, our gestures, our voices, our eyes, everything about us says we care and want to help. Enid Leahy, a psychoanalyst from Mt. Kisco, NY, used to say, "It's the love that heals. The rest is fluff." To a great extent that is true, and our loving intention can go a long way when expertise and technique elude us. This is especially comforting to know when someone you love is hurt or sick, and you want to help so badly that you may get tongue-tied, frustrated, brusque, and agitated. At such a time anyone can forget not only what to say, but what to do. It is therefore especially important to know that there is a specific way we can go about the business of helping—a way that increases not only our comfort level, but that of the injured person as well.

We show our concern and compassion by listening. Howard M. Spiro, in his important book, *Empathy and the Practice of Medicine*, bemoans the substitution of technology for relationship. "…doctors must listen to what the patient tells them, remaining open to be moved by the story, for that will clear the path to diagnosis. Listening goes straight to the heart and helps to create empathy. Empathy opens our eyes to let us see what the CT scan has missed." To nourish the development of empathy, he urges his young medical students to write first-person accounts of the way they imagine their sick patients live, so that they begin to feel what their patients feel.

Rapport is a foundation. It is *not* the house. The elements we've discussed so far are ways to build rapport or trust so that the rest of our work can be accomplished. Without the foundation of rapport, without gaining people's trust and willingness to go along with us, we can't offer them suggestions for wellness with any hope of having them accepted.

*Confidence*

If you are going to help, you need to *know* that, even in some small way, you *can help*. It is true. So just know it. Know it inside yourself. If you don't have a centering mantra already, then use this one: *I can help. I know that. I can help. I know it deep inside myself and as I feel myself connecting with the suffering person, I know that I am beginning to help already.* How can you be sure? Because there you are, on the spot. You're the next driver on that lonely stretch of highway when the car in front of you loses control and hits a tree. You're the one the man on a crowded bus turns to when he suddenly starts wheezing and gasping for breath. And so you find the strength inside of yourself, even if you don't have medical or first aid training, just by the words you use. *Know this. Have confidence in this. It is true.* The more you know it, the more confidence you have in this process and in yourself, the deeper the rapport between you and the other person.

Imagine, for a moment, you are in a hospital Emergency Room, or in a nurse's office at school. Imagine that you are in sick in bed and a doctor, a teacher, or a parent says they're there to help, but they're

86

not really sure they can. Can you sense their lack of confidence? What does it do to you? How does it make you feel? Are you as willing to go along with them, or their suggestions, if they don't seem to know what they're doing?

Now contrast this with another scenario, one in which you're not well and the person who comes to help you seems in control and fully confident. How does that feel? What is your sense about establishing an alliance or agreeing to a contract with that person? Quite different, is it not? People generally tend to resonate with one another, much the way we find ourselves walking down the street "in step with another," in unconscious rhythm or the way cars travel together in "schools" like fish. We consider it a form of *pacing*, a term first coined by the founders of neuro-linguistic programming Richard Bandler and John Grinder, and we will discuss its positive ramifications later. Sick and injured people seem to have enhanced capability to pace with those who are helping them. It is part of their altered state. If potential rescuers are not confident in themselves, victims tend not to be confident in them or in a *positive outcome* either.

The opposite is true, too. We can unwittingly reflect the emotional state of the person who is hurt or sick, a reverse pacing that can lead to our becoming hysterical, ourselves. We have to be aware of this tendency in both directions and be prepared to be the calm one, regardless of what the other person is doing or saying, if we want be truly helpful.

The question for us at the moment is what communicates confidence? Think of the confident people you know. What is it about their demeanor, body language, and voice made you feel they had confidence? What about them says, "I'm confident in my ability and I'm going to help you?" There's tone of voice, of course, which should be calm, clear, unhurried and firm. High-pitched, trembling voices, breathless and poorly paced speech are common indications of a nervous state, which would tend to make another person nervous as well. There's also body language, including posture. Our movements should be sure, smooth, and purposeful, whatever we're doing. Tentative, shaky, awkward movements speak volumes, which is why we emphasize the importance of getting centered as the first step in gaining rapport. Any time is the right time to take a breath, become calm and centered, and reinforce yourself. Once you are centered, your body language, voice, and breath automatically align with the calm strength you want to project.

### Credibility

Credibility is right up there with confidence. We discussed this in the section on communicating realistically above. Credibility needs to be maintained throughout, even after rapport is established. We always have to stay within the parameters of what is true, particularly for the injured/sick person.

We advise our trainees to "Keep it simple." Be selective with your words. Be frugal. It is better to say too little of the right thing than too much of the wrong thing. A breach of credibility could mean you would lose the rapport you worked so hard to achieve.

Because this book is about life-and-death moments, because so much of what happens in emergencies and serious illness seems out of our hands, we would like to mention *faith.* It is similar to confidence, but it is not related to one's personal ability to effect change. It is about the sick or injured person's capacity for wellness and healing. It is about our belief that the body has an inner healing mechanism and a wisdom of its own that can be engaged, that things can turn around, that the person can heal. And it is about our knowing that individuals—no matter how old or young they are, how sick or injured—have innate resources to alter their emotional, physical and spiritual states on their own. And in addition to saying the right word at the right time, it is about knowing that our loving presence can make a difference.

**Verbal First Aid Key – Chapter 4**
**Rapport: The Foundation for Healing Communication**

### Establishing Rapport

- Rapport is the foundation of empathy that we build so that suggestions for healing will be accepted. It is the foundation for all healing communication.

- Rapport is the state in which a relationship of trust, compliance, and healthy expectation can be developed.

- Three steps to gain rapport:
  Get centered
  Establish authority
  Gain alliance (e.g., I'm here to help you)
  Avoid contra-alliances (e.g., why did you do such a stupid thing?)
  Communicate realistically (e.g., the worst is over)
  Get a contract (e.g., will you let me help you?)

- The 4C's: Confidence, Credibility, Compassion and Concern

- If you can, have faith that no matter how dire things seem at this moment, they can turn around.

CHAPTER FIVE

# EXTENDING THE CONTRACT: STRATEGIES FOR MAINTAINING HEALING COMMUNICATION

*"Too often we underestimate the power of a touch, a smile, a kind word,*
*a listening ear, an honest compliment, or the smallest act of caring,*
*all of which have the potential to turn a life around."*
*–Leo Buscaglia*

Once we have established basic rapport, the next step is what Dr. Milton Erickson calls *utilization*. We want to *use* what we've built to further enhance healing and recovery. The following are key ways we can do that:

- Pacing
- Leading
- Yes set
- Soliciting their help
- Non-verbal approaches.

We have already seen several of these strategies in action. Now, let's take a closer look at them in greater detail to see how they work so you can feel comfortable using them whenever you need to.

## Pacing

In the last chapter, we described *pacing*, a term currently used by almost all hypnotherapists to describe our natural human tendency to tune in to others nearby by matching our words and our behaviors to theirs. Psychologists researching the nature of emotion agree that positive or negative emotional expression in one person will tend to produce a similar emotion in another. It seems that we pace by deeply ingrained instinct. The discovery of mirror neurons has shown the areas in our own brains that fire when we observe another doing an action. It explains why we smile when we're smiled at, yawn when others around us do, and open our mouths to spoon food into a baby's. Some researchers liken us to musical organs and our bodies to resonators, always responding to the energy or vibrations around us. We have all had the experience of walking into a room and feeling that we have made an awful mistake, judging solely by the *vibe* in the room.

Parents understand the more subtle nuances of pacing intimately and naturally. Heinz Kohut, the father of Self Psychology, used terms like "mirroring" and "twinship" to describe the longings we all have for someone with whom we can share our feelings freely. Mirroring is an essential aspect of the mother-child relationship, in which a mother attunes to her child, using subtle behavioral cues that provide the child with a sense of safety, a sense of healthy, positive self-regard, and the feeling that "we are the same." When we are wounded, frightened, and overwhelmed, we very often revert to our earliest longings for someone to take care of us, to make it right. "You are such a brave boy to help me clean that boo-boo," or "I can see what's happening. Tell me what's going on. What are you feeling? Tell me what you feel over here..." Pacing forms a significant part of mirroring and "*twinship*", whether through bodily or verbal expression, and gives us just the nurturing and reassurance we need.

Pacing, also identified as "joining in," is not only crucial to the mother-child bond, but to all successful relationships, including those we may have, however briefly, with someone in a medical emergency or a co-worker in a moment of grief.

One of our client's, Hannah, describes a moment with her daughter, Molly, who was in the throes of adolescent despair. Observe how Hannah read her daughter's subtle cues and how she conveyed empathy with her feelings even though Molly was too confused and overwhelmed to articulate them: "Molly had been depressed for a couple of days. At dinner, on the third day, Molly didn't have much of an appetite. When I questioned her, she began to cry, but didn't know why. I asked if she wanted to go up to her room and maybe eat later. She agreed. After dinner, I went to her room and asked if she needed to talk. Lying quietly on her bed, she shrugged her shoulders. This is a 'yes' to me, 'come rescue me.' I knew she didn't know why she felt badly. I sat down on her bed and asked her to crawl onto my lap. She began to cry and hold me. I rocked her and said nothing for a bit. Then, I said, 'Sometimes things really suck. It's hard to grow up and feel like you have no control. What I find helpful, in moments like that, is to do something that I do have some control over, like cleaning my room when everything around me feels like a mess or doing my nails, shaving my legs, taking a hot shower, or moisturizing with a pretty smelling cream. It can take your mind off some heavy things. You may not feel so helpless and lost.' I validated that she is dealing with a lot of grown up stuff, her dad and I separated, stresses at school and friends calling her for advice and support. Then we were quiet again. The tears slowly stopped and she seemed a bit lighter to me. The next day she told me she was feeling better. I was glad."

When you use these techniques, which we will from this point on simply call "pacing," people who are suffering come to trust your ability to understand what they are going through. Pacing ("Looks like that bandage feels tight and uncomfortable. Here, let me help you with that,") is an immense reassurance to people in pain or discomfort. It lets them know that you are sincerely *with* them and can respond to their needs. It communicates that you are sympathetic as well as empathic, because you have noticed a concern or feeling state before they have even mentioned it. Once again, be sparing with your words. If you are not certain how someone feels, it's better not to guess wildly. You do not want to suggest a feeling (such as being afraid) that a victim is not actually experiencing.

Here is a simple example of pacing in action. There has been a car accident and you stop to help. A woman is sitting by the side of the road. The ambulance and police have been called, but have not yet arrived. She does not seem to have any obvious injuries, but she is pale, clammy and may be going into shock. You might go over to her and sit beside her and say, "I'm Myra and I stopped to help you. I've got a blanket here that I'm going to wrap around your shoulders so you can feel more comfortable. How are you?"

"I think I'm okay," she responds, her voice and hands trembling. "But, God, the car just went out of control."

"The car went out of control," you join in, gently reaching out to touch her hand. The woman takes a deep breath and, as she does, you do so as well.

Donald Trent Jacobs, Ph.D., a pioneer in the use of language in medical emergencies, makes a fascinating point that can help to explain why pacing is such an effective way to gain rapport. At a time of deep emotion or shock, people often speak without remembering the words they just said. In her fear and confusion, this woman might not remember having uttered the sentence, "The car went out of control." So when you repeat back the words people in shock just said, it could seem to them that you are reading their minds. There is great comfort in being that deeply understood, and it creates an emotional environment in which suggestions for healing can be readily accepted.

### Body Language

Pacing is not only verbal, but can also be done with our bodies. Have you ever taken a walk with someone you really liked and noticed that you were walking "in step" with that person? Or noticed that the women in your office all menstruate at the same time of the month? This is a natural process. When you need to establish rapport, it is comforting to know that your body can do some of the work. Sometimes, joining in can be as easy as physically adjusting ourselves so that our heads are at the same level as that of the person in crisis. A wise doctor knows that standing over a patient's bed has a very different effect from simply sitting down next to the patient's bed and coming to the patient's level. By pacing a person's physical state–their posture, stature, motion, eye level, facial expression and breathing patterns–we consolidate rapport with people in order to lead them to a more comfortable, healthy state.

An important skill in pacing is paying attention to details. Pacing is so much more effective when you notice the little things a person does and may not even be aware of: the tapping of a foot, the twirling of a strand of hair, the catch in the breath, the slumped posture. When done properly—meaning with some subtlety and finesse—pacing can be exceedingly powerful precisely because it is a reflection of a connection in the moment. In our last scenario, Myra did that beautifully when she breathed with the accident victim. If the victim had been a child with a scratch or bruise, perhaps she would have pouted along with the child or subtly mirrored back some other facial expression. Simply assuming another person's position or facial expression not only helps the other person feel understood, it can also give *you* clues about what is going on inside them. In pacing, the emphasis is on awareness—both of what is happening to us and what is happening to (and with) the other person. To the part of the brain that is working overtime during an emergency or crisis, these strategies provide a visible connection that solidifies the positive connection we need.

One of the most wonderful things about pacing in trauma is its ability to ground someone in the moment. Because traumatized persons frequently dissociate and feel as if they were "not really here," pacing can serve as the rope back to a shared reality. When we are present enough to be able to reflect back and acknowledge emotions and behaviors in real time, we can stabilize someone in a moment that would be otherwise surreal and disconnected.

## Leading

Once we have begun to *pace* with the abnormal behavior of people in crisis or distress, we can begin to *lead* them back to a more normal pattern.

Breathing patterns are a prime example.

Recently we presented a symposium on Verbal First Aid to a group of pediatric interns and residents at Cedars-Sinai Medical Center in Los Angeles. We ran through a number of the techniques in this book. At one point we discussed the ways in which pacing and leading could help a person who was hyperventilating. We suggested that the helper, in this case a physician, breathe along with the hyperventilating person, exactly pacing the frequency and depth of the breath while looking into the patient's eyes. "Then," we told the physicians, "when you have their attention, slow down your breathing and they will follow."

One week later, the pediatrician who had organized the program, Dr. Sharon Young, called to report her experience with Verbal First Aid. "The first person I encountered after I left your talk," she said, "was a little girl having an asthma attack. I did what you said and it worked. Please come back and tell us more."

Dr. Milton Erickson was a master of pacing and leading. He was once presented with a patient who could not sit down. The patient came into Erickson's office and (no pun!) paced back and forth, reciting his history and detailing his problem. Rather than use verbal forms of persuasion or coercion, the very clever Dr. Erickson got up and literally paced the floor with his patient, gradually slowing down until at one point they were able to stand around the chair. They did this for a while until the patient was finally able to comfortably sit down.

We pace in order to lead someone we care about to healing.

### The Yes Set

The *yes set* is an important extension of pacing; once rapport is established, this technique involves generating a series of *yes* responses in the other person (consciously or unconsciously). It further confirms authority. It extends the *contract.* And it enables the victim to enter a pattern of affirmation, a rhythm of *yeses* that leads to a healing result.

For instance, on a nice day, we can safely look up into the sky and say, "What a blue sky." That gets a yes, even if the other person does not verbalize it. Why? Simply because it is clearly true. Paving the way for this strategy is one reason we have been emphasizing how important it is to avoid hyperbole and exaggeration. Keep it convincing, honest, simple. The essence of this approach is that the more *yeses* we get, the more likely we'll accomplish solid rapport and agreement.

*Truisms* are a way of utilizing the Yes Set. Truisms are statements that are so common to most people that they cannot be denied. As result, most truisms begin with, "Everyone knows…" "Anyone can see…" "We all know…" "It's easy to see…"

Here is a simple exercise you can do at any time. Wherever you are, stop for a moment. Put this book down and look around. Notice objects, people, the room, or the outdoors. Comment on one thing in the environment. Make one indisputably true statement without any interpretation. For example, John's eyes are blue. Or, you're wearing a gold watch. Notice things you haven't noticed before, such as the feeling of the air as it passes over your body as you move through the room. Hear things you haven't attended to before—distant traffic, birds, a dog barking, a neighbor's TV set.

Now, make three consecutive indisputably true statements. For example: "My name is John [true]. I'm a paramedic [true]. And I'm here to help you [true]." Or, "Mommy's here [true]. I see the boo-boo [true]. And I've got a band-aid right here [true]."

Finally, take those three true statements (all pacing) and then add a lead statement—a statement that takes the person from where they are to where you want them to go—at the end of it. The following example is one that can be used to relieve someone's pain:

"I'm Jim [pace]. I'm your neighbor [pace]. I saw what happened and I came to help [pace]. You can relax now *as I pull this blanket up over your shoulders [lead].*"

You can also add a truism at any point in the Yes Set as we do in the following example when we want to lead someone to pain relief:

"Everyone has had a finger or a hand or a leg fall asleep on them when they least expect it. You have fingers and hands and legs. You see them. But you may wonder now, are they falling asleep even as we speak?"

In the next chapter, we will explore lead statements and therapeutic suggestion in greater detail.

### Soliciting Their Help

We briefly mentioned this element of rapport in the previous chapter. Soliciting help from the person in an emergency or crisis is a straightforward technique that takes the established alliance and builds on it so the person participates in getting better. It focuses attention and it confirms the alliance through partnered action. It also *distracts* from the immediate peril. It is especially useful with children because they so often want to be included in everything. No one wants to be excluded, particularly when one's own health and physical well being are on the line, which is why this technique is so valuable.

Bobby is six years old and his arm is stuck in a broken wall in a construction site. A firefighter, Captain McMann, is on the scene.

"Hi. What's your name?"

"Bobby." (He is crying and afraid.)

"Well, Bobby, I'm Captain McMann and I'm a fireman and I'm here to help you. Now, I'm going to need your help...Have you ever seen a rescue on TV? (Yes or No) Well, I'd like you to be my partner here today, because you know best where I can help you. You can be my partner today, can't you?"

Bobby agrees, and becomes calm enough to follow Captain McMann's directions so that he can be freed.

Or, with adults:

"I'm Captain Peters with the Emergency Rescue Team. I'm here to help you. The best way to accomplish that is for *you* to help me. Can I count on you? Will you help me help you? You can just nod or signal me with your hand. I need you to scan your body in your mind and tell me what parts of your body need my attention."

### *Non-Verbal Approaches*

Sometimes words escape us. We are either overwhelmed, don't have time or opportunity, or we are too frightened ourselves to come up with the right words. Sometimes we don't speak a victim's language. For that reason, we would like to remind you of something you knew when you were young and reached up for a parent's or sibling's hand to hold. Maybe you were so little you didn't know how to articulate a thought or a need yet. But what you did know instinctively (and what you still know) is the *feeling* of reassurance and love.

When Jill's heart had been broken by a disappointing love affair, she could do nothing for weeks but weep. Although people said "Cheer up! You're so pretty and there are lots of fish in the sea!" nothing consoled her. One day, a friend, Kathy, came by and found Jill sitting on her couch, tears streaming down her face. Sincerely moved, Kathy's loving heart connected with Jill's. She sighed, sat down beside her and cried, too. At that moment, Jill recalls, "it was like a fissure had opened up in the wall of black clouds over me, and the light shone in again. I had forgotten what the sun felt like it. I realized that, despite the pain, I had not died. I could still feel love."

Even when language eludes us, rapport is still within reach. And even if we are lucky enough to be able to use words as healing tools, we can still utilize non-verbal techniques to facilitate and reinforce rapport. There are a number of ways to gain rapport with a person without speaking:

1. Eye contact, nodding
2. Physical contact (hand holding, stroking, embracing)
3. Transmission of emotional energy through soothing sounds
4. Breath pacing
5. Sending loving thoughts/prayer

Eye contact varies with different cultures, but in the United States, as in most of the Western World, to inspire trust and build rapport, eye contact should be frequent, direct, and steady. That does not mean inappropriate staring; it means a calm, clear, caring gaze that does not slip away or falter. Rightly or wrongly, poor eye contact conveys deceptiveness, lack of confidence, and fear.

Solid eye contact communicates honesty, trustworthiness, and ability. It also says something else, something amazingly simple that we shouldn't overlook. It says: I am here with you. It says: I have a relationship with *you*, not just with your wound or your disease. To a person in pain or fear, this is tremendously reassuring. It is said that the eyes are the windows to the soul. As such, they communicate our compassion and concern in ways so swift and effective that words sometimes pale in comparison.

A simple nod can also communicate support, conveying "I see, I hear you, I understand."

Physical contact is also an important ingredient in building rapport. A simple touch of the hand, a wet compress to the forehead, a squeeze of the shoulder—all these things say: "I'm here to help. I care."

In the late 80's, medical personnel were so frightened by AIDS that they strenuously avoided physical contact with AIDS patients. Those patients who did not have any family or friends to provide them with that nourishment suffered terribly, and     fared more poorly.

A recent study at Boston Medical Center documented that a mother's touch lessens pain in newborns. Half the infants in the study lay swaddled in their cribs for the routine procedure of pricking the heel to draw blood. The other half were given whole body, skin-to-skin contact with their mothers during the procedure. For those held in a loving embrace, crying was reduced 82 percent, grimacing by 65 percent, and heart rates were also substantially lower.

In a study of what he calls "the Mother Theresa effect," David McClelland, Ph.D. of Harvard Medical School demonstrated the profound power of caring touch, even when it is only witnessed. In his research he measured the levels of immunoglobin A (IgA) in students' saliva, then showed the students a documentary film of Mother Theresa ministering lovingly to the sick, then tested their saliva again. IgA levels rose significantly in the students after seeing the film, even in many of those who considered Mother Theresa a fake.

Transmission of feeling and intent similarly does not need words. Cooing and humming can easily soothe and reassure another person. We've all seen and heard a parent humming a lullaby softly, lulling a child to sleep without a word. This phenomenon is borne out by a burgeoning new industry devoted to music therapy, the notion being that sound—in the form of certain types of music—helps people to heal, promotes a healthier immune system, and reduces anxiety and depression. Researchers have studied the effect music has on the body as well. Certain vibrations have been found to shut us down, while others seem to stimulate us, or move us to tears, or to dance. The neurologic effects of music have been well documented, showing that music moves from the ears directly to the limbic system, the emotional center of the brain, which also happens to govern such involuntary processes as body temperature and blood pressure. In a study at Johns Hopkins University in Baltimore, Maryland, Dr. Noah Lechtzin found that people listening to the sounds of nature in addition to being given pain medication while undergoing invasive medical procedures experienced less pain than those given pain medication alone. During a diagnostic lung exam (bronchoscopy), nearly 30 percent of the group who viewed a static scene of a pristine meadow and listened to the sounds of a bubbling brook rated their pain control good or excellent, while only 20 percent of those on medications alone rated their pain control that high.

According to Edward M. Smith, TSgt, a linguist with the United States Air Force, no matter what language you are speaking, whether you are talking about medicine, natural disasters, having a phone conversation, doing an interview, there's a communication that occurs beyond the spoken word. What we say matters, but so does what we don't say. "For example, if I am listening to French but don't know the language, and they are talking about a medical procedure, I can know that although I don't know the language. I know they are talking about medical procedure since it has the same rhythm/pattern as someone who talks about medical procedure in English, Russian, German, or languages I DO know. There is a communication that occurs beyond the words themselves that we can understand."

Rapport-building techniques have the potential to be healing in and of themselves. As many physicians already know, up to 80% of the patients seen in primary practice are suffering from the cumulative and physical effects of stress, so anything that reduces that stress—whether a soothing sound or a loving gesture—can facilitate the biochemical changes necessary to begin healing.

Can a caring presence be conveyed non-locally, across time and space? Don Jacobs, who himself is part Creek and Cherokee, tells this mystical story of non-verbal communication in his book *Primal Awareness*. He had gone to Central Mexico to help the Raramuri Indians with their plight at the hands of the drug cartels who were robbing their lands and forcing them to grow opium poppies. With a guide, he traversed deep into Copper Canyon to meet with a renowned shaman by the name of Augustine Ramos. His translator failed to appear, so Jacobs decided to simply follow the Shaman around silently, which he did for days, hoping to learn from the shaman what he could do to help the people. The Shaman ignored him at first, but one day, he looked at Jacobs and "spoke to him" without actually talking. Jacobs just seemed to "understand" what the Shaman was thinking and the Shaman seemed to read his mind as well. These telepathic encounters continued for several days. Finally the translator showed up and through him Jacobs asked the translator to ask Augustine how they had been "talking" to each other. "Through our hearts," the Shaman answered.

Larry Dossey, M. D. has gained world wide recognition for his documentation of the power of prayer as well as other healing-at-a-distance occurrences he classifies as "non-local." As he puts it, "Empathy, compassion, and love seem to form a literal bond—a resonance or 'glue'— between living things." Dr. Dossey also states that distance is not a factor in the healing power of prayer and that love is the power that makes it possible. In research funded by a grant from the National Institutes of Health, Dr. Jeffrey S. Levin has uncovered more than 250 empirical studies published in the epidemiological and medical literature in which spiritual or religious practices have been statistically associated with particular health outcomes. Dr. Dossey found similar data. Not only would patients derive benefit when they prayed for specific outcomes, but also when they prayed for nothing specific. Some studies showed that a simple attitude of prayerfulness seemed to set the stage for healing. Overall, experiments have shown that prayer positively affected high blood pressure, wounds, heart attacks, headaches, and anxiety. The processes that had been influenced include the activity of enzymes, the growth rates of white blood cells, mutation rates of bacteria, and the healing rates of wounds.

Stephan Schwartz is founder of the Mobius Group and a parapsychologist involved in many projects involving psychic archeology, psychic criminology, and healing research. When his wife, Hayden, discovered she had cancer, Stephan asked the metaphysical people on his *Schwartzreport* list to participate in a prayer experiment for/with her. After she had surgery, he wrote to his e-list. "The experience has taught us something I, at least, had never considered: Therapeutic Intent/prayer expresses its influence not only in the body of the target recipient, but in the context of their lives. A critical person just happens to be in the hospital when needed, even though it is their day off. A nurse leans down and says just the right thing. It is very subtle, but very real. As Rand De Mattei said to me: Sixteen seemingly unrelated decisions combine to make a miracle. The healing you are sending puts Hayden on what she describes as *the plateau*, a subjective dimension where even something painful is accepted as right, and part of the process of healing. It's like a bubble around all of us involved, and I feel it, as well as do others."

Jason Aranda, R.N., works in the Intensive Care Unit at UCLA/Santa Monica Hospital. In his experience, spirit plays an active part in the healing of his patients. He tests the spiritual waters by watching to see if patients accept or reject the offer of a chaplain visit. If they seem so inclined, he sometimes asks them, "Do you want to pray together?' Sometimes it helps," he says. "You can see it on the heart rate monitors. And they're in a better mood. Lighter, somehow." According to Aranda, you can even see the difference on the monitor of comatose patients when relatives come in and talk to them, depending on what the visitors are saying.

Aranda describes one patient, an elderly woman smoker, who was on a ventilator. After many attempts it seemed clear to the staff that they would not be able to wean her from the machine. Her lungs had grown dependent on it. One night, Jason sat with her and asked if she would like to pray with him. She nodded that she would. The next day, to everyone's surprise, the nurses were able to remove her from the ventilator. Aranda believes that, when given a quiet opportunity to go inside, patients can do some of their own inner healing. "I became a nurse because I like the daily close contact with patients," he says. "You can't always cure, but you can always care."

Like other words, prayer has been demonstrated to have a powerful effect on healing. Whether you pray or you simply think, wish, or imagine, the idea is to generate as loving an intention as possible. Part of the benefit comes from rapport–with God, or a spiritual source, and with the object of the prayer, if you're praying for someone else. In some cases, praying for or asking for "whatever is in the highest good," keeps it on the level of rapport and caring, without any sense of interfering.

Rapport, however you achieve it—whether with a nod, a firm grasp of the hand, or a well-chosen word of assurance—is essential. It is truly the track on which communication runs. When we're agitated or fearful, we draw on the part of the brain that interprets things quickly and literally. When we're afraid or hurt, information is processed with an eye on survival. If a behavior, a word, an experience is open to interpretation when we're in *survival mode* it is usually interpreted negatively—which is wise. If we don't know what the dangers are and we feel threatened, it makes sense to take fewer chances. If we're walking through the jungle and we hear a heavy rustling sound, it's safer to think that it might be a tiger and prepare to fight or flee than to assume it's a parrot and possibly get a deadly surprise.

Rapport tells us we're in safe hands and that things from that point on can be interpreted positively to enhance our chances for survival and healing. Without rapport, the stress of assuming our life is endangered can trigger anxiety and panic so we can wind up fighting on two fronts—against the injury and against ourselves. With rapport, all our resources can be focused and utilized toward one goal—our comfort and well- being.

As we have seen, there are many ways to establish rapport. Use those techniques that best suit your style. Once you establish rapport, a person in extremis will follow your lead.

The next step is to master the suggestions that provide pain relief and comfort and set the course for healing.

**Verbal First Aid Key – Chapter 5**
**Extending the Contract: Strategies for Maintaining**
**Healing Communication**


Verbal Techniques:
      Pacing
      Leading
      The Yes Set
      Soliciting their help

Non-Verbal Techniques:
      Eye contact
      Nodding
      Physical contact
      Soothing sounds
      Breath pacing
      Prayer, loving thoughts

# CHAPTER SIX

# GIVING THERAPEUTIC SUGGESTIONS: LEADING THE WAY TO HEALING AND COMFORT

*"Whatever words we utter should be chosen with care, for people will hear them and be influenced by them for good or ill."*
Siddhartha Gotoma or Buddha

Establishing rapport opens the door for a therapeutic relationship with someone in crisis. Once that door is ajar, the power of suggestion provides access to real healing. This chapter establishes the basic rules for effectively communicating this healing effect. Up to this point, you have learned to achieve rapport by getting centered, establishing an alliance, and making a contract of one form or another. You have discovered the importance of confidence, credibility, compassion and concern and you have learned to use specific rapport-enhancing tools in an emergency: pacing, yes set, and others. Using these techniques, you now have the attention of people suffering a medical emergency. They are listening. They are waiting. They know you really want to help, and that the ambulance is on its way.

Now that all of this is in place, what do you say? How do you continue the good work you have started? How do you build on the connection you have formed? How do you lead the way to facilitate healing or pain relief?

The operative word is **suggestion**. The power of suggestion is difficult to overstate. It is the secret ingredient in the "placebo effect," whose power we demonstrate in every empirical trial run by the FDA and every study sponsored by the NIH. A little sugar pill plus the suggestion of symptom relief from a physician has been effective in 33-77 percent of cases studied. The "trouble" with placebos is that researchers want them *not* to work, even though they very often do. In research projects, scientists consider the placebo effect to be a problem that contaminates their experiments when people who just *think* they are taking a drug, but are not, improve simply on the basis of that belief. Let's consider the implication of that for a moment. *Patients heal in part because they are given permission, or because they believe it is the expected outcome.* And, as we explained in Chapter 2, the experience occurs not just in their minds, but also in their bodies, where the chemical changes that result from these beliefs can be measured. Verbal First Aid sees incredible value in this phenomenon. Not only do we honor the power of the placebo, we are counting on it. In many documented cases this power, with suggestion as its catalyst, opens the door to mind/body miracles.

Dr. David Cheek, M.D., a world-renown authority on medical hypnosis, is famous not only for his gentle, therapeutic manner, but for systematizing an ideomotor signaling approach (using fingers to signal to the therapist "yes," "no," and "I don't know," for instance), and for investigating emotional trauma, stress, and psychosomatic symptoms. It was Dr. Cheek who initially made popular the concept that severe stress creates an altered stated in which people are more suggestible.

"Hypnosis," he said, "occurs spontaneously at times of stress, suggesting that this phenomenon is a state-dependent condition mobilizing information previously conditioned by earlier similar stress. At such times," he adds, "the individual tends to revert in memory and physiological behavior to an earlier moment of great stress."

Trauma, by its very nature, creates instability and vulnerability. When we are scared and vulnerable, we invariably resort to instinct, which is why so much military, police and fire-fighting training involves endless repetition—to make new behaviors as instinctive as possible. For soldiers, police officers and firefighters to do their work successfully, their training requires them to deal with fear in a way that supersedes instinct and replaces old behaviors with new ones. When we don't have that training, we revert to whatever we already know—to those things that are "second nature" to us. This is not always helpful, as the following story from one of our clients illustrates.

Caryn, who worked with volunteer personnel in New York City, was assigned to Ground Zero shortly after the attack. Her training did not prepare her for what she saw or what she felt. Staggered by her experience, she went home uneasy, at best. Over the course of the following days and weeks, she began to suffer from irritability, her sleep was consistently interrupted, she was restless, hyper-vigilant, and her appetite diminished. When she watched television, she found herself compulsively twirling her hair around her finger. Wisely, she sought out a counselor and what emerged was not the incident at Ground Zero, but a trauma she had experienced as a child, in which she had been terrified and in horrible pain. That experience, unresolved, had lodged itself in her mind and her body, dormant until the attack on the World Trade Center. When she was presented with that new trauma, she resorted to what she had done when she was a child—suffering quietly, holding it in, twirling her hair around her finger. She didn't know what else to do with her fear until she found the support and the training she needed.

How different her story would have been if someone who knew the principles of Verbal First Aid had been there with her when she was a little girl. Her body memories underscore the importance of making therapeutic suggestions during the early moments of trauma. However, even years later, if we build rapport and give appropriate suggestions, we have the opportunity to create new, more healing patterns of behavior, so that old, unsuccessful ones do not re-emerge.

### *Suggestion Is Everywhere*

We give suggestions all the time. Almost all conversation is persuasive. Whenever we speak to people we are encouraging them to behave, think, or feel a certain way. Since this persuasion works in both directions, all of us are equally susceptible to being influenced by other people.

A friend comes up to you after not seeing you for a while, extends a hand or offers a hug, then steps back and holds you by the shoulders, saying, "You know, you really look tired. Are you okay?" If you're like most people, you begin to wonder, "Gee, am I tired? Maybe I *am* a little tired." Lo and behold, you are suddenly exhausted.

You go to work on Monday, feeling sluggish, disconnected. A coworker comes up to you and says, "What a great job you did on that project! Everybody's talking about it!" Suddenly, you feel just wonderful. You're galvanized by a sense of accomplishment, by support from your professional community. All that changed were a handful of words. It's quite astounding, really, when you stop to consider it. A few words. A cascade of chemicals. A different state of being.

Suggestion works both ways. While you are helping other people reclaim control over their bodies or become calm during a crisis, you are helping yourself to that relief as well. When therapists work with their clients hypnotically, it is very common for them to enter a trance state as well, receiving as well as giving, for when we tell a story to another, we also hear our own words. What goes around literally comes around. If you've ever taken a child by the hand and said, "Let's just go and see what made that noise in the basement," making believe, as the song goes, that you're brave, and discovering that "you may be as brave as you make believe you are," then you've felt this effect. When we "act as if" we were calm in order to help another person feel calm, often we end up truly calming ourselves as well. It is important to know and understand that suggestion is pervasive and powerful.

Dr. Lawrence Loeb, Senior Psychiatrist with expertise in mind/body work and trauma treatment, studied in the 1970s with Jean Houston and Bob Masters. Jean put Dr. Loeb into a light trance, during which a secretary was taking verbatim notes of everything that was said in the room. In trance, Dr. Loeb talked about the secretary getting a mark on her arm that looked like a raised red wheel, as large as a dime. As they watched, she developed a red mark on her forearm, shaped like a wheel, raised, as large as a dime. While she continued to take careful notes, Dr. Loeb talked about the welt disappearing. Slowly but surely it vanished, even though, presumably, he was the one in trance, not her.

### Basic Rules for Giving Suggestions

You will notice that the rules below for giving suggestions have some elements in common with the guidelines we created for establishing rapport. Now, however, our emphasis is on moving the healing process forward by providing specific directions. *Rapport got the body's attention and cooperation. Suggestion is the blueprint for action.*

The goal of suggestions is to stimulate images that initiate healing bio-chemical processes. Sometimes the directives are literal; other times they may be symbolic. A patient with a fever may be instructed to imagine being in a cool pond or feeling cool ocean breezes as he receives medication. A youngster who just cut herself in an art class can be directed to close down the faucet to help stop the bleeding. The possibilities are only as limited as your imagination and the constraints of your circumstances.

The following is a brief checklist of things to *avoid* when presenting suggestions:

* Avoid negative pictures ("hang on," or "don't die.") With the exception of what you are about to read right now, suggestions should *not* be negative.

THE WORST IS OVER

* Avoid blame or anger, as in "I *told* you, you would hurt yourself." or "How could you be so stupid?!"

*Avoid words like "pain" and "hurt" if you can and if doing so does not break rapport; sometimes a person truly needs to talk about the pain and hurt for a while. Most usually, though, whenever you use these words you are sending the mind on a mission to find and experience those feelings. While there are exceptions, especially in the case of emotional pain, it is usually better to use words like "discomfort" or "I see the area on your body that needs my attention."

*Avoid the word "try" if you want someone to take a specific action. "Try" is a word that implies failure; if you're trying, you're not succeeding. Show someone right now what it looks like totry and pick up a chair." You can't. You either pick it up or you don't. It is also more productive to use language in the present tense, e.g., "You are breathing..." "You can start to notice the tingling in your right wrist that lets you know healing has already begun..."

*Even if you disagree, build thoughts in a pacing mode; rather than saying," Yes, but," use "Yes, and..." to take people from where you find them to where they would be more comfortable. We'll explain in more detail as we continue.

### Principles of Therapeutic Suggestion

All of us give suggestions all the time, whether we are conscious of it or not—from asking someone to help clean the dishes, to calming the fears of a feverish child with a soft "shh...Mommy's right here," or reminding an ailing grandparent in chronic pain to take her medication. The following principles can help us to make those suggestions as healing, positive, and effective as possible.

1. Begin with the easiest and work your way up to the more difficult suggestions. In other words, start with something you know the person can accomplish, if at all possible. Positive reinforcement helps to build confidence and encourage continued compliance as well as reinforces rapport.

2. Create positive expectation. Teachers have known for a long time that when you expect success you often get it. Sometimes called "The Carrot Principle" by clinicians, it has been found that it is easier to motivate people from in front, towards a goal, than pushing them from behind.

3. Utilize imagination (yours and theirs). Be flexible. If one approach doesn't work, let it go and move on to another.

4. Make every thought and reaction a healing one. Take your time, think about what you are saying, and ask yourself, "Does this help?"

5. Congratulate even minor successes and use them to achieve greater ones. Stay solution-focused and goal-oriented, reminding people of their own needs and desires as a way of motivating them.

6. Focus on the stronger emotions. The Law of Dominant Effect states that emotions with the most gravity or force will take precedence over the weaker ones. Love, fear, disgust, anger—all these are an intimate part of the human experience and are strong motivators for change.

### Guidelines for Giving Suggestions

There are certain guidelines for giving suggestions. Though this list is not comprehensive, it will give you a working understanding of how to communicate therapeutically.

## 1. Suggestions Should Be Clear and Specific

Remember that in altered states, particularly those spontaneously achieved in a crisis, we hear things literally. If there is more than one possible interpretation, when we are in danger we will opt for the more negative of the two. For instance, saying you are putting the baby to sleep has one meaning. Saying you're putting the dog to sleep has quite another. If you think a phrase or a word can be interpreted in more than one way, don't use it. Find another, less ambiguous one. Make your language simple and accessible. Unless you know the person will understand you, avoid medical terminology. Refer instead to general body processes. If you do not have an understanding of medicine, keep it even simpler, speaking only about "feeling better," "doing whatever your body needs to do to heal itself and begin to recover," or "experiencing comfort and security."

Clarity is context-specific. What is clear in one situation changes in another. What is important is that you are understood. One of the pediatricians at Cedars-Sinai Medical Center inadvertently got into trouble by telling a five-year-old child's parents within his earshot that his abdominal pain was due to "gas." This explanation provided the child's active imagination with a picture of his insides filled with gasoline and about to explode. The doctor found the frightened child sobbing quietly in his room that evening and had to clarify the matter before the child could relax and go to sleep. If you are in doubt about what to say, or if the circumstances are confusing, remember you can always simply hold the person's hand and make soothing sounds.

Words are tools for making your intention clear, and your intention should always be focused on creating a calm, safe environment in which healing can begin. You may be communicating clearly to yourself, but if you are speaking to a child, a person in shock, a person with limited intelligence, or a person who does not speak your language, you may want to simplify your suggestions and rely more on non-verbal supports.

## 2. Suggestions Should Be Firm

This is really a function of confidence and authority. You must feel sure that you are making a positive contribution, that you are truly helping. The last thing a person in pain or shock needs is to depend on someone in doubt, panic, or distress. This just adds to their confusion and compounds their fear.

A kind but firm tone of voice is the quickest way to let people know that you are in control, you've got it handled, and you can really help them. As stated earlier, we are biologically programmed to follow directions in an emergency, when we are ill or upset. Speaking with authority establishes you as the leader whose suggestions should be followed.

The same strategy of establishing authority that we applied to rapport also holds true for the delivery of suggestions. It is not a technique so much as taking a position and an attitude that needs to be consistent throughout.

## 4. Suggestions Should Be Positive and Affirming

Affirming here means two things: it refers both to the statement itself, which should be optimistic within the boundaries of truth, as well as a way to phrase a suggestion, and the bias that phrasing reveals. If you have ever heard someone make the positive statement, "It's going to be fine," yet you walked away feeling dismissed and frustrated, you can see that it is not in the statement alone that the suggestion lies, but also in its underlying attitude. It is also true that being affirmative is not the same thing as being a cheerleader. Positive suggestions are founded first in reality and then offer the opportunity to lead the person to expect something better, like comfort or safety or even recovery, whatever that looks and feels like to that person. Positive suggestions do not deny what is evident, nor do they deny what is possible. The idea is to be and remain consistent. There has been an accident or a sickness or a medical emergency. So, things are not pleasant. Pretending they are creates resistance.

Use words that affirm the ability to accomplish things, rather than words that only suggest the possibility. Rather than saying, "Try to eat something to get stronger," instead say, "notice how much better you're beginning to feel now that you've taken those few bites of good food." Using the "ing" (gerund) form of the verb is often a good idea in that it is active and present.

Technically speaking, an affirming suggestion is one that starts with "you can…" or "you may…" or "begin to notice…" Thus, a simple affirming suggestion is: "You can be more comfortable with each breath." It helps the person or patient focus on a desirable outcome. An affirming suggestion, by definition, offers something the person *can* experience or believe. It is not negative. Many clinicians feel strongly that the mind is so quick to process images that a "not" is skipped over; therefore, if you mention an image, it will come up for better or worse. If you say, "don't die," the unconscious mind hears only the vivid "die." If you say, "Try not to think about the burn on the roof of your mouth," instantly the inner mind sends the tongue to explore. These are automatic responses. To avoid a potential problem, keep things simple and positive. Do not call up images of anything you do *not* want the person to picture and imagine.

While we all naturally believe that statements like "This isn't going to hurt," are positive statements, they do not have that effect on the frightened, irrational part of the brain. That part may hear only the word "hurt" in the statement. And the negative suggestion is implanted. It takes some effort and time to translate out the negative words making it less likely to happen, particularly in moments of stress. Furthermore, because this aspect of creating suggestion is far from intuitive, we strongly advise that you practice it before you actually need to use it. We are very reliant on "nots" in colloquial usage. Breaking that habit takes some time and practice.

In hypnosis training, this phenomenon is demonstrated with the following example:

"Close your eyes and imagine any animal in the animal kingdom, any animal you can imagine, except the elephant. Don't imagine African elephants with their large, graceful ears and their beautiful ivory tusks. Don't imagine them walking through the open Serengeti plains eating leaves and grasses as they go. And don't imagine Indian elephants with elegant carriages on their backs as they meander through steaming jungle...Don't imagine elephants and their babies in a large herd...Or circus elephants balancing on their trunks.... Okay, now what animal comes to mind?"

Our minds instinctively respond to images, particularly when we are hurt, frightened, or in an altered state. Rather than saying, "Don't breathe so fast," isn't it more effective to say, "You can breathe slowly and comfortably now"? You can feel the difference by just reading these words. Stated in a calm, reassuring way, the effect is amplified.

When Judith Simon Prager created a series of CDs for the cardiothoracic surgery unit at Cedars-Sinai Medical Center, she recognized that even under anesthesia patients would be aware that their chests were being opened, that the body was being invaded. The words she used acknowledged that the operation was going on, but then proceeded to suggest that, "Every touch that you feel is a healing, loving touch taking you closer and closer to the time when you feel better and better. Every sound that you hear is for your highest good...."

## Practice

Here are ways to take the following statements (which contain negatives) and make them positive. You might want to try this for yourself.

| Not this... | This. |
| --- | --- |
| This isn't going to hurt. | You may feel a slightly cool pressure as the serum flows into your vein. |

| | |
|---|---|
| Don't die. | Focus all your energy on healing. |
| It's not so bad. | You have so many skills to handle this with. |
| Don't be afraid. | You can feel safe, knowing I'm here. |

### 4. Suggestions Should Be Believable

In an emergency the truth may often be quite harsh. Yet people's recovery can depend on their ability to see a hopeful future. People with no hope or in great fear can slip into despair. They may also panic. These states—which, as we've seen, have both emotional and physical aspects—can interfere with their recovery.

Let's illustrate this with a story.

Someone is working on a construction site. He falls from the scaffolding and his arm is mangled, but he's conscious. He is in a panic: "I can't feel my arm, is it still attached, will I ever be able to use my arm, oh God, I need my arm…"

The arm, in fact, looks terrible. What does one say to him to be most helpful? What are the options? How do you tell the truth and keep it positive? Do we sugarcoat it? How do we tell the truth, maintain rapport, confirm what he already knows (that something is very, very wrong with the arm) and still leave room for hope?

One thing we can do in a situation like this is to admit to not knowing, which leaves doors open. We can also remind him that medical science is fully capable of the kinds of miracles he's already heard of or seen in the media. You might say, "I can see your arm has been injured and I'm not sure how badly. But, thank God we live in a time

118

when medical science can rise to occasions like this. Every day you read about cases like this with positive outcomes."

We feel that people in crisis do not need a litany of damage read out loud. They need to be assisted and led toward recovery. Tell the truth when asked a question, but don't give more information than you've been asked for, don't go into lots of specific details, and frame the news hopefully. Be direct. Avoiding the person's questions will just exacerbate a person's fears.

If you have children, this may remind you of dealing with their early questions about sex. When they first asked, "where do babies come from" they weren't interested in lots of specifics about human mating practices. The simple answer "from Mommy's tummy" was usually satisfactory. In that situation, as in this, it's important to respond to questions with accurate, straightforward answers, but there's often no benefit in providing additional information. Keep it simple. Less is more.

*5. Suggestions Should Be Rich in Imagery*

In an altered state, we are talking to the right brain. We are drawing pictures of hope, possibility, healing. The right brain doesn't understand or process analytic language. It sees, it feels, it reacts. The best way to reach this part of the brain is to utilize multi-sensory, descriptive language. For instance, instead of saying, "Your breath is getting nice and even now," you might say, "Notice how your lungs are beginning to enjoy that natural ebb and flow, carrying your breathing in and out in a smooth, even rhythm like the waves on the shore. In and out. Ebb and flow."

Imagery speaks volumes very quickly. Describing an icy, soothing stream of water to a burn victim can literally prevent swelling and scarring. What images could you envision that could help the healing of someone with a broken bone? Pain? Bleeding?

*6. Suggestions Should Be Gentle and Kind*

Forty percent of communication is nonverbal. Our intention and degree of empathy are communicated in a dozen ways before we open our mouths. We continue to communicate them through our words as well as our tone, eye contact, and touch.

Kindness has a healing effect in and of itself. When Judith Simon Prager does a presentation with a slide show, she slips in a surprise shot of her grandson, Jack, when he was two years old. And she tells this story: "Jack is a very active little boy. He's jet-powered. Sometimes he runs and falls and hurts himself. One time he had to have stitches behind his ear. Whenever he falls and hurts himself, he cries. Then his mother picks him up and kisses him. Then he stops crying. That's both a placebo and the power of kindness."

### Basic Rules in Practice

1. Practice changing your tone of voice and see how it affects both people you know and people you've just met.

2. Pay attention to the change in your style, tone of voice, and vocabulary in different situations. What do you notice? When do you change? Why?

3. Listen to other people's tone of voice and notice how it makes you feel. What gets you upset? What soothes you?

### Types of Suggestions

There are many different types of suggestions we can create for people. While they often overlap and weave into one another, there are two basic styles of therapeutic communication: direct and indirect. They sound contradictory but in fact they are often used together. Furthermore, each type of suggestion will vary in its degree of directness. The examples given here often address emergency situations, but can apply across a wide spectrum of conditions. Keep in mind as you learn these techniques that the goal is to make the protocol your own, to begin to imagine how *you* would say the words that would open the door to healing. As we have established, rapport must be firmly in place before healing suggestions will be accepted.

## Direct Suggestions

Because injured people are already in an altered state, they can accept suggestions given in a very straightforward manner. Keep it simple. Say it straight and with authority.

## Positive Direct Suggestion

You can begin to feel sweetly sleepy.
Your foot feels numb, like when you fall asleep on it.
Remember when you were lying on the warm sand at the beach in Hawaii.
Experience each hour as if it were only a minute.
Close your eyes when I count to three.
Stop bleeding and save your blood.

## The Power of "Because"

Direct suggestions are most effective with people who respond to authority and respect it—like children, or people in a medical crisis. With this population, the word *because* can have magical properties, even if the suggestion style is less *directive.* You can tie it together with a healing proposition, even if it is not really connected, using trance-logic. Tie it to a past truth, and it works even better, such as:

"Because you have a habit of healing so well every time you've been hurt before, you can become more relaxed knowing that your body knows how to heal itself."

We all recognize the "*because* clause" from childhood. Our mothers used it in response to our continuously asking "why?" (even if they sometimes replied "Because I say so"). This association is another good reason to call upon its powers in times of crisis.

"Because the ambulance is on its way, you can begin to feel more comfortable right now."

"Because you are breathing easier now, you can begin to imagine feeling even better tomorrow."

*Indirect Suggestions*

Sometimes we can take the conscious mind by surprise by bypassing it entirely. By using indirect suggestion, what we are really doing is speaking to the unconscious mind and giving it the guidance it needs in a crisis. While the conscious mind is busy *figuring* things out, the unconscious mind can choose healing.

There are various styles of indirect suggestions. Clinicians may recognize them under different rubrics.

"I know that everyone knows how to feel tingling and numbness in his arm when it falls asleep."

"I wonder what you will think of that will allow you to comfortably close your eyes now."

"Isn't it nice to be able to sit easily and let one's breathing do all the work?"

"Some of us remember very well what it's like to be in a snowball fight and have so much fun we didn't even know we weren't wearing gloves and that our fingers were already numb."

"I once knew a person who became violently ill every time he put a cigarette to his lips."

With both direct and indirect suggestions, we are appealing to the unconscious mind's worldview. Because the unconscious is less defended and more powerful than the conscious mind, we want to occupy or distract the conscious mind while engaging the resources of the unconscious, something hypnotherapists have done for decades.

**Indirect Suggestions**

As I/You Can;
As You/You Can
Apposition of Opposites
I Know A Guy Who…
Truisms
Visual Imagery
The Illusion of Choice – Double Binds
Implied Healing/ Presuppositions or Future Pacing
Leaving the Scene
Metaphors
Reframing

*As I/You Can;*
*As You/You Can*

Sometimes called a *conjunctive* or *contingency* statement, this connects a positive outcome with something you are already (or will soon be) doing. The first part of the suggestion is the indirect suggestion to do something, and the second half of the suggestion then asks for a response.

"As I hold this compress on your leg, you may notice a tingling telling you it's starting to heal."

"As I call 9-1-1, you can focus on your breathing."

Some of these statements can involve trance logic or be "translogical," which means that we suspend the cause and effect connection generally required in a logical thought process. There may be no real connection between the two statements, yet people take the logic at face value because they believe you and want to get better. Some "As I/You Can" statements do have a logical connection, such as "As I put this ice compress on your hand, you can feel cooler and more comfortable." Whether a contingency statement utilizes trance-logic or not depends on your circumstances, your comfort level in using it, and the person to whom you are speaking. As you may have already surmised, this suggestion style works just as well with an "As *you* /you can" format:

"As you begin breathing more slowly, you can notice how much more relaxed you feel."

"As you hold your arm still against your body, you can be-gin to notice that it feels light-er and more comfortable."

### Practice

Create one or two state-ments that use an "As I/you can" format that would lead to healing or comfort. Here are some additional exam-ples to start you off.

Logical Examples:

"As I walk with you and you pedal the bicycle, you can feel all your muscles getting more and more comfortable, more and more sure about how to balance…"

"As you hold this bandage over the wound, you can feel the bleed-ing slowing down and the clotting beginning…"

"As I get your water, you can imagine a cool, cool breeze on your forehead, cooling your skin."

Trans-logical Examples:

"As I straighten your blankets, you can begin to breathe even more easily."

"As you swallow this pill, you can experience yourself as you are when you are young and strong." (Notice the modifications in grammatical tense, which suspends logic even more.)

"As I take your temperature, you can begin to feel sleepy."

Can you use one of those statements in ordinary conversation in a manner so natural that it goes unnoticed? For instance, take an ordinary event, using ordinary logic:
"As you're doing your homework, you can feel really positive about yourself."

"As you lie still and I call the ambulance, you can be anywhere else but here...anywhere you want in your mind..."

Now, can you practice a contingency statement using trance-logic?

"As you sit with me, you can consider all the times you've experienced a feeling of numbness..."

*Apposition of Opposites*

A form of contingency statement, this is particularly useful with people who are oppositional or who need to maintain control. In this technique, we offer suggestions that create distinct polarities of experience within a person. For instance, "As your left hand clenches into a tighter and tighter fist, the rest of your body can become softer and more relaxed." Or, "As your fingers become pleasantly cold and numb, you may notice that your wrist is actually quite warm and responsive."

*I Know A Guy Who...*

It's often very helpful to tell people in medical emergencies a story of someone who was in a similar situation and made it through okay.

You can start with "I know a guy [or woman] who…" This allows them to have a picture in their mind not only of the healing but also of a better future. It encourages them to think, "If someone else did it, I can, too."

Speaking of pictures, remember what we have said about using mental imagery. Be selective. Don't dwell on the negative. Keep it simple. "I know about a guy who had a burn like this. I saw him in a television report. He was in an ambulance and his arm looked just about like yours does now. And then I saw him released from the hospital and he looked as good as you did before this happened. And he was smiling."

Another general way of giving someone a picture of survival might be to say, "There are great treatments at the hospital these days for this. Those doctors and nurses have seen it all before, and they know just what to do about it."

*Truisms*

The yes set, which was covered in the section on pacing, now incorporates a *lead* statement to utilize the power of suggestion. Recall that the yes set simply consists of a series of *truisms* in a pattern that moves the person in the direction of *yes*. A truism is a statement of fact that someone has experienced so often that it cannot be denied. The strategy here is based on the theory that if you can get someone to unconsciously say "yes" to three consecutive propositions, they have essentially built up an inner momentum of agreement and can continue to do so in ways that are healing and helpful.

"Everyone dreams at night. In your sleep at night your mind can drift and dream. Of course it can. And it does, even if you don't remember those dreams. And in those dreams you can hear, you can see, you can move. You can be comfortable. You can have any number of experiences, **just as you can now.**"

**Practice**

1.  Make up a story starting with "I know a guy who..."

2.  How many times a day do you start a sentence with "Y'know, a friend of mine just..."? How does it affect the other person's understanding of what you're saying? Can you use this technique of illustrating a successful outcome in another case to clarify a point or to lead the other person to a conclusion?

3.  Imagine an emergency. Then make up a healing story that begins with "I know a guy..."

A famous example of leading with a "yes" by Milton Erickson, M.D.:

A new patient walked into Erickson's office saying that all psychiatrists were &\*&^\*^\$%#! So, Erickson said, "You undoubtedly have a damned good reason for saying that and *even more!*" The italicized words were not consciously recognized by the patient as a direct suggestion to be more communicative, but they were most effective.

With much profanity, frustration and resentment, the patient related his futile attempts to secure psychotherapy. Erickson replied, "Well you must have had a hell of a good reason to seek therapy from me."

Or, for pain relief:

"Everyone gets numb...we all know how to develop anesthesia in just about any place on the body...just the way you've forgotten all about the soles of your feet or the back of your neck [choosing places that are clearly comfortable and pain-free]...or the way you listen to someone talking and you're really motivated to hear what he's saying...so you forget about the chair you're sitting on or the book in your lap, you're so focused."

127

**Practice**

Yes sets and truisms by their very nature often utilize phrases beginning with "Most people...", "Everyone has seen...", "It's common knowledge...", "Sooner or later everyone..."

Develop three yes sets that end with a lead statement, such as:
"Sooner or later we all need to hold on to someone. You are holding my hand and you have a very good reason for holding my hand...I'm here with you and I am staying with you...The ambulance is coming, so you can breathe more comfortably now and let your head rest back on the pillow..."

*Visual Imagery*

Creating specific imagery is a technique that can be used either to focus on the situation, to improve it, or to help the accident victim focus elsewhere. An example of using imagery to focus on the present moment through imagery is: "Imagine that arm resting in a cool, clear mountain stream, getting colder and more numb and more comfortable every minute."

Here is an example of changing focus to distract the person: "I wonder if there's someplace where you wish you were right now, someplace you love to be. I wonder where that is, and what it's like...how it smells, the colors, the sounds...what you love best about it..."

"I know a place where the nights are so clear you can see shooting stars streaming across the sky like fireworks, where the air is so clean you can take a deep breath and smell the lingering sweetness of sage and rosemary, a place as close to heaven as we mortals can know where there are flowers so colorful they look painted. Every morning the moisture beads up on their petals, all you can hear are the hooves of wild horses; it's a place where your heart wants to sing and all you feel is safe…"

## Practice

Begin with "I know a place where," and describe it to yourself or a friend lovingly, using all the five senses. How does it taste, feel, smell, look, and sound? Make it vivid and become acutely aware of how imagining it changes your autonomic functions: your breathing, your blood pressure, the tension in your muscles.

### The Illusion of Choice/Double Binds

Make an offer of healing that can't be refused. Let the victim choose between two ways to be more comfortable. These are sometimes called double binds by many clinicians and are known intimately by mothers around the world. "Would you like to go to bed now or in five minutes after you've put away your clothes?" This gives children a choice, and with it the all-important illusion of control, but either way the child goes to bed. Making a choice also means investing in that choice, so in this way the person you're helping commits to the desired end without argument.

In an emergency situation, this is a technique you can use freely. For example:

"Does your arm feel more comfortable this way or this way?"

"Are you more comfortable lying down or sitting up?"

Either way, the sufferer has agreed to feeling "more comfortable," accepting a relative improvement in discomfort— which is what we want. If people respond negatively, saying "Neither," give them two more choices.

"Here, we have an ice pack that can help give you some comfort. So you might want to use it here, or maybe here? You can take it and show me where you want it to give you the most comfort."

Any choice you give should lead to the desired outcome, in this case, improved comfort.

If a person does not reply at all, you can feel free to suggest your preferred option more directly, giving a simple "bind" instead of a "double bind." "Would you like me to hold you up a bit so you can breathe more comfortably?" or "It seems you want the pressure decreased in your bandage..." In the altered state created by the emergency the patient will be receptive to your direction.

The illusion of choice can also be phrased as follows, to see if you can elicit a reaction:

"I don't know which way this will feel better, this way or this way..."

## Practice

Try the illusion of choice technique at work with your employees, at home with your family, with friends, wherever it might be appropriate. Think of a desired outcome and then offer two choices, two real choices, both of which lead to agreement with that outcome. See how this works and how you can modify your technique to make it more effective.

*Implied Healing/Presuppositions or Future Pacing*

Implied healing involves a bit more intricate wordplay and is often woven into other forms of suggestions, such as double binds. It is also very effective. Some people call these suggestions presuppositions, because essentially that is what they are: they presuppose or assume something to be true. We believe that this type of suggestion is the most important and powerful, particularly when used by someone with a great deal of confidence and authority. In many ways, it forms the basis for all other suggestions. When we imply healing, we presuppose what we do not want to have to be questioned: that the wound will heal, you are feeling more comfortable, grief is temporary, and things are already changing. When you presuppose, you are making it clear that you expect success. Some people are naturally anxious to please, especially when they are sick or hurt. If they know that you expect improvement from them, they make every effort to comply, which is exactly what we want. Good teachers know this technique instinctively.

"I'm not sure exactly when you can start to feel better. You can let me know as soon as you do." (This suggests you will start feeling better sometime, it's just a matter of when; since it's something we can discuss, there's that incentive for it to happen soon.)

"When you're ready, you can notice a comfortable numbness around that finger."

"Itching like that is a sign that the healing has begun."

"Have you noticed the soothing effect of this music yet?"

"Before you breeze through this exercise, I'd like you to take one deep breath."

"When you get out of the hospital, you can give me a call and let me know how well it all turned out."

**Practice**

*Implied Healing/Presuppositions or Future Pacing* assumes positive outcomes. The only questions are how and when.

For example: "And how happy and surprised you'll be to discover that you have healed in the way you hoped to heal and look around to see that it's real." Or, imagine that you're at the scene of an accident. A woman has been injured in her car and is waiting for an ambulance and you are assisting her. When she explains that she is upset because she is a singer and she won't make tonight's performance, you can create a presupposition that allows her to move in the direction of healing. "Oh, I'd love to hear you perform. When you're feeling better and performing again, would you please let me know so I can come?"

These suggestions can be used anywhere you would like to encourage a positive outcome, at home, at work, or in a medical emergency. Suggestions can go anywhere the mind can go, here and now, or there and later. Imagining a "better later" can mobilize a person's healing resources. It suggests and motivates at the same time.

You can practice by casually dropping a presupposition or an implied healing statement into an ordinary conversation so that it flows naturally and credibly.

*Leaving the Scene*

This technique is also called *dissociation*. It is one of our most important defenses against trauma. People naturally and spontaneously dissociate when they are in pain or very frightened so they can avoid experiencing those negative feelings. We want to utilize this natural response and redirect it toward healing.

With certain types of suggestions we can help make the injury a separate entity so that "it" can heal, while the person can think of other things. Basically what we do is keep the person from identifying with the problem. When the focus is on the injury, the person can be overwhelmed by the anxiety and pain. Changing the focus can provide temporary pain and stress relief.

Recognizing that you are more than your circumstances can have a profound effect on your entire life. In an emergency situation, we naturally dissociate. It is a way our minds protect us. This technique utilizes what the person is already doing.

Let's take a look at some examples.

"While that leg **over there** continues to heal, the other part of you that's here can rest comfortably with me."

"You can take your mind any place you'd like to be, while we take care of that wound. If you could go on an all-expenses paid vacation right now, where would you go?"

"And even as I sit with you right now, your unconscious mind is already busy at work, on its repair mission, going through your whole body, it's already taking care of business and the healing has already started without your having to do a thing…"

"You can experience all you need to experience right now without being able to consciously make any sense of it…or even really feel anything at all…but you can have all the experience you need to begin healing now."

"A part of you can watch comfortably while a part of you can experience what you need to in order to promote your healing."

While every altered state involves dissociation and every suggestion utilizes it to some extent, we can also specifically encourage it, especially for pain relief.

*Metaphors*

Stories have been used to convey insights about the human condition since the dawn of spoken language. In the beginning was the
word, and then we told a story with it. All good stories contain hidden
messages, have layers of meaning. *The Odyssey, Moby Dick, The Ugly Duckling:* every story brings to life new possibilities, unforeseen directions,
new understandings. Often this happens without our knowing about
it. And that's fine. We do not need to learn everything consciously.

In an emergency situation, stories and metaphors can be used in
conversation to weave in healing suggestions. Use any information you
have about the patient to create a story that is relevant or meaningful
to that person.

When psychiatrist Milton Erickson, met Joe, the gardener, Joe was
at the end of his days, suffering painfully from terminal facial cancer.
Dr. Erickson talked to Joe and learned that Joe was a retired farmer
who had become a florist. Joe was experiencing a pain that was un-
touchable by medication and intolerable. Joe had been sleepless for
weeks. Joe's children begged Dr. Erickson to use hypnosis, although
Joe had his doubts. One day, Dr. Erickson came to visit and sat with Joe
for a while, communicating to him by his manner, tone and presence
that he was genuinely interested in helping. Thus he began: "Joe, I
would like to talk to you. I know you are a florist, that you grow flowers, and I grew up on a farm in Wisconsin and I liked growing flowers.
I still do. Now, as I talk, and I can do so comfortably, I wish that you
will *listen to me comfortably* as I talk about a tomato plant." Dr. Erickson
spoke to Joe for quite a long time about tomatoes, how they grow, put
out flowers, give forth fruit, interspersing his monologue with indirect, embedded suggestions for comfort, relaxation and freedom from
pain. Joe's response was positive. He slept, gained weight and strength.
Only rarely did he need any medication for pain. As a result of his

two, lengthy sessions with Dr. Erickson, Joe lived comfortably until his death three months later.

Giving suggestions through metaphor is fairly straightforward. For example, if you know the person likes sailing, you might say, "I like sailing, too…I'll tell you, I wouldn't mind being out there right now, you know, the fresh air and the water, enjoying that feeling when the wind is just right and it carries you so smoothly, effortlessly really, like you're floating on a cloud. That reminds me of this amazing weekend I spent sailing in the Caribbean…and you can feel as if you're *sailing through everything*, right now, just by thinking of it."

*Reframing*

Reframing is the "if life gives you lemons, make lemonade" technique. It is used to find a more positive context for a situation that is a problem—oops, not a *problem*, but a *challenge*. Whereas always finding the silver lining is not for everyone, there are times when repositioning *suffering* into *courage* can help all concerned.

We know a woman who bumped her head and developed serious headaches as a result. She refused to see a doctor. Sometime later, a friend accidentally bopped her on the head and the headaches grew worse. Then she went for a check-up and it was discovered that she had a small growth behind her eye that could easily be removed, not related to the bumps, but had she not banged her head, it would likely not have been discovered until too late. She had a choice about how to interpret this set of incidents. She could have said, "How unlucky I am. I got hit on the head twice, and, as if that were not bad enough, then they found a tumor in my brain." Instead she said, "How lucky I am. I ignored the first wake-up call, but I 'felt' the second attempt to get my attention in time to save my life." That's reframing, and when we see things in a better light, we're helping ourselves to a better quality of life.

*Putting it All Together*

Obviously, these suggestions are basic building blocks. You won't use all of them every time. But you can utilize several at once or in a sequence. Combining them usually improves the effect. The more familiar you are with each one in theory and practice, the easier it will be for you to improvise and adapt them naturally and conversationally.

Here are some ways to put what you have learned together and to add impact to your suggestions.

"I know someone this happened to and he used his imagination to soak his arm in an icy pool, and by the next morning his arm was dramatically better. Research studies have proven this technique really works. Give it a try. Then, when we get you to the hospital and all those doctors and nurse begin to work their high-tech miracles, you'll already be way ahead of the game."

"The ambulance is on its way. As I cover you, you can begin to feel comfortable with your arms outside the blanket. As you relax, maybe you'd like to imagine yourself somewhere else that you'd like to be, somewhere that…"

Although we've formalized these techniques here, they are more than likely very familiar to you in one form or another. The best thing you can do is begin to use them in everyday life, using the suggestions for practice so they become second nature, and so you can develop conviction and confidence in your own skill and instinct.

*Sending Your Voice With Them*

Dr. Milton Erickson used to give his patients a simple directive when they left his office after a hypnosis session: "You can take my voice with you wherever you go." After you've gained rapport and made healing suggestions, you want to help the person keep a sense of calm and control even when you are no longer with them. In a less personal, more chaotic environment, they may be overhearing a number of inadvertently harmful suggestions. Here are a few strategies we can offer to keep the work going.

*Anchors*, or *cues*, are signals strategically used as a physical reminder of the relaxed state. At the moment of greatest calm, have patients put the pads of their forefinger and thumb together sort of in an "okay" sign or as if they were picking up something tiny and ask them to squeeze and lock in the feeling. Tell them that every time they put those fingers together, they will recall the sense of calm they are experiencing at that moment. If their hands are injured, you can still provide them with a physical anchor, using other body parts, such as putting their tongue on the roof of their mouth, or wiggling their toes, even something they do naturally such as blink or swallow, so that they do not have to consciously remember to choose it. With a child, you can use a toy, a stuffed animal or a blanket to anchor those calm feelings. "Every time you hug Teddy, you can feel as safe and calm as you do right now as we sit here together, nice and quiet and easy…"

No matter what the circumstances, you can always just tell the person you're helping this one simple statement: "Wherever you go, whoever is with you, you can continue the healing you started with me. You don't even have to think about it. It will just happen."

## Verbal First Aid Key – Chapter 6
## Therapeutic Suggestion

Suggestion is everywhere, since all conversation is at least somewhat persuasive.

Suggestions should be:
>   Clear, firm, positive and easy to understand
>   Believable
>   Rich in imagery
>   Gentle and kind

>   Say what you want to have happen, not what you don't.

Suggestions should avoid:
>   Using negative visuals along with an admonition not to do it, such as "Don't die'"
>   Words like "try," since trying means "not doing"
>   Any implications of blame or anger

Two major types of suggestions: Direct and Indirect

Techniques to deliver suggestion:
>   "Because"
>   "As I/you can" "As you/you can"
>   "I know a guy who…"
>   Truisms
>   Implied Healing/Future Pacing
>   Visual Imagery
>   Illusion of Choice
>   Leaving the Scene
>   Metaphors
>   Reframing

PART THREE

# Putting It All Into Practice

# CHAPTER SEVEN

# VERBAL FIRST AID FOR MEDICAL EMERGENCIES

*When written in Chinese,*
*the word 'crisis' is composed of two characters—*
*one represents danger and the other represents opportunity."*
*–John F. Kennedy*

The piercing sound of the siren, the throbbing lights, the ambulances, stretchers, hoses, ladders, oxygen tanks—all the signs of a medical emergency. Someone lying helpless on the ground. Unless we're professional rescue workers, this is a scene we hope against hope we'll never to have to encounter. The sight of a stranger—or, even worse, a loved one—lying unconscious, or panicked and gasping for breath, can be overwhelmingly frightening.

Chances are, however, given natural disasters, violence intended and unintended, and the stresses and diseases of modern life, some day we will find ourselves in an emergency situation with someone we know and perhaps love, a situation in which every moment—and every word—counts.

Emergency situations are unique. They happen fast. The victims are clearly in an altered state. Fortunately, just as there are established medical protocols for emergency care, we also have protocols for using Verbal First Aid techniques in medical emergencies. This chapter gives you specific scripts for using Verbal First Aid in common emergency situations, such as bleeding, burns, asthma and breathing emergencies, heart attacks, poisoning, broken bones, and childbirth.

When you are at the scene of such an emergency, it's easy to be overwhelmed by the realization that there is so much to do. You may feel that you're not up to the task. It *is* daunting, even for trained personnel. After a futile day of searching through rubble or under debris for lost or trapped survivors, even specially trained rescue dogs are often demoralized and depressed by their failure to make a difference. The only way to keep up their morale is for human rescue workers to volunteer to take part in a staged rescue so that, finding the volunteer alive, the dog has a renewed sense of competence and professional pride.

Verbal First Aid was developed initially to support the vitally important work of rescuers by providing them with flexible, portable, effective new tools they could always have at their disposal: words. As we've seen, research indicates that saying the right words at the right time in the right way can change the outcome of critical care, and can set the course for recovery for people before they even arrive in the emergency room. The protocol for Verbal First Aid has been used by paramedics, first responders, fire fighters and police officers in the field. Now it is time to make it available to everyone, because everyone will, at some point, deal with a medical emergency, large or small.

Verbal First Aid provides an emergency tool kit that anyone of any age can use anywhere, at any time. Having read the previous chapters, you now know how to establish rapport and give therapeutic suggestions. The next step is to review a few scripts for medical emergencies. We don't expect you to memorize them, but rather to understand the theory behind them and to become confident that, should you be confronted with a medical emergency, you will have a good idea of how to help.

In any medical emergency, we recommend that you call 9-1-1 immediately, and follow their instructions. You probably will also want to refer to a first aid book if you have one on hand. If you don't have one, buy one and keep it where you keep this book. Verbal First Aid is **not** a substitute for physical first aid. It will not replace any proven first aid techniques, but it will complement them.

What follows is a standard script for medical emergencies in general, with a variety of alternative phrases to encourage you to make the healing words your own. You will also find Verbal First Aid scripts and information on bleeding, burns and other emergencies including asthma, heart attacks, poisoning, broken bones and childbirth. At the end of the book, there is a chapter about you, the person on the scene who has also been thorough a traumatic experience. It is about how you can help yourself in the aftermath, after you have been brave and helpful and have to sit with your feelings about it all.

**Standard Scripts for Most Medical Emergencies**

Although every emergency and every person is unique, we have developed some protocols that you can use in any situation after you've called 9-1-1 (if necessary), while you wait for medical attention. It is especially important to use the general protocol when you don't know what is wrong with the person and you aren't absolutely sure what to suggest to them.

Remember not to move people who you even suspect might have a spinal injury. Always be aware of the possibility of back, neck and head injuries if you come upon a person who is unconscious, who has been thrown or fallen in an accident, or who has been in a motor vehicle collision.

We strongly recommend that you avoid referring to specific bodily functions unless you're certain that you know what needs to be addressed and how to do so. It's easier and safer to say less in this regard. Your support will still be felt—even if you say nothing at all.

One of the techniques we use in our more advanced trainings is to have the students practice putting each other into deeply relaxed states using only soothing sounds—no words at all. It's been amazing to watch tough, seasoned firefighters and police officers whisper to their peers, "sh...sh...," or hum a lullaby and see the positive responses they get. After the awkward giggles and tentativeness passes, they do it and they do it very well. Even more importantly, they are delighted to see how it works.

In all circumstances you can use this general approach for gaining rapport and giving suggestions for comfort and healing:

"I'm _____(name and health care title if appropriate) and I'm going to help you. The worst is over. I've called 9-1-1 and the ambulance is on its way. I can see that your [whatever body part or injury] needs attention. Why don't you scan the rest of your body now to see that everything else is all right. Let your body do what needs to be done to protect your life and begin healing. As your body tends to the healing, you can allow your mind to go someplace else, someplace you really love...and you can be comfortable being in that place right now."

## Making It Your Own

While circumstances and specific words may vary, this protocol is useful from the smallest emergency to the most awful tragedy. In the devastating emergency of September 11th, as they ascended the stairway up the Twin Towers, the firefighters of Ladder Company 6 found themselves trying to reassure people—some burned, some crying, some all right but confused—who were rushing from the building. Sal D'Agostino told us he had been saying, "It's going to be all right." But then he heard Mike Meldrum saying, "People, it's over for you, now. Just make your way to the lobby and keep on going. Go home. It's over," and, Sal told us, watching the faces of those who heard Mike, he realized that that was a good thing to say. For those people leaving the building, Meldrum's words were both true and reassuring, allowing them to experience more calm and less fear, and to recover from the trauma more comfortably

We've given you our interpretation of Verbal First Aid, but if it doesn't feel natural to you, you might want to look over this list of other ways of expressing the same thoughts. It's the idea behind it and the intention of caring that gives Verbal First Aid its power. Feel free to experiment in your mind with different language. Just keep it positive and keep it simple.

### Gaining Rapport with Adults

Establish an Alliance: " I'm _____ and I'm going to help you."
"I'm here to help."
"It's okay. I'm here."

Get a Contract: "Will you do what I say?"
"Will you come with me?"
"Will you let me help you (your arm/leg etc..) feel better?"

Be realistic: "The fire is out."
"The danger is past."
"The worst is over."
"I see what's happening here."

Pace/Join In: "I know. I can imagine how it feels right now."
"I can see the burn."
"I know. That was quite an accident."
"Mmmm."
"I can see that your [body part] needs attention."
(You can also repeat their words back to them.)

| | |
|---|---|
| Show compassion: | "That *is* frightening."<br>"That's an impressive cut. I've called for an ambulance and they're on their way. I'll stay right here with you."<br>"I understand. I'm right here." |
| Solicit their help/shift their focus through distraction: | "I'm going to help you, and to do so I need you to help me by scanning the rest of your body and telling me what else is going on. What about here? [Ask about unaffected body parts to give them a sense that some things are all right]." |

### Gaining Rapport with Children

| | |
|---|---|
| Establish alliance: | "I'm (your name) and I'm going to take good care of you."<br>"Mommy's here. I'm going to help you, sweetheart, we're going to make it better." "I've got you, [child's name], and I'm going to help you." |
| Get a contract: | "Will you be my partner and help me now so we can get this all better really fast? Good." "It's important you do what I say so I can help you. Will you do what mommy says?"<br>"For me to help you, you've got to help me. Like a team. Will you do that? Good." |

| Show compassion: | "I can see the boo-boo and that it hurts a lot. I know."<br>"I know how burns can make you cry sometimes." |
|---|---|

**Don't forget that with a child, a look, a gesture and a touch can go a long way to show that you care. Small children may need to be held. This is fine so long as there is no danger of a neck, head or spinal injury or unless you suspect internal bleeding. Please don't move or pick up an injured child if there is any doubt.**

| Distraction: | "Does it hurt here? [Point to where it's obviously not injured]. Does it hurt there? How about here?<br>What does this part feel like?<br>Does it feel better over here?" |
|---|---|
| Soliciting help: | "I'm going to put a cool towel on it now so that it feels really cool and comfortable. You can be my partner, like [cite their favorite cartoon character]_____, and help me by holding your arm right like that, can't you? Good girl!" |

Note: Please keep guilt, anger, blame, and "told you so's" out of the dialogue. If anger or fear needs to be expressed, wait for a more appropriate time, when the healing crisis has passed. If people are angry with themselves or others for the accident, try to refocus them and reframe the situation. It's important for injured people to understand that they are suffering enough and that, "*for right now, it's easier and smarter to just focus on the healing.*" There's always time to go back to the other feelings, if they still choose to do so.

## *Therapeutic Suggestion for Adults and Children*

Direct Suggestions:

"In just a moment (or when the wound is cleaned) you can stop your bleeding and save your blood."
"Look at me and begin to breathe with me. That's right."

As I/You Can:

"As I put this cool, clean, wet towel on the burn, you may notice that your skin is beginning to feel better and that your whole body is starting to relax a little... and a little more...."

"As I call 9-1-1, you can focus on your breath, making each one longer and smoother and easier...

Truisms:

"Everyone knows that the best medical practice is to just hold the bandage firmly, just like you're doing; as you do you can take a deep breath with me now and focus completely on how much more comfortable it is..."

Yes Sets:

"I'm sitting with you, right here, and we're breathing together and we're starting to relax and you can notice how much more comfortable it is..."

I Know A Guy:

"Remember [Freddy]? And how he [had that accident] and now he's still running around annoying everyone..."

"I know a guy who had this same thing happen and he's doing great…"

Illusion of Choice/
Double Binds:
"I don't know which way this will feel better…this way or this way?"
"Are you more comfortable with me sitting here talking to you or just sitting here quietly?"

Leaving The Scene:
"While that part of you *over there* is beginning to heal, you can tell me about…[something positive or neutral]."

"Some people experience a feeling of looking at things from outside of themselves…"

"You can hold your arm up like that and forget that it's there as you put your attention over here with me…"

Implied Healing/ Presuppositions or Future Pacing:

"You may have already noticed an improvement in your [injured area]…"

"You know that itching like that always-signifies the beginning of healing…"

"You may wonder which side you're more comfortable on…"

"When you're feeling better, you can let me know how you did it…"
"How surprised the doctor will be when he sees that it has already healed over…"

"Won't you be pleased to say 'I told you so' to everyone when you walk on your own…"

## Verbal First Aid for Injuries Involving Bleeding

Of all the welcome benefits of Verbal First Aid, none is as dramatic or extraordinary as the ability to help people slow or stop their own bleeding, even bleeding from small arteries and veins. For many of us, even those familiar with the power of suggestion and our capacity for self-healing, this particular phenomenon is so pronounced it can seem magical.

The body has tremendous healing capacities and they are intricately connected, consciously or unconsciously, to the mind. The British Broadcasting Company aired a program about the mind/body connection several years ago, which featured dental surgery on 200 hemophiliac patients. Those who were given no hypnotic suggestion to "save their blood" required as many as 35 transfusions during the procedure. Those who were hypnotized and directed to control their bleeding required only two to three transfusions.

There are various theories about how and why the power of suggestion can affect even this, the most basic biological process. You're cut, you bleed. How much simpler could it be? How could the mind play a role here? Fortunately, as the studies with the hemophiliacs showed, it can. David Cheek, M.D., a pioneer in medical hypnosis, proposes that the phenomenon that allows for the control of bleeding might be related to the relaxation of the muscles surrounding the injury, a process that then helps to produce epinephrine, a hormonal secretion from the adrenal gland that increases the speed of blood coagulation. Others suggest that there is an emotional component to the process: having someone in authority nearby to take charge of the situation allows the injured person to relax just that small amount necessary to slow down the heart rate, thereby altering blood pressure and flow.

In the video, *Hypnosis for Medical Emergencies*, Dr. Cheek relates a story about a traffic accident in which two women are injured. One woman was thrown from the vehicle and one was pinned under it, bleeding and unconscious. Dr. Cheek approached the unconscious woman under the car and, touching her forehead with his hand, said

151

to her, "I'm Dr. Cheek. I'm here to help you. Stop that bleeding, don't waste your blood. The ambulance is on its way. Just relax and breathe evenly." The bleeding stopped and Dr. Cheek moved toward the other woman to see if she needed his assistance. As he examined her, he overheard onlookers near the unconscious woman making frightening comments about how dangerous it was for her to be lying under that car. He asked them to leave and returned to the unconscious woman's side. He discovered that, as a result of the onlookers' conversations, she had begun to bleed again. He put his hand back on her forehead and said to her in a firm, confident and authoritative tone: "Stop your bleeding. You did it the first time." And she did.

To anyone who is not familiar with Verbal First Aid, this scene would seem surreal at the very least. However, you already know some of the mind/body mechanics that make such miracles possible.

Dr. Cheek says, "It's very hard for people to believe there can be that much control of hemorrhage. This was a small artery, but venous bleeding also can be stopped…. I know that as this practice is extended, as more credibility is given to those who are dealing with emergencies, there will be many lives saved that otherwise are lost because of fear, because of hemorrhage, and because of panic."

There is an important point we'd like to make here, before we proceed. Although blood makes some people uneasy, it has a uniquely important purpose in a laceration or abrasion. Blood can clean the wound from the inside out, or push debris from it. Therefore, before you give a directive to *stop the bleeding*, you'll want to allow the blood to do its job. This is a simple idea that's quite easy to accommodate in your suggestions to the injured person. We'll explore it further, but a statement such as the following works very nicely: "As soon as your wound is sufficiently cleansed, you *can stop the bleeding and save your blood.*"

Captain Frank Neer, EMT, Marin County Fire Department, tells an amazing story about a young man who had fallen off his bicycle and suffered a deep laceration on the scalp, which was filled with dirt and debris from the road. "Upon our arrival, even though the bleeding had stopped, we were unable to tell the size of the actual wound itself and how bad it actually was because of the debris. On command…he was made to start this bleeding process again thereby cleaning out the wound and then a few moments later was told to stop the bleeding again. It was nothing short of spectacular to see something like that actually occur."

The late Dr. Peter H.C. Mutke was a medical doctor and surgeon whose experience in the kinds of processes described here actually changed the direction of his own life. Several years ago he told us this story. He and his wife were on vacation in a ski resort in Europe miles from any town. When she began feeling ill with nausea, vomiting, and acute back pain, he grew concerned. Although she hadn't mentioned it until then, she had been passing blood in her urine all day long and now the bleeding was growing severe. For all his medical knowledge he felt helpless, as the last train to town had already left and continually falling snow made any passage treacherous. Then he remembered a clinical demonstration he had seen by Dr. Milton Erickson in which the patient was told to control his bleeding. He was able to recall the procedure, and "I induced a hypnotic trance in my wife, gave her the proper suggestions for the contraction of the blood vessels that were causing the bleeding, and within a few minutes the nausea, pain, and bleeding had stopped and she was asleep."

Because of this and other successes, Mutke gave up his career in surgery, studied psychotherapy and psychosomatic medicine, and personally demonstrated for us the value of his new mind/body practice on a friend whom he relieved, in large part, of the symptoms of Crohn's disease.

### What to Do:  The First Aid Protocol

As always, the first step in any first aid process is to check to see whether the injured person is conscious or responsive, and how serious the injury is. Remember the ABCs of CPR: Check the **A**irway, **B**reathing, and **C**ardiac function. This will help you assess what your next steps are. When in any doubt, call 9-1-1 and follow their directions. Always go to the emergency department for any wound that has glass in it, is on the face, hands, or bottom of the foot, or occurs in a person with poor circulation or diabetes.

While a minor cut will eventually stop bleeding, it would be foolish to rely on suggestion alone to stop the flow of blood. If a laceration or bleeding abrasion is all you are dealing with, applying pressure to the wound and elevating the affected area is the best way to physically halt the bleeding. Contrary to what you may have thought, tourniquets are not often recommended as they can cause unnecessary *tissue* damage as well as negatively affect blood pressure, particularly if applied improperly.

NOTE: If possible, especially when dealing with a someone whose medical history you don't know, wear a pair of latex gloves or put a layer of plastic between you and the blood if you don't have access to those gloves.

1. If it is a minor wound, clean it with soap and water, then hold the wound under running water for five minutes to remove dirt and bacteria. Gently pat it dry, apply a small amount of Bacitracin ointment, and place sterile gauze pads or a clean, thick, cotton cloth on the wound.

2. If it is a gaping wound that is bleeding heavily or spurting blood immediately place a sterile gauze or clean cotton t-shirt on top of it and apply firm, direct pressure by holding your whole hand evenly over the wound and pressing down hard, for at least three minutes. Do not remove any foreign objects sticking out of the wound, and if possible, avoid jostling the object as you dress the wound. If blood soaks through it, don't remove the dressing. That could re-open the wound. Instead, add more layers of cloth and apply even firmer pressure.

3. Tie the bandage in place without cutting off circulation—firmly, evenly apply pressure—so you can free your hands to attend to other things. One way to do that is to wrap roll gauze over sterile gauze pads (or cotton cloth), letting the elasticity of the ace-type bandage maintain the pressure for you.

4. Elevate the wound, if possible. If it is not possible, please refer to a more comprehensive medical guide for information regarding the use of pressure points for bleeding.

5. If you suspect internal bleeding, call 9-1-1 and follow their directions explicitly.

**What to Say: Verbal First Aid for Injuries & Bleeding**

Some people are more sensitive to bleeding than others, but we assume that if you are in a critical situation, you can put whatever thoughts you used to have about bleeding into another part of your mind, where it cannot interfere with the work you have to do. The quickest way to do that is to remember to center yourself at the outset and stay centered throughout. Take a deep breath before you approach the patient, and remember to do so at any time you wish while you are attending that person.

Sometimes bleeding, especially from a head wound, can be profuse. Seeing it can be a bit frightening both to the rescuer and the patient. Avoid commenting on its appearance to the victim, and keep in mind that it can look worse than it is. The body holds a considerable amount of blood. If you've ever been a donor you know from experience that you can spare quite a lot without any ill effects. Stay focused on what you have to do.

Please don't hesitate to take care of yourself. Don't worry about hurting anyone's feelings by putting on a pair of latex gloves, for example. Whenever you are dealing with another person's blood, if at all possible avoid direct contact with your skin, particularly if you have an open wound yourself. If gloves are not available, use any plastic bag to form a barrier. Even plain leather gloves are better than nothing.

Finally, remember that you are helping even if you say nothing. If all you do is continue to hold a clean cloth over the wound with some pressure and provide support with your steady presence, you've done a great deal. If you do speak to the victim, please remember to keep your voice calm, even, clear, and low-pitched. And remember to breathe!

The following scenario is an example of a common household emergency. The Verbal First Aid presented is but one possibility.

You're working on a friend's country house. It's a weekend, off-season. He slips on a stepladder and his arm goes through a window-pane. He suffers multiple lacerations and there's a lot of blood, but he's conscious and able to walk. You put a call in to 9-1-1 or the volunteer fire department. They say they'll be there in a few minutes.

| What To Do | What To Say |
|---|---|
| 1. Call 9-1-1. | "John, I called 9-1-1. They're on the way." |
| 2. Get John away from the glass and to safety. | "Let's get you to a safe place where you'll feel better." |
| 3. Get latex gloves or a piece of plastic and some gauze or clean cotton. | "John, I'm getting some bandages to clean you up...." |
| 4. Apply pressure directly over the wound(s). | "and as soon as your wound is sufficiently cleaned, you *can stop your bleeding and save your blood.*" |

5. If possible, wrap an ace bandage around the gauze so your hands are free to assist in other ways. Have John holds the bandage while you roll it around his arm.

"John, can you help me by just holding this down here while I wrap? Good, just like that."

6. Have him raise his arm up.

"Here, John, that's good, so as we wait for the ambulance, you can keep your arm right here so you can continue to stop the bleeding and save your blood. That's good. Very soon, you'll have a whole medical team here to help."

**Verbal First Aid for Burns**

This protocol can help reduce the inflammatory response of the body that accompanies fever, pain and blistering, and can assist people with serious burns recover more rapidly, sometimes without surgery, significant pain or disfigurement. Burns can be caused by overexposure to the sun, fire, a hot substance (such as cooking oil or coffee), a chemical or an electric current and are classified according to their degree of severity. The risk of infection increases proportionately with severity as well as the extent or surface area of the burn. Always seek medical attention if the burn is larger than the size of a hand, if it occurs on the face, genitals or hands, or if it was caused by an electric current or a chemical. Both the elderly and very young children should be taken for immediate treatment.

*First-degree* burns appear as red areas on the skin and involve only the top layer. Often these burns may be tended to at home, with washcloths soaked in ice water to cut down the flow of blood to the affected area and reduce damage done to the tissue by the burn.

*Second-degree* burns can be both red and blistered, and they involve deeper layers of the skin. Even if you can tend to these at home (also with icy, cool cloths or running cold water), it is highly advisable to have a physician look at them to determine whether any further measures are indicated. Do not break blisters or remove clothing that is stuck to the skin. If possible, elevate affected areas above the heart.

*Third and fourth degree* burns are the most severe and appear raw, charred, often white, and involve the full thickness of the skin. Underlying blood vessels and nerves may be destroyed. With these burns, have someone call 9-1-1 and check airway, breathing, and circulation or get to the nearest hospital immediately. While waiting for the ambulance or in the car, you can protect the burned area with clean, cool towels and cover the individual with a clean sheet to help reduce loss of body heat. If the nerve endings are entirely destroyed, surgery may indeed be necessary. Still, nothing is lost in giving good and positive suggestions whereby the patient's overall sense of well being and comfort are enhanced. Verbal First Aid may be delivered while you're on the way to the hospital or while you're waiting for the ambulance. Suggestions, as we'll show you, should always focus on "cool and comfortable."

*Chemical burns* can quickly burn through several layers of skin and tissue. Make sure you are wearing gloves to protect yourself against contamination. Flush cool running water over the affected area for 15 to 20 minutes. If you can find the chemical's original container, make sure you show it to the attending physician or EMT/Medic to arrive on the scene.

*Sunburn* can be addressed with the same techniques we use with general burns. If a person has heat exposure or sunstroke, first elevate their feet slightly so that the blood can return to the head. Symptoms of shock include loss of skin color, cool moist skin, thirst, weak but rapid pulse. Call 9-1-1, apply cool compresses, and proceed with verbal first aid as follows for general burns.

The following examples can be easily altered or expanded to suit your own needs and/or style as you become more proficient and adept with this healing communication. The first aid protocols themselves have been adapted from published First Aid materials and do not substitute in any way for a doctor's intervention when indicated.

**What to Do: The First Aid Protocol**

1. As always, first things first. *Stop the burning.* Put out the flames or remove the source of the fire/burn. If the burns were caused by electricity, safely make sure the power is off. For electrical burns, check breathing and pulse, if unconscious. Cover burn with a clean, dry dressing.
2. Cool the burn. Use large amounts of cool water. Do not use butter or any other ointment, unless directed to do so by a medical professional.

3. Cover the burn with dry, clean (preferably sterile) dressings.
4. If the burns were caused by chemicals, flush the skin or eyes with large amounts of cool running water.
5. Call 9-1-1 for immediate medical attention if the burn:
   - involves breathing difficulty,
   - covers more than one body part,
   - involves the neck, head, hands, feet or genitals,
   - is to a child or elderly person (other than a very
   - minor burn),
   - is caused by chemicals, explosions or electricity.

### What to Say: Verbal First Aid for Burns

Jerrold Kaplan, M.D., Director of the Burn Center at Alta Bates Hospital in Berkeley, California, states in the video, *Hypnosis for Medical Emergencies*, that using words to help facilitate healing is "Simple, effective and may be used by anyone at any time. It gives pain relief from injury, decreases the possibility of progression of injury and makes the patient more comfortable. The techniques are well documented and they effectively decrease burn injury."

Dr. Kaplan relates a story about his son returning from bad sun exposure during a ski trip. "We talked about cool and comfortable on his face. The next morning when he woke up, his face showed no effect from the sunburn, so you might think he wasn't going to have a burn, anyway. Except that his ears, which were not mentioned in our cooling conversations, and which he did not internalize as part of his face, were bright red; the face, which we talked about, had no significant burn injury; the ears were burned bright red."

All images and suggestions should move the patient toward *cool and comfortable* to constrict the flow of blood to the affected site. Such suggestions, when given within one hour post-burn, can have tremendous impact on autoimmune response and on the nervous system before it begins reacting to the burn with inflammation on its own. Much of the damage in burning is caused by the body's own response to the burn. Our intention in Verbal First Aid is to avert this inflammatory response.

Remember to get centered and stay centered. Take a breath whenever you need to. Keep your voice low-pitched, even, and clear. Know that you are helping, even if you say nothing and keep the cool water running. If all you do is keep applying cold compresses or hold the affected area under cool running water, noticing the coolness ("the cool water is helping it now...the water is so cool and clean..."), you've helped a great deal.

The following scenario is an example of a common home injury. The Verbal First Aid presented is but one possibility.

**The Scenario**

Phil & Mary are in the kitchen. Phil is standing by the stove. He turns to say something to Mary and he bumps into a pot of hot oil. Part of it lands on his forearm and part on the floor. The gas stove is still on. Phil screams, "It hurts. God, it hurts!" Mary jumps up.

| What to Do | What to Say |
|---|---|
| 1. Turn off the stove. Remove cause of injury. Lead Phil away from the scene. Take a deep breath and get centered. | "I know how you must be feeling now. Leave all of that—I'll take care of it. The worst is over, Phil, and I know what to do. I'm going to help you. Come with me, okay? Good." |
| | (Now, as you walk with Phil from the kitchen continue to help him by making simple, soothing sounds, if you're comfortable with that. If he's complaining about the pain, supportive feedback is the right thing to do):"I can imagine how much |

it does feel right now." Keep your voice calm, clear, low-pitched and firm.

Take a deep breath and refocus as often as you need to.

2. Move to a safe place with cool, running water. Collect towels or sterile bandages.

2. "I'm going to check your arm now and put it under cool water to clean your arm and start the healing. As I hold your arm, Phil, you can begin to focus on that coolness and how it's already starting to soothe your arm. It's starting to feel more comfortable, the cold water can do that very, very quickly. Even before you realize it, the swelling is going down and it starts to feel cooler, and you can feel that coolness working its way down into every cell, every layer of tissue. If you want to you can close your eyes and be even more comfortable as the cool water cools off your arm all the way deep down."

3. Call 9-1-1.

3. "Phil, now that you're safe, I'm going to call 9-1-1 just for a second opinion, and as I do, you can go on sitting there with your arm resting comfortably under that cool, clean water with your eyes closed. Just focus completely on the cool water

and how it's cleaning and cooling all the way down to the deep-down cells. And you can do that, can't you? Good. I'll be right back."

4. Apply bandages or wet, cold cloths as indicated.

4. "I called 9-1-1 and they're on the way. While we're waiting we can help your arm heal even a little more by putting some cold compresses on your arm so the cold goes even deeper. You can take that feeling with you, you know, Phil, wherever you go and whoever you're with, whatever is being said to you or around you, you can take that cool feeling with you in your arm until you don't need it anymore…"

5. 9-1-1 comes.

5. "Phil, whenever anyone comes to look at your arm or examine you or asks you about it, your conscious mind can answer them as usual, that's fine, but your arm can just go right ahead being cool and healing, doing what we started here."

The important thing is to keep the mind focused on the cool and comfortable condition. The real water is only part of it. Even in situations when cool, running water is not available, the suggestion of cool and comfortable can be very helpful. Continue to reinforce that suggestion. Allow the victim to "go" to a mountain stream and immerse the burned area in it indefinitely.

## Verbal First Aid for Breathing Emergencies and Asthma

With the possible exception of massive cardiac arrest, few emergencies are as critical or as frightening as breathing emergencies. Once a person has stopped breathing, we have no more than a few minutes before brain damage or death. Unfortunately, respiratory difficulties are becoming increasingly common in this country, with some doctors describing an "epidemic" of asthma, especially in certain urban populations. This means that you are more likely than ever to be confronted with a breathing emergency.

There are numerous types of respiratory ailments: asthma, pulmonary edema, croup, epiglottitis, hyperventilation, suffocation or choking. We will focus primarily on asthma, since that is the most common problem at this point, but we believe that these Verbal First Aid techniques are useful in any situation in which people are having difficulty breathing (other than acute foreign object obstruction blocking the airways). Please remember that Verbal First Aid is not a replacement for proper medical treatment and in the event of a respiratory problem, you *must always* call 9-1-1 or your physician immediately.

Asthma is a condition in which the bronchioles (the small airways in the lungs) become narrowed, making it difficult to breathe. During a severe asthma attack, there is often tightness in the chest, sweating, and a rapid heartbeat. The person may be unable to speak. In situations in which people are not receiving enough oxygen, they may become *cyanotic*, a condition in which their lips turn blue.

Most asthma attacks are headed off by bronchodilators, drugs commonly delivered in the little pumps that people inhale. If people suffering an attack do not respond to the prescribed inhaler, doctors may place them on oxygen and give corticosteroids. If they go into respiratory arrest, doctors may assist their breathing by inserting a tube down into the trachea and connecting it to a ventilator.

Asthma, more than other respiratory problems, has a distinctly emotional component and has been shown to respond to various psychological interventions. A study in the *Journal of the American Medical Association* tracked two sets of asthma sufferers. One group wrote about the most stressful event they had "ever undergone" for 20 minutes on 3 consecutive days. Researchers found significant improvements in lung function up to 4 months later, compared with patients who spent the same amount of time writing about neutral topics. In less clinical terms, dealing with their pain, their disappointment, and their hurt by writing about it helped those patients breathe. Writing about this study, *New York Times* writer Erica Goode concluded that, "these findings add to increasing evidence that attention to patients' psychological needs can play an important role in the treatment of many physical illnesses, a view shared by many doctors and nurses...."

*Please remember:* We don't suggest that you make any attempts to diagnose or medically treat a breathing emergency without proper training. It's always best to call 9-1-1 immediately and follow their instructions. Of course, learning CPR is the wisest course of action and we absolutely recommend it. Verbal First Aid is supplemental to any recommended medical procedure and should *never* be used as a substitute. The Verbal First Aid techniques suggested here are designed to be general enough to be used in most breathing emergencies.

### What to Do: The First Aid Protocol

The initial steps are the same: call 9-1-1 and check your ABCs: Airway, Breathing and Cardiac Function.

It is always a good idea to stay on the phone with the 9-1-1 operator in case there are changes in the victim's condition that require specific actions on your part as you wait for the ambulance to arrive. That may include giving CPR or rescue breathing.

### What to Say:  Verbal First Aid for Asthma and Respiratory Crises

Asthma attacks and acute respiratory difficulties in general are frightening, and people can easily aggravate their own condition with their fear. Aside from the complicated emotional components in chronic asthma, in acute attacks a person's entire attention is focused on getting the next breath. Your greatest strength in a breathing emergency is your calm, clear thinking and your ability to get the person's attention. Pacing and leading are the most useful tools to have in your Verbal First Aid kit, especially when they are interspersed with healing and life-saving suggestions.

### Scenario

You've been walking with your best friend. You just went up a really big hill and she starts to wheeze a bit. She checks her pockets and finds that she forgot to bring her inhaler. She becomes frightened. You are quite some distance from home and you don't have a cell phone with you. Her breathing becomes more shallow and strained.

| What to Do | What to Say |
|---|---|
| 1. Put your hand gently on your friend's shoulder, helping her to face you squarely. Breathe along with Nancy, pacing her as you speak to her. (Make sure you get enough air yourself!) | "Nancy, I'm right here…I can see…it's a bit hard to breathe…right now… and that it can be scary… I can help you if you do as I say. Just nod your head. I'll be right here… and you may begin to notice… |
| 2. Keep breathing with her | "that your breathing is… (start to slow your breathing down) right now…just a bit slower… |

and deepen your breath.

"and easier...you can breathe slower and easier...

3. Have her make a fist and grab your thumb...

"I'm going to take your hand, now, and ask you to squeeze my thumb...that's right...make a fist now...real tight...Squeeze real hard...

4. Have her squeeze and slowly release as you pace her breath and slow it down.

"And as your breathing begins relax you can gradually begin to ease your grip on my thumb now as your breath slows and *your bronchial tubes relax*...that's right...

5. Continue pacing...as you lead Nancy to slow down her breath and relieve any inflammation.

"...as you find it easier and easier to breathe...letting the muscles in your chest relax...letting air flow...coolandcalm...inandout... soft and easy...soft and easy... that's right...letting the muscles and bronchi relax...

6. Continue pacing and leading with your breath.

"...so you can allow the air out... so you can allow the air in and you can turn off the wheezing any time you need to...letting the natural chemicals in your brain and in your adrenal glands ...do what they know how to do...you can see that clearly in your mind... and begin to feel that in your chest... as surely as using your inhaler... that's right...and you can begin to recall with your mind and your body what it feels like to breathe easily...and comfortably...just like you were doing before...right over there...stay with my voice, Nancy.

7. If Nancy can walk, help her get to a physical place where she was able to breathe comfortably before

"Let's go over there, Nancy, where you breathed comfortably just a while ago...and your body has a habit of breathing comfortably, does it not?
And it remembers that habit... as you become more relaxed...

This can continue until Nancy has relaxed and her breathing has returned to normal, or to at least a state in which you can get her home or to a hospital. Pacing and leading with your breath should be interspersed with suggestions. Direct suggestions may include simple commands to "breathe in and get a full breath out" or "soften your bronchial tubes," or "imagine your inhaler filling your lungs now," or similar imagery that specifically addresses the dynamics of asthma.

Obviously, you don't have to memorize this scene. It's the idea here that counts—breathe with the person where they are, then slow down your breath and lead them where they need to go, which is to be breathing normally.

## Verbal First Aid for Heart Attacks

According to the National Institutes of Health, coronary heart disease (CHD) continues to be the leading cause of death in the United States, despite a remarkable decline in CHD mortality over the last 30 years. Statistics vary, but by some accounts as many as 700,000 people die of acute myocardial infarction (AMI) each year. Heart attacks occur in almost every population no matter how you break it down: race, age, and socio-economic status. It is increasingly likely that at one time or another you will witness another person suffering a heart attack.

It is a life-threatening emergency. In a classic and most common heart attack, a sudden arterial blockage prevents blood from reaching the heart. As a result, the heart muscle begins to die. Angina is a milder form of the same process, but instead of a full blockage, the arteries in an angina attack are only partially obstructed; the pain, which is prominent, though less severe than a full heart attack, usually dissipates after a while. In a full attack, the individual may experience a crushing pressure in the chest that lasts for several minutes, radiating through the chest, face, jaw, shoulders, stomach and down through one or both arms. Because the person may sweat, have difficulty breathing, feel nauseated, vomit, or belch repeatedly, a heart attack is often mistaken for indigestion and dismissed.

Shock, poisonings and hemorrhage may place a great strain on the heart as well, causing circulation to fail. When the heart stops receiving blood, it stops receiving oxygen. The result is what is called a cardiac standstill—the heart stops beating. The heart can also simply stop beating in the elderly or those with severe congenital heart disease due to muscle failure and an inability to carry on normal processes.

There are numerous early warning signs. If you see any of the following signs and you have any suspicion that a heart attack may be in progress, *call 9-1-1 immediately.* Do not hesitate. The earlier you can get emergency medical assistance to the individual, the greater the chances for survival.

In a heart attack, time is of the essence. Heart tissue is at risk with every moment wasted in hesitation. However, as you assess the situation, remember that people tend to be in denial about what's happening to them.

### *Signs of Heart Attack*

- Intense pressure, tightness or squeezing in the center of the chest that persists for 5 minutes or more.
- Pain that spreads across the chest to the shoulders, arms, neck or jaw.
- Pain in the chest that is accompanied by sweating, nausea, shortness of breath, and faintness.
- Unconsciousness with no respiration or heart sounds and skin color that turns pale, gray or gray-blue.

After you have called 9-1-1 what then can you say?

- Center Yourself
- Establish Rapport
- Authority/Alliance/Empathy: e.g., I'm here to help
- Get Contract: Will you do as I say?
- Give Therapeutic Suggestions

### Scenario

You and your old college buddy, Tom, are in a restaurant enjoying a plate full of fries, a couple of burgers and a beer. Suddenly, he feels nauseated, belches repeatedly, and turns pale. "I don't feel so great," he says, clutching at his chest. He is breathing, but in pain. *Have someone call 9-1-1 immediately.*

## What to Do

1. If the patient is conscious, separate him from extraneous noise and distraction if at all possible and help him into a comfortable position with feet horizontal

Wrap him in blankets or anything available to keep him warm.

2. Keep him shielded from unnecessary noise/distractions. Current medical wisdom is to offer an aspirin if one is available to help thin the blood and promote an easier flow of oxygen to vital organs.

## What to Say

1. "Tom, I'm right here with you. I've called 9-1-1 and help is on the way. I'm putting these blankets around you to keep you warm and help your heart to function properly…"

2. "Tom, I had a friend who had chest pain a little while back, right in the office. We took him to the ER right away, gave him an aspirin, like I'm doing with you, now, and he was fine. He's back at work, now."

"Tom, with every breath, focus on the oxygen moving through your lungs and into your blood stream, moving smoothly through your arteries and into heart, opening what needs to be opened, relaxing the muscles."
Keep your friend focused on what needs to occur in his body to help direct his recovery.

"To focus even more, you can squeeze my hand, if you'd like, with every breath...keeping your focus on the oxygen and the way the body can heal itself."

3. Keep your friend focused on the future:

3. "Imagine us next June, you and me, our fishing poles dangling from the dock at the creek and the fish jumping like popcorn and you telling the guys what you went through to get there..."

4. If the patient is unconscious, begin CPR according to standard First Aid Protocol.

4. "Tom, I'm going to help you. And you will do as I say.
As I breathe for you...all your body's resources...everything inside you—your lungs, heart, brain—can work to help you be well...and to help your heart pump your blood freely and comfortably...

5. If you can speak at the same time that you perform compressions, you can say:

5. "As I do this, Tom, you can help by directing the blood in your body to the places that need the oxygen most: your brain and your heart.

With every compression and every breath I breathe into you, send that oxygen into your brain.

"You can do that just by hearing my voice.
And I know you can hear my voice even when you are not conscious...

"When I breathe into your mouth, I'm breathing out 16 percent oxygen. It's more than enough to feed your brain and heart and keep you alive.

"You're doing a great job, Tom. Just keep staying with my voice, okay?

"People are saved with CPR all the time, Tom. This works. It's keeping your brain and heart alive. Every time I press down on your chest, I'm helping your heart keep working—every compression keeps your blood flowing to where it needs to go.

"You can take a lot of comfort in knowing that this kind of thing happens to a lot of people. The paramedics and doctors really know how to handle it and will help you be well and comfortable again soon.

> "Until they get here, you can stay with
> my voice, keep squeezing my hand
> with every breath. I'm right here."

6. Continue CPR until the ambulance arrives. If you are too winded from the CPR or too nervous, continue the compressions and artificial respiration in silence. Try to keep others away from the scene. Silence can be enormously helpful. And don't forget, as you work, you can pray.

**Reminders**

Avoid phrases like, "Don't die!", "How could you do this to me?" or similarly negative or accusatory remarks. Keep all your statements positive, focusing as much as possible on the specific things you want the person's body and mind to do.

If you do not know CPR and the victim is conscious, after calling 9-1-1 you can use some of these Verbal First Aid techniques.

*Future pacing/Implied Healing*

It is always a good idea to give people who may be fearful of the future a picture of their ability to recover. "The ambulance is on the way, and all you have to do now is remember that your body has a wisdom of its own, that it has ways to protect you. And just as you body has healed before, from an illness, like when you had a cold and your body recovered quickly, you can rest easy now, knowing that you'll be in good hands in the hospital and that your body can do its part in your recovery."

*Guided Imagery*

You can also use a script like the one above that directs the body to maintain the blood flow to the heart: "With every breath, focus on the oxygen moving through your lungs and into your blood stream, moving smoothly through your arteries and into heart, opening what needs to be opened, relaxing the muscles."

Obviously, emotions such as fear and panic that send the blood soaring and the pulse racing are not good for heart patients, so helping them to relax can take the pressure off their system until help arrives. As always, guided imagery can be a valuable technique to use in this situation. If you know the person, you can help guide him or her to a favorite place. "Wouldn't it be nice to be back in Hawaii, right now, Sue? Remember that little beach by the cove where we went snorkeling...."

If you don't know the person well enough to suggest a specific place, you could simply say, "The ambulance is on the way, so now you can just take a nice easy breath and just let yourself remember a place that you love to be, some place that makes you feel so peaceful and comfortable. Maybe by a beach, or in the mountains..."

*As I/You Can*

Use the contingency directive that suggests that as you perform an action, the victim has the desired reaction. "As I lift your head up onto these pillows, you can begin to notice how much more easily you are breathing." "As I call 9-1-1, you can begin to relax a little knowing that help is on the way and that I'm right here with you."

*I know a guy who...*

If the person is in fear of the outcome, and you know a story with a happy ending, this would be a good time to recount it. "Just last week I met my neighbor, Joe Bingham, do you know him? He's had two of these heart attacks, and he was out there riding his bike, passing the younger kids and waving! They've got great techniques, these days, at the hospital for getting people right back on their feet, you know?"

## Coming From The Heart

Sometimes in the drama of the moment, something unexpected happens. One woman we know actually knelt beside her husband as he was having a serious heart attack. She put his hand in hers and said into his ear, over and over: "Stay in your body. Stay in your body." He recovered and later they both attributed his survival to his hearing those words and *deciding* not to leave.

### First Aid Protocol for Heart Attacks
Call 9-1-1 if:

   *Patient has chest pain lasting more than five or ten minutes, shortness of breath, sweating, or nausea and prescribed medicine doesn't relieve.

   *Follow directions given by 9-1-1.

   *Make the patient comfortable.

   *Check for nausea and vomiting, light-headedness, sweating, shortness of breath.

   *Check for pain in the chest, abdomen, lower jaw, neck, or either shoulder.

   *If patient has medications, assist with them.

### Verbal First Aid For Poisoning, Broken Bones, and Childbirth

There are as many medical situations as there are individuals in the world, making it difficult to address that wide variety here in this one book. However, because we understand that being in a medical emergency can be so frightening and overwhelming, we wanted to give you as many specific examples as possible to help the right words come more easily to you when you need them most.

Please remember: In all the following cases, *call 9-1-1 first*, then proceed according to the accepted First Aid Protocol or the 9-1-1 Operator's guidance. It's always better to do nothing if you are not truly sure of what to do.

Then, remember the Verbal First Aid basics:

Center Yourself
Establish Rapport
Authority/Alliance/Empathy: e.g., I'm here to help
Get Contract: Will you do as I say? Will you let me help you?
Give Therapeutic Suggestions

## Poisoning

Every year, tens of thousands of people die from accidental poisoning. If you include drug overdoses in the calculation, the numbers are staggering. The ingestion of a toxin, whether a harmful chemical, an overdose of something otherwise helpful, or even a snake bite, is frighteningly common. With the proliferation of over-the-counter pharmaceuticals and under-the-sink cleansers, it is easier than ever to suffer an accidental poisoning. Aspirin, lye, bleach, weed killers, detergents: they can all cause respiratory arrest, coma, convulsions and even quick death.

If you come upon someone who appears to have either ingested, injected, or come in contact (inhalation, absorption) with a toxin, identify and isolate the suspected toxic agent and call 9-1-1 immediately or your local poison control center. Do not induce vomiting unless specifically instructed to do so. If all you can do is wait for the ambulance to arrive, there are still some things you can say.

"Lucy, it's me. I've called 9-1-1 and they're coming to help you. I know what's happened. I also know that my words can reach deep down into the most essential parts of you to help you survive and get well, so listen carefully. You have vital organs that are especially designed to protect and defend the body against any toxins. They work like strainers to filter out the bad chemicals and keep the good ones. That's right. You know what a strainer does. Stay with my voice, now. All the parts of you, every cell is now listening and taking direction from my voice—to clean your system and protect you. Your body knows exactly what to do and it can do that now."

Essentially, anything you say in a case of poisoning, whether accidental or not, should direct body resources in a process of cleansing and purification. You can also remind the individual to protect vital organs, making sure that blood and oxygen continue to be supplied to the most essential organs to keep them alive.

### Broken bones

When someone's elbow or head makes an unexpected and unintended impact with our soft tissue, bones seem amazingly hard. However, they break frequently in people of all ages, although with increasing frequency and severity in the elderly.

Broken bones can involve numerous medical problems: lacerated skin and open tissue, hemorrhaging in internal organs, ruptured lungs, brain injury. These fractures can be simple, compound, or hairline. Symptoms may include pain, swelling, bleeding. If you are with someone who seems to have a broken bone, do not move that person unless absolutely necessary (meaning life-or-death urgency). *Call 9-1-1*, immobilize the affected area if you can, and speak in a clear, calm, and reassuring voice.

"I'm Jane and I've called 9-1-1. I'll stay with you and help you get more comfortable until they get here. Is that okay? Good."

### Give Therapeutic Suggestions

*Distraction*

If people suffering a broken bone can speak without great effort or pain, you can begin to use distraction techniques to get their attention away from the afflicted area.

"I see your arm has been injured, and I've got that immobilized now so it can start healing right away. While your arm starts to heal, I'd like to see how the rest of you is doing. How's that?" (Point to or touch a clearly more comfortable, uninjured area.)

You can continue using distraction until the ambulance arrives, interspersing suggestions for continued healing.

"While we go through your whole body this way, your arm has begun the healing process all on its own...and *it can continue to do so*...no matter where you are or who is speaking with you...

*Stories*

If the ambulance takes a while to arrive, you can tell stories:

"We have the most amazing healing capacities...my 80-year-old mother broke her hip, recovered fully, and just last week she was doing the mambo at her granddaughter's birthday party. Nearly gave everyone else a heart attack, but she had a great time."

If you feel that the person would not respond positively to humor or story telling, you can be directive and concrete:

"There is a technique I know that can help you with any pain you may have. It's called dialing-down. It's really simple. In your mind's eye, you can imagine a huge control room with beepers and buzzers and dials to monitor everything that's going on in your body and mind all the time. It's a busy room, but you can go there now and find the dial that is just for pain...go ahead and signal me with your [right] finger to let me know you've got it...good. Now, notice the level of your pain. Dial it down one notch, not too much, not too quickly...just one notch. Good. Now one more."

Be patient, consistent, firm and willing to repeat the process if necessary. We discuss this particular technique in greater detail in Chapter 8, on pain.

## *Childbirth*

Childbirth is not an illness and, in many cases, it is not a medical emergency. While we have romanticized the childbirth process in the media, it is in truth a magnificently messy process. It may also involve pain for many (though not all) women. Not all deliveries are easy and a few have dramatic and dangerous complications, requiring extraordinary life-saving measures for both mother and child.

If you are confronted with a situation in which a woman goes into labor and you are unable to get her medical assistance, there are specific ways you can help.

*First and always: Call 9-1-1.* There is usually ample time to prepare for the birth and the odds are that the ambulance will get to your side before the baby is actually ready to emerge from the birth canal.

If it looks as if you'll have to assist with the birth, here are a few basic steps to keep in mind:

- o Find a private, quiet, warm place if possible.
- o Ask the mother to empty her bladder.
- o Cleanliness is essential. No one with a cold or infectious disease should assist in the delivery. If you can, scrub your hands or use an anti-bacterial solution.
- o Have available clean towels and sheets as well as boiling water, scissors and cloth tape.
- o Follow accepted First Aid protocols or the advice of the 9-1-1 Operator.
- o In Verbal First Aid, it is always helpful to know as much as you can about the process you are addressing because it allows you to make strong, confident, factual statements that can help alleviate the mother's anxiety and make sense of everything she is going through.

For instance:

"Emily, I'm right with you and I'm going to stay right here and help you through this. Hold my hand, that's right, squeeze it. That was another contraction. Good, you did that beautifully...and each contraction pushes the baby downward and dilates the birth canal just a little bit more until it is wide enough and relaxed enough to allow the baby's head to pass through."

"As your uterine muscles contract to give the needed push, your cervix can begin to become soft and flexible, opening like a basketball hoop through which your precious baby can slip out, just as nature intended."

However, if you do not have such specific information to convey, you can still use words beneficially in a more general way.

"The body knows what it has to do and just how to do it. Before we built hospitals women used to have their babies in the fields as they worked and, even after having them, were able to continue working with their newborn infants suckling them."

And you can future pace;

"Just imagine holding your sweet baby in your arms, looking into your baby's eyes, very soon, maybe in just a few more contractions..."

You can also use distraction to help lessen the mother's discomfort and plant therapeutic suggestion even if you don't know her:

"That was a terrific contraction...Okay, you can let your body soften now. Tell me how this pillow feels under your head like that…What about your pulse? If you count out loud for me, I can take your pulse. Would you do that and as you say, 'one-one-thousand, two-one-thousand,' you can let your vaginal canal relax and soften…"

## Verbal First Aid for Medical Emergencies

Remember that a person in crisis is already in an altered state. Careless words can harm but well-considered words can help them heal. Verbal First Aid can connect with the autonomic nervous system and help begin the healing process.

---

### TO DO

**First Things First**
- *Call* 911 or
- *Go* to the nearest hospital
- Keep the patient still
- If possible, *consult* your first aid book for details on treatment for shock, bleeding, burns, etc.
- *Use* Verbal First Aid to promote more rapid healings as follows
- *BREATHE!*

**Establish an Alliance, Authority**
Let the patient know you are here to help and that they can trust you.

**Get a Contract**
Get them to agree to help themselves and be helped.

**Be Realistic, Confident, and Compassionate**
Don't over-promise. Keep it truthful and simple. Stay grounded in compassion and remember you can be confident that this works.

---

**TO SAY**

"I'm [name] and I'm going to help you." Or, "Mommy's here and we're going to make it better."

"Will you do as I say?" Or, "Will you help me to help you by [doing x, y, z.]?" Or, "Will you relax as I help?" Or, to a child, "Will you be my partner, like the Power Rangers or Dora and Diego?"

"*The worst is over.*" Or, "I called 911. Help is on the way." Or, "You've been hurt and the healing's already begun. Your body knows how to heal itself." Or, "I'll be right here until the paramedics come."

## TO DO

**Pace/Join In**
Connect with the other person. Be where they are so you can help lead them to comfort and safety. Sometimes just a gentle touch is enough.

**Distract for Pain Relief**
Get their attention *elsewhere*, for pain relief, take the focus off the injury.

**Solicit Their Help**
Get them to actively participate in their own healing. Make them feel there is something helpful they can do.

**Give Healing Suggestions**
The following are examples of what to say once you've gotten their attention and agreement.

**Direct:**
Say it straight and clearly with authority. Be *directive*.

**As I/ You Can:**
Connect a positive outcome with an action you are performing. Say it clearly and firmly, but allow for flexibility.

## TO SAY

"I can see that your [body part] needs attention." Or, "That *is* frightening, but I'm right here." Or, "I know." Or, "I can imagine how that feels." Or, "I understand."

"I can see where your body needs attention, there and there....Would you scan the rest of your body now and let me know what else is going on?" Or, "How does it feel here? Here?" (Point to a place that is clearly uninjured.)

"Would you hold this while I wrap the bandage around your [arm/leg]?" Or "As I move [this]...breathe deeply to the count of three." Or, to a child, "You can play Robin and I'll be Batman, so you can help by holding that right there. Good!"

"Relax now. Help is on the way." Or, "Take three breaths and on the third breath, feel your body becoming more comfortable." Or, "As soon as your wound is cleaned, *stop your bleeding* and save your blood."

"As I [hold this compress/wash that cut] you may notice a tingle telling you it's starting to heal." Or, "As I get up to call 911, you can *focus only on your breathing*

## TO DO

**I Know a Guy Who…**
Give them a reference to healing as a model. Help them to anticipate a future beyond this incident. An easy lead into stories with embedded suggestions for healing and comfort.

**Yes Sets:**
Get them to say "yes" to the obvious, and it's easier for them to agree with the next suggestion and come to the conclusions that will help them.

**Future Pace/ Implied Healing:**
Point their thoughts to a time in the future when things are already better. Help them to imagine a time of healing, comfort, joy. Make it clear you expect success. Presuppose acceptance of your suggestions and of their healing, both now and in the future.

**Visual Imagery:**
Give them images of healing to focus on or help them recall pleasant scenes to distract them.

**The Illusion of Choice:**
Also called *double binds*. Make them an offer of healing they can't refuse. Let them choose between two ways to agree to be more comfortable.

## TO SAY

"I know a guy who [had a burn] like this and he thought about *cool* and *comfortable* and the swelling disappeared." Or, "When I had that surgery, they kept telling me it would take weeks to feel better, but I was up and about in a day..."

"You are holding my hand...I am talking to you...the ambulance is coming *and* you can breathe more comfortably now."

"You can give me a call later and tell me how well it all turned out." "I'm not exactly sure *when* you can *start* to feel better..." Or, "When it itches it means it's healing or you might just feel a kind of numbness to indicate that."

"I wonder if there's some place you wish you were right now, some place you love. Where would that be? What's it like?" Or "Imagine that arm resting in a cool, clear mountain stream, getting colder and more numb and comfortable every minute."

"While that leg/arm over there continues to heal...you can rest comfortably with me." Or, "You can take your mind to any place you'd like to go while we take care of that wound."

"Does your arm feel more comfortable this way, or this way?" Or, "Would you be more comfortable sitting up or lying down?"

CHAPTER EIGHT

# VERBAL FIRST AID FOR RELIEVING PAIN

*It is easier to find men who will volunteer to die,*
*Than to find those who are willing*
*To endure pain with patience.*
*–Julius Caesar*

Pain and suffering. These words underlie some of the most fearful aspects of medical emergencies and of any kind of illness, including chronic conditions. This chapter on pain relief lies at the heart of the book because it applies to so many conditions. Whether you are helping to relieve the agony of someone in an accident or providing comfort to someone in constant pain, Verbal First Aid techniques can give you, and those you tend to, powerful tools for creating relief.

How can words help with pain relief? As we've established, people in medical emergencies are in an altered and particularly receptive state. Although hypnotherapists and biofeedback experts often use altered states to relieve pain, we know that sometimes pain actually *causes* people to go into an altered state. Martyrs, saints and holy men from many ancient practices have been known to use pain, starvation and thirst to go into a state in which they can reach a metaphysical experience. It is an accepted definition among hypnotherapists that an altered state of consciousness is a condition in which our consciousness has been fixated and focused to a relatively narrow area rather than being diffused over a broad area. Pain is transforming. It shuts out the outer world and narrows one's focus.

Like emotional problems such as anxiety and depression, pain is both subjective and invisible. We can see bleeding; we can pay witness to a broken bone, and respond to the visual cues of a fainting spell or a choking response. Pain, on the other hand, is impossible to quantify. But it is very, very real. And it can be one of the biggest obstacles to healing.

Alleviating pain is a large part of helping someone through a crisis. There are several techniques that can be used to help relieve pain, or distract a person from experiencing it. Pain is real but it is also an interpretation of neurological events. Therefore it is mutable; we can use our minds to change the way we experience it. This is why we have placed so much emphasis on strategies such as avoiding words like "pain" and "hurt" as much as possible, referring instead to specific neutral—or even positive–sensations ("you might feel the pressure of this bandage..." or "the area that needs attention").

In 1990 the U.S. Agency for Health Care Policy and Research undertook a major review of studies on chronic pain, including cancer pain. It found that the evidence clearly substantiated the effectiveness of relaxation techniques and hypnosis in alleviating chronic pain. Hypnosis was also effective in ameliorating the discomfort of such difficult ailments as irritable bowel syndrome, oral mucositis (inflammation of the mucous glands), temporomandibular disorders, such as TMJ, and tension headaches.

Before Morton's discovery of anesthesia, those who were unfortunate enough to require surgery were left to a bottle of strong liquor and their own devices. While many obviously suffered, the records indicate that there were others who did not. Hypnosis has a long history of being used to alleviate pain on the battlefield when no other means were available. In 1846, James Esdaile, a Scottish doctor in India, performed almost 350 major operations without any chemical anesthetic. Ether had only just been discovered in 1846 and chloroform would be discovered in 1847. In those days, many patients undergoing surgery died of shock related to pain. Generally, the mortality rate of those undergoing surgery had been a devastating 50 percent. Under Esdaile's use of what was then termed "mesmerism," the mortality rate of his patients was dramatically reduced to 5 percent.

The word used by physicians of the mid-19th century to describe what happened to those who went through the procedures stoically and later denied feeling pain was "insensibility." Baron Larrey, the principal surgeon to the French Imperial Guard under Napoleon, was present during the amputation of General Caffarelli's arm. He wrote in his journal that the General had "extreme courage" and did not speak a single word, perhaps due to what he called, "much concentration."

In this chapter, we'll show you several techniques to help reduce or control pain in a medical crisis:

> **Pain is the great motivator *and* the great communicator!**

- Object metamorphosis (concretizing and manipulating)
- Control room/Dimmer switch
- Glove anesthesia
- Changing focus/scanning
- Dissociation
- Visualization

Like other Verbal First Aid techniques, these work best when the victim or patient is in the healing zone, which is so often the case with those in pain.

*The Value of Pain—Please Note!*

When we see people in pain, we naturally want to help them. We want to ease their suffering and bring them relief. There's an important caveat, however, as you try to help. Please keep in mind as you are helping someone in pain, that *pain is also a signal that something is wrong*. When the emergency rescue people arrive on the scene, or when the doctor appears at the bedside of a seriously ill person, the patient has to be able to communicate which areas need attention and why. Pain can be tremendously informative, so while we want to ease it, we also want to allow the pain to communicate its vitally important message.

What that means is that, as we are successful in mitigating pain, for example during a long wait for an ambulance, we can also build in a little alarm that sounds when something must be attended to, an override that allows the pain to call attention when needed. You might say something like, "and while you are feeling this comfortable numbness and your body is beginning to heal itself, whatever needs to get your attention, or the attention of the paramedics or doctors, will signal by letting you feel what needs help, even as the rest of your body remains relaxed."

Chronic pain, however, may continue far past the point of usefulness, causing incapacitation and depression. Pain, when no longer productive (in that it points our attention to a problem), can have deleterious effects on the heart, kidneys, gastric and colonic processes, and blood pressure.

According to R.A. Sternbach, an expert in the field, pain can be defined by the following:

1) A signal or something that points to the source of pain as a potential problem;
2) A pattern of neurochemical responses that allow the pain to be recognized by someone else, such as a doctor;
3) the subjective sensibility or suffering. Pain, however, remains a mutable, inconstant, and slippery companion. It is very common in cases of intractable pain for examinations to reveal no organic causes.

There are many pains that give us confusing information, such as phantom limb pains, referred pains, and psychosomatic pains. When presented with more complex situations, it is wisest to rely on the most basic of Verbal First Aid procedures: pacing. For instance, Donna is attending to Pete, an elderly relative with diabetes who has recently suffered a right leg amputation. He complains that his right leg itches terribly. Instead of reminding him that he has no leg, she goes to the bed and asks him to point to where it itches. "Over there," Uncle Pete points to a fold in the sheet. Mary responds, "Would you like me to scratch it so you can be more comfortable?" Pete nods and relaxes as Donna scratches his phantom itch.

Keeping in mind the communicative value of pain, when using any of the following techniques you can suggest to the patient that he "keep only enough discomfort at the site so that you can inform the doctors what needs attention and what's working."

The techniques you are about to learn can be used to keep the patient comfortable and safe until the ambulance comes, and they can provide chronically ill patients with skills to control their own pain, whenever they need to—not just in emergencies. In both cases the gift they bring is invaluable.

*Object Metamorphosis*

One very useful strategy calls on the victim to imagine a feeling as an object and then do something to change the nature of the object so that you can, in turn, modify the feeling. For example, Bob is hurt in a fall and says that he feels a tremendous pressure on his abdomen. He is clearly in great discomfort. At this point, we can ask what that pressure feels like, and encourage Bob to describe it. Once he has articulated the pain as a specific image, our goal is to change it into something less painful, less frightening. The following is one potential scenario:

"The pressure on my stomach feels like a big, heavy rock.'
"Okay, now that you see it as big, heavy, rock, what color is it?"
"I don't know.... It's red."
"It's a red, big, heavy rock. You can obviously see it very
clearly. Now let me ask you a question: what color does it have to
be to feel better?"

Oddly enough, perhaps to his surprise and yours, Bob knows the answer to that question. At this point, you can continue to use his imagination to change the rock's color to a cooler tone, such as blue or green, and then ask him to change it from a rock to a balloon. Get him to describe that balloon. Once he's got that image firmly in his mind, you have several options, either of which will help relieve the pain. Either the balloon can float away, or we can let the air out of it until it disappears.

*Control Room/Dimmer Switch*

Although we have suggested that you avoid the word "pain" in most of these protocols, this one addresses it directly. In Chapter 1, we told the story of Timothy Trujillo and how he helped a man in a motorcycle accident while waiting for the paramedics to arrive. This is the pain-relief technique he alluded to. It asks the patient to imagine a *control room* in his mind, perhaps like the cockpit of a jet fighter plane or a scientist's lab with lots of knobs and buttons to push. In one area, there is a rheostat with a control button that slides horizontally, from a low of one to a high of ten. Under it is a sign, *pain control.* Ask the patient to assign their pain a number along this spectrum. In an emergency situation they are likely to respond with nine or ten, to which you reply, "Fine," or "Right," or "Okay."

Next you ask them to reach over and slide that control button down to eight, or seven. Difficult as this is to believe (and to their total surprise), they will be able to do so and the pain will actually diminish. Then ask them to push the control switch down to six or five. The effect might come a bit more slowly this time, but it's likely they will be able to do this, as well. Have them indicate when they are at "six" by moving a finger. This is called an *ideomotor* response and it helps keep the patient in the altered state that furthers this process. Here's the difficult but important part. To make the most of this technique, you then have to ask them to take the pain back up to eight again. They may resist, but if they comply, they will make a dramatic discovery—that they are in full control of their own pain! Then ask them to take it back down to a five or six or even lower if it is possible. The lower they can slide that knob, the better.

As we saw in the Trujllo story, when the patient with the corkscrew fracture in his leg said that he no longer needed the pain medication because it "was at zero," this is a very powerful pain-control tool. It teaches patients that they are in control, and can therefore turn the pain down whenever necessary. Having experienced it for themselves, they know it is true. As its name implies, this approach and the one that follows, give the patient a sense of control, which is especially valuable when one's entire life suddenly seems to have been turned upside down.

Dr. Don Jacobs uses the metaphor of electrical wires and a light bulb in the brain to accomplish pain control. He suggests that people experience their "distress" as their body's way of telling them that something needs attention. Once they've gotten the message, then can turn down the signal. He asks people to imagine that electrical wires of various colors run from whatever part of the body is experiencing the distress to a light bulb in the brain. Then he has them imagine that there is a *dimmer switch* that allows them to dim or brighten the light. Then he says, "Go ahead and begin to dim the light a little now... Good. Now you control with the dimmer to whatever level you need..."

*Amnesia*

When pain is of a more episodic nature, we can help people to forget it. Half of the problem with chronic pain is the memory of pain past. The other half is the anticipation of pain to come. Of course, that anticipation is replete with anxiety, tension, and fear—the ingredients for an altered state. Remembrance can be dulled with suggestions for amnesia: *Everyone forgets things, just like we forgot what we were arguing about the other day...we can forget where we put our socks, where we put our jewelry...and who hasn't forgotten where they put their keys??? We can forget anything...even where we put pain... and pain can move and change so fast...we can forget where it was last...and have no clue what it may have felt like...* Interestingly, in forgetting past pain, we forget to fear future pain. The memory seems to be linked to anxiety about the future. When the dread is reduced, so is any pain in the present.

Ernest Hilgard, M.D., and Josephine Hilgard, Ph.D., distinguished researchers out of Stanford University, feel that amnesia is one way to help prevent the discomfort associated with nausea and vomiting from chemotherapy. They have worked with patients whose anxiety is so intense, they begin vomiting even before they enter the hospital for treatment. By helping them to forget the discomfort of their past experiences and simultaneously suggesting other interests to distract them, they have helped their patients to find renewed comfort. Many clinicians combine suggestions for amnesia with suggestions for time distortion so episodes of pain come as complete surprises and the expected 20 minutes of discomfort can seem like 10 seconds.

*Displacement*

No one would mind having a disease quite so much if they didn't have to have any of the symptoms and would never have to know it was there. The same holds true for pain. If we could only have as much pain as we absolutely needed in order to properly care for ourselves (so we don't lean up against hot stoves and burn ourselves to the bone) but no more, or could limit it to one part of our body so it was manageable, most of us would agree that would be satisfactory. Displacement works with that agreement.

Displacement takes the pain from one area, where it has caused undue distress and interrupted our lives, and puts it in another area, so we can feel more comfortable and go about our business. One man experienced such terrible back pain, he walked practically doubled. During the time when the origins of the pain were being explored both medically and psychologically, he was out of work, the sole supporter of his family and desperate to get back to the job. We asked, "Would it be all right if the pain continued in another part of you? In a part of you large enough to remind you of the work you need to do with yourself, but small enough to allow you to get back to the job and make a living?" He agreed to it and it worked.

Another person had migraine headaches which kept him from accomplishing much in his life. But he was so identified with the headaches that he could hardly imagine life without them! Who would he be if he didn't have to arrange his schedule around this limitation. Yet he knew that he wanted to be free of them most of the time. When it was suggested to him that he could "store the migraines in his pocket and have them when he felt he had the time for them," he nodded slowly. He felt them sit in the palm of his hand, as if they were a live, throbbing little being, and put his hand in his pocket. Then he knew it was there if he still needed to identify with it. This is a combination of Object Metamorphosis and Displacement, as you concretize it and change its form, place, and timing.

A kinesthetic way of achieving displacement is by asking people to clasp their hands together very tightly so that attention is focused on the sensations generated there, rather than in the more grievously affected parts. Some clinicians use this technique in childbirth, asking patients to squeeze their hands or some object as tightly as they can with every contraction. Attention gradually shifts from the more painful contractions in the abdomen to the less difficult sensations in the hands.

*Glove Anesthesia*

This simple technique has a long history in hypnotic anesthesia. The practitioner asks patients to imagine that all sensations are leaving their right hand and moving into their left hand. The idea here is do this as vividly and specifically as possible. You could say to the person in pain, "Have you ever reached for a drink in a cooler full of ice? Remember how cold that feels? Or maybe you've had your hand in an icy mountain stream, or you can remember making a snowball when you forgot to put on your mittens. Remember how it feels when your hand begins to tingle when you fall asleep on it. You can feel that tingling now. Hold your hand in that icy water until it is numb…tune in to that feeling that there is no feeling in your right hand as it grows more and more cold, frozen, numb."

Then ask the person to "place that frozen, numb hand very gently where you are experiencing the discomfort and notice how that part of your body becomes numb, too." Oddly enough, once the hand is numb, it can transfer this numbness (lack of sensation) anywhere it comes to rest, providing pain relief. It's one more testament to the amazing power of the mind!

*Changing Focus/Scanning*

As we mentioned in the chapter on *rapport*, pain is at its most powerful when it is the object of attention. Simply asking people to turn that attention elsewhere can be a source of pain relief. Suggesting that they "scan the body to see if anything else needs attention" is one way of moving the attention away from the injury. This technique is fundamental and easy. All we have to do is ask about an uninvolved part of the body and draw the attention there, and we've created a certain amount of comfort.

You can also help people to focus on another priority, such as getting away from a burning building or any other external factor, effectively displacing awareness of the pain. Everyone can recall a time when they were having so much fun or were so in love or so involved in their work that they completely forgot about that headache or those menstrual cramps or that aching back. It happens all the time. When something else is a priority, pain takes a back seat.

*Dissociation*

Some people are able to separate themselves from their body's experience, especially in the altered state of an emergency situation. It is a natural, protective instinct. In an emergency situation, indeed, wherever the heart is vulnerable, the experience of our life space can be radically altered. There is a narrowing of focus so that what is ordinarily available to the conscious mind gets shut out. Certain areas are given priority and other areas are not even recognized as existing. This opens the door to making suggestions that allow the person to float apart from the situation, as if they were resting in bed or floating in a calm pool of water, thereby obtaining some relief from pain.

Some people, when given suggestions for specific sorts of pain relief such as displacing the pain from the abdomen to a more tolerable place, like the tip of the finger, will spontaneously dissociate. One woman we know reported a feeling of floating out of herself, watching the pain, but not feeling it. She admitted that she didn't understand it herself and wasn't even sure she was describing it properly. We suggested she could just take that awareness with her wherever she went so that her experience of the pain would be altered permanently. "You can have the pain as long as you need it," we assured her, "but you never have to actually feel it." When presented with such a gift and such relief, understanding is hardly necessary.

*Visual Imagery*

Depending on people's ability to use their imaginations, you have a variety of approaches to visualization from which to choose. Working on the more concrete level, you could tell the victim that our body knows how to make its own endorphins for comfort and invite them to picture those pain-relieving neurochemicals in any way they can, mobilizing the endorphins to do their work—filling the victim with feelings of comfort. In addition to providing comfort, this visualization can also help stimulate repair and recovery.

You could suggest that the victim imagine T-cells inside their blood, working on the front lines of the immune system, rushing to fix whatever needs attention. Cancer patients can use guided imagery for chemotherapy, imagining the chemo attacking only the weak and confused cancer cells, while the rest of the body rejoices in the help and remains healthy. As we've seen in research studies, burn victims receive not only pain relief, but often suffer less edema and scarring when told to imagine themselves cool and comfortable in clean snow or a cold spring brook, where they float calmly, noticing how their body temperature already is beginning to lower.

Imagery can be as specific as your understanding and the situation allows. For instance, R.K.S. Lim researched the chemical reactions that stimulate the perception of pain and found that there are specific substances to which our organs, tissues, and muscles respond. Many of these are amines or peptides, the most familiar being a peptide known as bradykinin that develops in blisters when skin is burned. Knowing this, we can utilize it in our suggestions if the context permits. For instance, "Tom, I see the burn and, yes, I can see that you're feeling it. I'm going to help you now. Come with me to the sink. Good. Now [as cool water is running], as the cold waters starts to cool your skin, you might imagine microscopic peptides getting the signal to turn off so that your skin heals smoothly ...and as your fingers continue to feel the water cooling them all the way through the layers of skin to tissue, you might imagine your body choosing the quickest way to heal...."

Sensory visualizations can invite people to *go* to a safe place, such as the beach, where they can see and feel themselves being cradled and soothed by waves of comfort, where the waves can carry away anything that might stand in the way of comfort. In 1999, Dr. Elvira Lang at the Beth Israel Deaconess Medical Center in Boston, embarked on a study involving 241 people who were being operated on to open clogged arteries, nerves, and blockages in the kidney drain system, as well as to block blood vessels feeding tumors. One-third of the patients were guided through visualizations of scenery they loved. One-third received extra attention. One-third were the less fortunate *control group*. While those receiving extra attention fared well—confirming that your loving kindness *is* good medicine—the guided visualization group fared best. Those patients had less pain, fewer problems with blood pressure and heart rate throughout the operation, and their operations finished 17 minutes earlier than the control group.

Children have ready access to their powers of imagination. To help them facilitate the healing process, you might simply say, "Remember the last time you played a video game?" In seconds, they are off in another world. Another good strategy is to ask children to "see" their favorite TV show in their minds and describe it to you; ask frequent questions to stimulate the process. Then, find a way to bring the characters to help in the present situations. "What do the characters do? How do they 'fix' things when they get hurt? Ask Dora the Explorer. Ask Barney. Ask Elmo. They'll know."

*Pain & Emotions*

Sometimes people in accidents expend precious energy being angry at themselves for having made a mistake, or at others for their thoughtless actions, or even railing at fate. If you suspect that the victim's anger and frustration is sapping their energy, help them in any way you can to let that go *at least for now*. Forgiveness is the best medicine, but if time is pressing, you can give accident victims permission to suspend judgment now, knowing that they can review the accident in their mind later. For now, they can help themselves best by concentrating on sending healing messages to their body.

Any and all of these techniques can help you help others in pain. You can follow any of these suggestions without interfering with the rescue effort, or with any aspect of appropriate medical care. You don't have to move, or even touch, the victim.

And, always remember, for both yourself and the injured person, becoming aware of breathing and slowing it down creates an environment of relaxation in the body that, by relieving stress, helps also to provide pain relief.

What follows is a sample visualization designed to help a person experience the sensation of "numbing." Please feel free to reprint it and keep it with you.

*Numbing Visualization Scripts*

"As I hold/put cool water on your arm/leg [affected body part] now, you can rest comfortably knowing that I'm going to take care of everything and you can focus completely on feeling the cool water... you can even close your eyes for a moment or two and see deep, deep down how fresh, how clean, how cool the water is, even feel it like new fallen white snow, so cool, so comfortable, packing gently around your [leg/arm etc.], cooler and cooler. And you may remember the last time you felt cool, cool, clean snow..."

or

"You may remember the last time you put your arm into a bucket of cool, clean ice water to reach for a cold can of soda pop and you had to fish around in there and it was so cold, your arm almost got numb... yes...just a little like now..."

or

"In a cool mountain stream or lake in early spring with bubbling, icy water running over the rocks and washing your arm clean, making it feel so cold now it's almost numb...but not quite...but really close... you know that feeling don't you...everyone knows that feeling of an [arm/leg] being so cool, so comfortable that you can hardly feel it... and you can feel now that your [arm/leg] is in that bucket of clean, clear ice or that mountain brook, clean, fresh and freezing cold...can't you?"

or

"You know the feeling of the air conditioner blowing on your face as you sit in the car and at first it's cool but then it seems cold and you feel it tingling and cold on your face? And you can remember that feeling as the water runs cool and comfortable over your [arm/leg] of the air conditioner blowing so that your face is feeling so clean and refreshed and so cold and almost...but not quite totally numb..."

*Changing Focus for Pain Relief*

"Maybe in all this excitement, you haven't noticed how relaxed your foot [unaffected, un-tense body part] is, lying there, just relaxed and uninvolved, as we have tended to other parts of your body. Now, tense it up just a bit, make it into a muscle now, and then that's right... relax it again...Good. And you can keep your eyes closed as you consider that foot and how relaxed it is, and from time to time you can tense it, just to see what it can do, you know...whether it's kidding or not...or just pretending to be relaxed...and then you can let it go again and be curious about it...how can a foot be so relaxed with so much going on all around it...and if one foot can be so relaxed, what about the other foot...Now, what about that other foot...

"And go ahead, now, close your eyes and take a really good look inside there inside that foot and see how relaxed it is...and we don't want this one foot getting away with something the other one can't so, go ahead and tense this foot now and feel the muscles tighten and then... in just a moment...okay...go ahead...let it go. Good. Now you know. And you can enjoy that you know, just a little and start to allow yourself to let that relaxation move up through the rest of your body...through your legs...through your torso... [follow through unaffected parts first and ultimately through to affected body part]...

"And that feeling of relaxation with all the rest going on around outside you can bring just the smallest of smiles to the corners of your lips, the kind of smile you have when you've got it and you'd like to laugh, but maybe you'd like to keep it to yourself for now...so you can take it with you wherever you go..."

There are some questions among professionals about whether hypnotic suggestions to relieve pain work with people who are not in formally induced trances, meaning when suggestions are given to them in the waking state. To demonstrate the power of communication, even without a prior hypnotic induction, M.B. Evans and G.L. Paul, Clinical Psychologists who study pain, conducted an investigation that was reported in *The Journal of Consulting and Clinical Psychology* (1970). First, they measured the hypnotic susceptibility of the volunteers. Then they gave half of the group a hypnotic induction and left the other half in an "ordinary" state. When they gave both groups suggestions for pain relief, they found that both groups reduced their pain by an equal amount. From this they concluded that suggestions for pain relief work in "ordinary" and "extraordinary" states of consciousness when there is sufficient motivation. We see the possibilities in their investigation in a slightly different light: Aside from showing the power of suggestion, it also alludes to the point we make all along—that pain and stress can, in and of themselves, create the alterations in consciousness that make us more open to suggestion, particularly when those suggestions contribute to what we want: for the pain to stop.

# CHAPTER NINE

# PHYSICAL ILLNESSES AND CHRONIC CONDITIONS

*"Don't deny the diagnosis; try to defy the verdict."*
*–Norman Cousins*

Up to this point in the book, we have taken you through the dramatic, sometimes terrifying world of the medical emergency. The techniques we have shown you for helping people before the rescue teams arrive can provide pain relief, promote calm, and influence the healing outcome for the better. But what about the perhaps less dramatic–but still debilitating–world of physical and emotional illness? What are the words that can make a difference, that can promote healing in the non-emergency scenario?

It is one thing to address a person you might not even know while waiting for the ambulance and quite another to speak to your beloved grandmother who is suffering with Alzheimer's disease or cancer. There are not only different things to say and different processes to address within the other person, but you, yourself, will be in a very different frame of mind. It is another thing altogether to recognize the looping, negative thought processes in your own mind as you move through a crisis or a series of crises, and then change them into thoughts that serve you and promote your own physical and emotional well being. All these issues have to be taken into consideration as we adapt our protocols to fit this different situation.

As you have seen, the protocols for Verbal First Aid in medical emergencies are very prescriptive. People in a medical emergency can be expected to be in an altered state, which makes it possible to communicate directly with their autonomic nervous systems. Things happen fast in a medical emergency. In terms of the time frame, decisions are urgent and there is not much flexibility. What we have discovered, though, is that much of what has been developed for medical emergencies is easily adapted for non-critical physical and mental illness. As we move into the protocols for various forms of illness, scheduled surgery and even dying, let's take a look at how those situations are similar and how they differ from what you have already learned in Verbal First Aid for medical emergencies.

1. While pain and fear may cause an altered state in people with physical and emotional illnesses, that state is not as acute, not as obvious, and not as predictable as it is during an actual emergency. There may be moments of extreme pain or anxiety when we get signals that the person's unconscious mind is available for suggestion. Sometimes, however, the receptive altered state has to be evoked in non-emergency situations with imagery and/or stories (See Chapter 3, The Healing Zone).

2. Although there is always a sense of urgency when pain, terminal illness or threats of suicide are involved, in general the time frame for dealing with physical illness or emotional distress and pain is distinct from that of a medical emergency. No ambulance is arriving in ten minutes. You have time to practice and improve (and improvise) your general techniques. Rather than having to manage immediate survival needs, the focus in working with the physically or emotionally ill becomes comfort, reframing, and acceptance. These conditions offer the opportunity for genuine, deep-down healing that can be facilitated and enhanced by words.

3. There is less need for a script. Patient contact takes place over a longer period of time, allowing for greater understanding of the complexities of personality and the conditions surrounding the specific illness.

What is most interesting, however, are the distinct similarities between critical care and longer term health issues, since these provide opportunities for using much the same techniques for establishing and maintaining rapport, and for using the power of suggestion, which you have already learned. In this chapter we will show you how to adapt these techniques for use with physical illness and scheduled surgery.

Here is a quick review of the techniques we have discussed for gaining rapport.

- *Getting Centered.* In an emergency, when panic is in the air, getting centered is a basic survival technique. Without it, a person attempting rescue can fall prey to the hysteria of the moment and be unable to think as clearly as the situation demands. In physical and emotional illness, it is also wise to center yourself before you begin, because this contributes to a sense of calm, empathy, and insight that can mightily benefit your work.

- *Establishing Empathy.* While this is a valuable technique in emergency situations, it may be even more important in non-emergency situations because of their longer duration. Long-term healing rapport requires patience that only empathy can provide. This is not the same thing as sympathy (which implies, "I'm sorry for you," but suggests that it's *your* problem, not mine). Empathy means, "I feel what you feel," and gives an ill person that all-important feeling of being understood. In an emergency, long-term bonds are not necessary, nor, for the most part, are they established. In on-going illness, however, you can establish a relationship that allows you to gain a real sense of what is going on inside the other person.

- *Establishing Authority.* As you know, this is a necessary part of ensuring that your suggestions will be followed in a medical emergency, especially when you're dealing with strangers. This authority, together with the receptivity of the victim, lends tremendous power to statements like "I'm here to help you," and "the worst is over. Will you do what I say?" In on-going illness, establishing authority may not be such an important issue, but it is still very useful when you begin to give therapeutic suggestions.

    o   Your *presence*, which consists of your complete attention, focus, and caring interest, is your most valuable healing tool. In simply being present, you are already providing the love that is the most important form of Verbal First Aid. There is ineffable magic in such a gift—partly because it is, unfortunately, so rare in our experience. It is as if we've been lit up by a spotlight. We become the center of someone's attention, and in that light dormant parts of us awaken—parts that suddenly realize we may be worthy of notice, may be worthy of life, may be worthy of health.

    o   *Conviction* is simply belief. But with conviction comes a certain authority, a sense of leadership. Conviction states clearly, without equivocation: "I know this to be true." When you have conviction, your tone, your body language, your touch, and your heart stand behind every word you utter. Everything you do and say has more power. Conviction literally convinces. It moves mountains. It gets people to do things they might not ordinarily do.

- *Establishing an Alliance* in this case this may simply mean that you wish the person the best, that you share the same objective for their recovery. You are there to help.

- *Communicating Realistically* means being honest, but finding ways to reframe a situation so that an ill person can more comfortably live with the illness, benefit from the wisdom that can result from experiencing it, and move deeper into a healing mindset.

- *Avoiding Contra-alliances* is probably most important over the long haul. It *never* does any good to be part of blaming people for their illnesses. To say, "If you'd only quit smoking when I told you to," does not advance the cause of healing one bit. This caution is both obvious and remarkably easy to forget, especially in frustrating situations.

- *Getting a Contract* in a medical emergency means asking, "Will you do as I say?" Over the long term of an illness, it means confirming with patients that they understand that you are trying to help, and that they will agree to participate in that effort. You may have to renegotiate that agreement many times over a longer period of time. This is to be expected.

- *The four C's, Confidence, Credibility, Compassion and Concern,* are critical components to Verbal First Aid in physical and emotional illnesses as well as in acute care. The steps for gaining and utilizing rapport are essentially the same, but need to be maintained over time much the same as you would in any relationship.

Once you've adapted the rapport-gaining techniques to non-emergencies, you will want to turn to the *therapeutic suggestions* that help patients with pain relief, calming and healing.

Here is an important element to remember in all situations. Your facility with therapeutic suggestion, whatever form it takes, is based in large measure on your conviction that it can and does work. You have almost certainly had the experience of trying to convince someone of something you didn't fully believe in and felt the futility of that. When you use visual imagery, your tone should reflect both your conviction and your compassion. Speak softly, firmly, intimately—let your conviction resonate with every syllable. This is a shared process; you're not doing this "to" anyone. You're doing this in concert *with* someone. You facilitate the images *they* conjure.

All communication is participatory and refractory, whether we are aware of it or not. What we say to someone else, in the final analysis, is something we are saying to ourselves. Here's perfect example: When one of us was still smoking cigarettes, a businessman came in for help to quit his own habit of two packs a day. While taking his case, we learned that he smoked in "binges"—chain smoking for several hours, then stopping altogether while he attended a meeting or sat on a six-hour flight across the country. When asked, "How do you do that?" he replied, "I forget about it. If I can't smoke, I just make myself forget." That moment, combined with an understanding of utilization and the knowledge that one could develop a state of amnesia around something as specific as smoking, led to a series of hypnotic sessions with that fellow focusing repeatedly on "forgetting to smoke." What is most interesting and pertinent is that not only did *he* stop smoking but so did his therapist, going out night after night for a week to pick up a pack of cigarettes only to arrive home realizing that she had forgotten to buy them, and had instead gotten side tracked in the literature aisle of the store. What goes around does indeed come around. Words said are words heard—one more good reason to say them lovingly and with care.

## Guided Imagery for Healing

You can use these techniques and ideas to help people with most chronic and life-threatening illnesses. Because each person's mind, history and experience are different, images will be highly individual. We do not actually have to suggest specific images, but we can provide the context for them. Images can be literal or metaphorical. Dr. Carl Simonton, when using visualization techniques with his patients, originally suggested conjuring up the image of white blood cells as little Packmen, from the early video game, eating the cancer cells. This worked for some people. However, others objected to the violence of the image, so they were allowed to suggest their own imagery, with Dr. Simonton providing the metaphorical framework.

There are many ways to employ imagery for healing. Once you understand how they work you can select the ones that best suit your temperament and that of the person you are helping.

### Simple Relaxation Technique

If the person is willing, you might begin with this simple relaxation technique:

"You may notice the bottoms of your feet now as if a soft, soothing light—any color light—were shining on them, softening, soothing, warming the cells that need to be warmed, cooling the cells that need to be cooled and you may notice that feeling begin to move up through your arches and your ankles, softening and soothing in the same comfortable and safe way. It's moving into your calves, your knees and your shins…slow it down so you can spend just a moment enjoying that softness and that safety, that warmth and coolness as the light moves through you, into each cell, taking in what is healthy and alive, sloughing off what is useless to you now. It's moving along like a soft breeze down the street, just like a soft breeze on a lazy, easy day, taking the leaves that have fallen off the trees down the street with it, taking the dead leaves away, leaving the street clean, clear, open, full of light…"

This sort of imagery can continue throughout the whole body, spending time where the patient needs it, providing the opportunity for open-ended suggestions for healing and comfort. For instance, you might say, "As you become more aware of your kidney [substitute with the organ in question], you might notice the light spending a bit more time there, softening and surrounding the area, cleaning…nourishing…healing." At the end, it is common practice to send the light back out again through the top of the head, "leaving behind the goodness and grace and softness and love, taking with it anything you no longer need and that keeps you from full well being and comfort."

Many chronic sufferers need to let go—not necessarily of life (although at some point that may be the case), but of resentments, entitlements, angers, and regrets. Mostly, they need to let go of trying to control that which is beyond their control. Here's a simple, but very effect guided visualization for letting go.

**Letting Go and Flowing Visualization**

"I'm going to tell you a story about the river. You know how a river flows, don't you. It just flows, from its source to its destiny. Sometimes there's a rock or a boulder in its way, and the river just flows easily around it or over it. Over time it will effortlessly wear any obstacle down, just by doing what it does best: flowing. Sometime the river takes on a heavy load, like a boat or a log, and the river carries it easily as it flows from its source to its destiny. Sometimes it rains and the river absorbs that water and it becomes more river. And the river just flows on. And sometimes the river gets caught in eddies, and it whirls around and around, until it straightens out. And then it just flows. And sometimes the sun shines. And the river dances with it and reflects it in

214

a million little diamonds on each little wavelet. And the river just flows, from its source to its destiny. And the river just flows."

This example of guided imagery can be easily amplified or modified to suit the person to whom you're speaking. Notice the many suggestions for allowing: objects in the way, burdens to carry, confusion to spin you around, floods, shining moments. And through it all, just flowing is the answer. (At this moment you may be thinking to yourself, "How wonderful to be a river." It seems that way to us, too.)

If you're working with someone who seems not to be interested in using guided visualization, you can also casually intersperse visual imagery in ordinary conversation. You might comment, "I can just picture your white cells getting stronger and beating up the cancer cells every time you take this medication, can't you?" We suggested to one friend whose cancer was so advanced that she was almost bereft of white blood cells that she imagine her while blood cells multiplying like little white rabbits every time she took her medication. "Rabbits with Uzis!" she said enthusiastically.

All suggestion involves utilizing the resources of the unconscious mind, whether that is directly ("Take a deep breath") or indirectly ("It's a wonder, isn't it, why sometimes there are clouds and sometimes not, but there's always the blue sky behind it, no matter what the weather looks like today."). Whether you choose direct or indirect suggestion depends on the personality of the person to whom you are talking. Rarely does arguing change the way a person feels, especially if that person has a more assertive style. We have found that knowing whom you are talking to and being able to quickly assess their motivation often makes the difference between suggestions being accepted or rejected. For instance, we would never tell new, frightened, or hypervigilant clients to just "close their eyes" without helping them to first feel safe. The more resistant a person is, for whatever reason, the more indirect the suggestion should be.

Many hypnotherapists believe that direct suggestions work best with obedient or highly motivated people. People in acute pain or in medical emergencies often are tremendously motivated and can benefit from more straightforward directives. "Just do it!" or "Just say no!" are highly publicized examples of simple directives. Some clients are so motivated to change that all they have to do is make the appointment for a session and by the time they get in, they're feeling "surprisingly better." In fact, one of the questions on our intake is "What's different since you phoned us?"

Direct suggestions deal with the problem at hand overtly and usually offer very concrete, detailed instructions.

"You are tired. You want to sleep. Notice how heavy your eyelids are feeling. Notice that heaviness moving to your hands. You feel your muscles softening in your face. Your neck muscles are softening. You think of your pillows. Imagine yourself in your bed right now. Remember the last time you fell asleep so easily. Remember being asleep before you knew it."

Not everyone is so open, and, in most cases, more subtlety is required.

Indirect suggestions appeal less to the logical, conscious mind than to the unconscious mind. In fact, indirect suggestion can leave someone consciously wondering what you're talking about, while at the same time, the unconscious mind is already making good use of the information, paving the way for healing and change.

An example of indirect suggestion might be: "Everyone knows what it's like to be reading a book and then finding the book lying flat on their chest in the morning, having no recollection of falling deeply asleep. Without any effort at all they nodded off quickly and easily."

An indirect suggestion is more open and less "instructive." It leaves the interpretation up to the other person. In guided imagery, we might offer this indirect suggestion to someone suffering from a burn, "It is so easy to remember that moment of shivery anticipation before you put your toe in the cool, cool lake. After all, it's still only April, and everyone knows how cool the water is in April. And as you take another deep breath, a part of you—perhaps your toe, perhaps your whole foot—is already in that water, feeling how icy it is…"

One woman we worked with had a growth on her tongue that had developed after someone had disappointed and betrayed her. In her visualization she saw that if she imagined pouring sugar on the growth, it would go away. She felt that if she repeated this visualization three times a day for three days, the growth would dissolve. When she went for surgery, the growth had already disappeared. It occurred to us that the growth was born of bitterness and had to be "cured" with sweetness. This metaphor emerged from her spontaneously once she was provided with the tools. *Metaphorical imagery* is the use of symbols to represent ideas and body functions, manipulating them toward wellness and healing.

*Personal resources* are people's own historic strengths, the parts of their story that they forget in times of illness, but of which they are most proud. Within the metaphor or imagery format you use, it can be very effective, at some point, to refer back to a time when the patient was able to do something well, when the patient felt different—strong, clear, healthy. This subtly reminds us who we are, and of the abundant resources we have within us, no matter what our circumstances. It tells us that we are not our diseases. We are not our fears. We are not our discomforts. We may *have* them, but we **are not of** them. We are so much more than the sum total of our ailments and body parts, and we can draw great strength from that insight.

### Verbal First Aid for Physical Illness and Chronic Conditions

Verbal First Aid can help you talk to a person suffering from a debilitating illness in ways that will lead to emotional relief, physical comfort, and, as a result, even measurable biological improvements. These techniques do not claim to cure, but they can create the conditions in which real healing can take place. The word healing comes from the Old English word "Haelen" which means to make whole. It does not mean to cure, to fix, or to mend. Wholeness, then, may not necessarily get rid of the disease itself. It may, however, integrate it in such a way that the person lives fully and dies more comfortably.

Most healing involves the body/mind mending itself, restoring itself to balance. Tapping in to the body's intelligence and reminding it of its ability to regenerate, achieve homeostasis and rebuild, can lead to relief, peace of mind, and, as you will see, sometimes the elimination of the disease. Whenever we talk about the body's ability to heal itself, we always remind people of the simplest and most miraculous ways in which the body does this every day, in recovering from razor nicks or paper cuts or bruises. Each day we watch our skin knit itself together without benefit of needles or threads, and our bruises gradually restored to normal.

As Dr. Michael Samuels, author of *Healing With The Mind's Eye*, points out, you will not find a description of the body's own healing capacities or mechanisms in any medical textbooks. But just because medical training overlooks this miraculous capacity doesn't mean that *we* should. Our bodies *are* absolute miracles of design. Quite aside from everyday wonders the body performs are the miracles of spontaneous remission; perhaps you yourself have had the experience of a serious medical condition just *go away*. What does *go away* mean, anyway? Where does it *go*? Why? How? What have we done differently when things just *go away*?

We once had a friend whose husband, Burt, walked into the hospital for an operation on his prostate. The operation went very smoothly, but when it was over and time for Burt to stand up and walk, his legs gave way. Something was very wrong, something the doctors labeled "a spinal infarction." The prognosis? They had no idea if Burt would ever walk again. Burt's wife decided to call in her own support system. She had an herbalist, a Native American healing circle, an acupuncturist, and a physical therapist rushed to her husband's side and asked us, as well, to come and help. By the time we got there, Burt had had enough. He turned to his wife and said, "Honey, you're healing me to death! I don't want to see any more of these people. Please get rid of all of them." All of them? Fortunately, all but us.

We asked Burt to go to his favorite place in his mind, which turned out to be a picturesque old ghost town in the southwest. We asked him to picture an old saloon with a rickety, once proud staircase in it, and we invited him to imagine he could fix that staircase and to make it functional and safe again. He worked at it. And he promised to continue to work on that staircase in his mind until he was satisfied that all was well. Burt is walking today, despite his physicians' prognosis or lack of one, and we like to think it was a harmonic concert of the healing team that paved the way for us, and the guided imagery which contributed to Burt's ability to cure himself.

There is no question that visualizing bodily functions actually generates chemical reactions that have both short- and long-term physiological consequences. Working from our essential premise that the mind and the body are one, pictures in the mind *are* pictures in the body. They are not related. They are one. You cannot think a thought and not feel it. You cannot feel a sensation and not have it perceived as thought, albeit subliminally. There is no seam. We are a continuum of mind, body, and spirit.

### Turning Point/Healing Zone Opportunities

One way in which long-term illnesses differ from medical emergencies is that there are shifts and changes all along their course. Sometimes, for long periods, one is just coping. Other times bring moments of crisis—the diagnosis and naming of a disease, new medications and surgery, for example—when survival issues and treatment concerns rise up. It is at those moments that the techniques derived from Verbal First Aid can work their magic most notably, as the healing zone opens up. In that sense these moments provide us with opportunities to say things that help shift fear into hope and even change the trajectory of an illness or concern.

A principal task of Verbal Fist Aid in non-emergency situations is to identify healing zone opportunities, in which people are more ready to accept therapeutic suggestion. The healing zone turning points we will discuss in this chapter include: The shock of diagnosis, iatrogenics, chronic pain, and surgery.

## The Shock of Diagnosis:  Do I Have to Listen to This?

When people receive a diagnosis of a life-threatening, or even a life-altering, long-term disease, something inside of them changes. In societies that believe in magical ritual, the naming of the disease in this way might be considered a curse. From now on, and because the doctor (or an X-ray, or a blood test) says so, the patient has been placed under an evil spell. .

The shock of this blight is akin to being run over by an SUV and left on the medical roadside to emotionally bleed. Thereafter, the patient, not unreasonably, is looking to be rescued. The situation, in terms of Verbal First Aid, is similar to that of an accident victim. From the moment of diagnosis, the person may be considered to move in and out of a state not unlike post-traumatic-stress-disorder. This means that often the patient is in that semi-altered state that can lead to the healing zone, in which the techniques of declaring with conviction that one can help, and making suggestions that begin inner healing can be very useful.

## How to Defuse the Diagnosis

Some years ago, a group of women in a small community, all farmers' wives, were been diagnosed with serious and terminal diseases. Researchers tracked them in order to understand what, if anything, might contribute to survival past the doctors' expectations. What they found was both shocking and amusing: Every woman who survived had met the initial proclamation by her doctor with a solid "So *you* say!" Because of the town's already long-standing negative relationship with the corporate authorities who ran the town's only large business, some of the women had never established a positive rapport with their doctors and simply did not trust or believe them. While we would never suggest that patient-doctor rapport, with all its potential for healing, be undermined deliberately, in this case it is more than of passing interest to notice how that fractured rapport saved the lives of these women. The appropriate Verbal First Aid technique here would not to be to disagree outright with the physician's diagnosis, but rather to assist the person who is ill to place the diagnosis into an overall context. This way, the shock of the negative diagnosis can be overcome without destroying the medical authority. Curiously, it seems to be possible for people to disbelieve the prognosis and still believe in the competence and goodness of their physicians, allowing them to participate in treatment and recovery.

The effect of a dreaded diagnosis is that people feel they have been sentenced to death, or worse, to a life of pain and imprisonment. From that moment on, for many people, nothing is the same—not for the people who have the disease nor for the people who love them. Everything changes. Now life must be lived around doctor visits, pill schedules, dietary needs, bathroom availabilities, and fatigue.

A woman we know, Edie, was diagnosed with a benign fibrous growth in her brain that had to be removed because it was attaching itself to the nerves in her ear and would continue growing, threatening her other functions. As a result of a fall some time before, however, her neck had been compromised and the surgeons felt it was absolutely necessary to operate on her neck before they risked the brain surgery, because the position in which they would have to rest her head during the brain surgery might otherwise leave her paralyzed. They also told her they she would likely emerge from the brain surgery deaf in one ear and perhaps with facial paralysis. All of this was very grim and the woman—who, until that time had been walking around feeling all right, not paralyzed, not deaf—was traumatized by this terrifying prospect.

It just so happened, however, that she had come to see us several years earlier with a growth on her tongue that the doctors and her dentist had declared might be fatal. "They have me with one foot in the grave," she had said at the time. She had used guided imagery before that operation, and not only was the mass much reduced by the time of surgery, but the catastrophic pain they had promised her also did not materialize.

We decided to use both that experience and guided imagery once again to help her through this case. If 50% of the people who emerge from this operation are deaf, we reminded her, then 50% are not. We also reminded her that she had been able to use guided visualization to great benefit before, so we know her body responded beautifully to that technique. Not only did both surgeries go well, but her spirit was revived and, by remembering her own strength, she moved into the future with renewed confidence.

We will discuss the importance of attitude—the physical effects of belief systems—shortly. For now, we are addressing only that turning point, that moment when the shock of the diagnosis throws a person into the Healing Zone and allows your words to be heard at a deep level, where they may be accepted as healing suggestions.

**Scenario**

A friend, Maria, calls and asks if you have a minute to talk. React-ing to the tone of her voice, you say, "Yes," even if you have to literally drop armloads of files or diapers to listen. "I just came back from the doctor," she says. "I had this funny, you know, numbness in my right side and I couldn't use my hand, and I got panicked. He ran tests, ruled out everything else, and now they say I have MS. **MS**! How could that be? I eat right. I do what I'm supposed to. And now the doctor says that I might end up in a wheel chair!"

"That means," you say, *reframing*, "that you might not?"

"Well, yes. He said about 1/3 of the people have one episode and that's all."

"That would be good," you say.

"And about 1/3 have, you know, episodes and remissions, off and on. And the rest—right into that wheel chair."

"So that's not even most people. I know a woman who works out in my gym who was diagnosed with MS and I don't think it slows her down one bit." (Here you're using the "*I know a guy who...*" technique.)

"What am I going to do?" she cries.

"You can talk to your body about it. It's just a mistake made by your own immune system. It thinks your own nerves are foreign invaders and it attacks the myelin sheath around them. You can use your mind to picture little post-it notes on them saying 'me' or 'self' or 'friendly,' and then send your immune system on an errand to fight the real invaders. Then you can imagine yourself joining the one-episode only group. You'll have an exciting story to tell while we're out there playing tennis again," (you *future pace* and help her with *imagery*).

"You think?" she says

(*Truism*) "Two out of three people never get near a wheel chair. Why would you think you..."

"But the doctor said—"

"Maria, doctors have to cover their bases, they have to mention all the possibilities, they're bound to do so by law. He can't tell you that everybody recovers fully from this because some people don't. It doesn't mean that it's true for you. You just accepted it because you were scared. Really, the doctor meant well, but he doesn't know *you*. He doesn't know you are an amazing woman. I know you and I know that about you. And amazing women can do amazing things."

(Recount some of the more miraculous or "lucky" things in her life, if you know them, anything she overcame in the past. Get her to agree. Get a *yes set* going. Then *future pace* her into healing so that she agrees with that, too.)

"Yeah...that's true..."

At this highly emotional crisis point, you can remind your friends of their whole selves, before fear takes over and makes them accept a label, before they succumb to what Andrew Weil, MD, calls a "medical hex."

**Practice**

You might want to take a moment to think of how you would defuse a devastating diagnosis with a friend or loved one. You might:

- Remind them of their strengths, resources.

- Find information to provide significant truisms.

- Recount examples of others who have survived.

- Help them picture a future in which they have overcome the illness.

**Iatrogenics**

"I have to tell you," says your doctor, "that one of the side effects of this new prescription could be nausea." You take the pill and proceed to throw up.

Doctors are in a bind. They are required by the laws of informed consent to let you know everything that could go wrong with a procedure, a pharmaceutical, or a treatment. By so doing, are they, as authority figures, inadvertently *prescribing* those outcomes?

One woman we know, Jeannie, went to speak with her doctor about what she believed to be truly minor surgery. She had even anticipated it being an outpatient procedure. However, she was soon told that the procedure would be performed in the hospital and that she would have to "prepare" for it. Lists were provided for her, detailing her responsibilities and rights, and she had to sign an informed consent form that included a litany of possible gruesome outcomes. From a routine event the surgery turned into a major production. Negative suggestions were flung around unintentionally, from the well-meaning warnings that "this will hurt," to the interview with the anesthesiologist who told her "I'm putting you under just in case anything happens," to the admonitions of the staff that there would be lots of swelling and pain and that she would have to stay in bed. Jeannie truly believed in the competence and goodness of her physician despite the iatrogenics popping like popcorn all around him, so she was able to overcome the negativity and to utilize Verbal First Aid, telling herself that all would be well. There was in fact, almost no swelling, no pain, no need for painkillers, and she was walking around within a few days.

When Andrew Weil, M.D calls iatrogenics—doctor-induced illness— a "medical hex," he blames "medical pessimism" for its prevalence. As wonderful as contemporary medicine is in emergency situations—much of it was born on the battlefield—it is easily frustrated by its limitations in chronic illnesses. When medicine runs out of options, when the chemo- therapy or the drugs don't work, a doctor may fall into that pessimism. Weil quotes a physician telling a patient with ulcerative colitis, "Listen, I've got nothing more to offer you, and chances are you'll eventually develop colon cancer." That prognosis can be self-fulfilling unless the "hex" is somehow broken. And it is at this time that a person moves into the altered state that might be used as a Healing Zone if the right words are poured on like a liquid antidote.

However the problem of iatrogenics can also be seen in a positive light. Psychiatrist Milton Erickson, ever mindful that we have the power to see things differently and therefore alter the outcome in medical situ- ations, wondered about the possibility of *physician-induced wellness.* If iat- rogenic illness is possible, he thought, isn't it also reasonable to propose that iatrogenic *health* is also possible? If it is within the realm of science to use suggestion in placebo trials, why not offer a therapeutic sugges- tion in the ambulance or in the waiting room to a doctor's office?

## Scenario

Your mother brings home a bottle of little white pills to forestall her osteoporosis. The doctor has told her that she has to take them in the morning on an empty stomach with eight ounces of water and not lie down nor eat anything for a half hour, during which time she her stomach might get upset.

MOM

Every morning. I'm supposed to get up and get an upset stomach.
Nice way to start the day, right?

YOU

Is this a *guaranteed* stomachache or a *maybe* stomachache?

MOM

He said *may*. You *may* get a stomachache.

YOU

So, then, you may not. (*Reframing*). You may get strong bones, instead.

MOM

No, I'm *supposed* to get strong bones. I *may* get a stomachache.

YOU

When was your last stomachache?

MOM

I don't usually get—

YOU

Yeah, I know. So why should this little white pill change
the habits of a lifetime?

MOM

It probably won't. Only he said—

YOU

He *has* to say that. Or the side-effects police will come and get him.
(*Humor*)

MOM

Those side effects. *Everything may cause something.*

YOU

Yeah. That's just legal talk. Did you ever get a side effect?
(*Resources*)

MOM

No, actually…

YOU

Do you know anybody who ever got a side effect?
(*"I **don't** know a guy who…"*)

MOM

No.

YOU

Did a pill ever make you sick?

MOM

No.

YOU

Is this one gonna make you sick?

MOM

(laughing)

No.

And you've just done a *positive **no** set!*

## Side Effects

*Side effects* has been a useful phrase in terms of public relations, but examined closely, it turns out to be meaningless. There are no *side effects*. These are the *effects*, unwanted though they may be, of the treatment. And, not only can a prescribed medicine cause, say nausea and vomiting, but the doctor is obliged to tell you as much, so that nausea and vomiting also become iatrogenically part of the prescription. It's useful to know if it "may cause liver damage," so you can monitor your liver. But, in terms of the iatrogenic part of the side effect, an important Verbal First Aid technique involves placing those warnings in context, thereby removing the hex. Something as simple as, "Oh, Margaret takes that every morning and she has no problem with it at all," will often help to keep stress about that factor from interfering with healing.

## How to Help Alleviate Chronic Pain

You can hardly watch commercial television without encountering myriad advertisements for products that offer pain relief from even minor distress, so anxious are we all to avoid it. In this cultural context seemingly endless pain can seem catastrophic. People suffering from chronic pain often turn away from the world and focus inward, because the pain seems to be all there is. From time to time, even in that state a Turning Point/Healing Zone opportunity comes to light.

Ray is in chronic pain. He says, "I just can't stand the pain anymore. I just can't take it." Mona sits down beside him, takes his hand and says, "I'll sit here with you with you for a while. You know what I wish? I'm wishing that I could put a tap on your side, a little faucet like the one in the bathroom sink, that I could turn on and drain the pain out from you. I'd turn it on, like this, and maybe the pain would come out a color—I don't know what color the pain looks like to you, but you probably do—and you could just let it flow out until that color was gone. [Pausing. And then I would imagine that that place was filled with a different color that felt better. I don't know what color that is, but you do, the color that feels better. [Pausing.] And I thought maybe I'd leave that tap there, in your side, so you could turn it on if the color that isn't good for you ever comes back, and you could let it drain out again so you could be more comfortable."

For more specific pain relief techniques, please see Chapter 8. You might want to practice them on yourself or with someone who is suffering discomfort, so you can build your confidence, which will allow you to project even more authority.

**What to Say to People About to Undergo Surgery**

With the possible exception of some elective surgery, most surgery has a great many fears associated with it. There is the fear of "going under" anesthesia, fear of the knife, fear that something might go terribly wrong and you might not survive, and, the fear of a long, painful recovery. The mental images we associate with surgery are plentiful, and few of them are pleasant.

An accident or a medical emergency takes us by surprise. We have no chance to get caught up in the anticipation, only in the event itself, its repercussions, and recovery. However, people who know they are going to undergo surgery have time to worry before the event. And worry they will. That concern may put them into the healing zone so that the effect of your words may be especially helpful and contribute to a speedy recovery. One young woman, who is scheduled for surgery within a few weeks of this writing came in tense and trembling with anxiety. She had known about her surgery for a few months and waited through several postponements. With the date finally upon her, the fears flooded forth—the what-ifs that had been filling her mind now overflowed. Because she was so anxious, she had unwittingly put herself into an altered state (what some therapists call a *negative trance*) in which all she heard were the voices in her own mind and all she saw were her worst fears projected into the future. With

Verbal First Aid, it was possible to reach behind those barriers to provide the reassurance of another voice and another vision. When she left our office, she felt calmer, clearer, and secure.

One woman we know had delivered her third baby by caesarian section and had experienced dire consequences when her colon was inadvertently ruptured. She was scheduled to have an operation to repair the situation but was in great fear that something else might go wrong and she wouldn't wake up after the surgery. A few days before the scheduled procedure, her six-year-old daughter began to wake up at night with a stomach ache, even vomiting, having picked up the worry that filled the house. Helping the mother involved not only helping her relax and future pace a good outcome, but suggesting that she write a picture book with her daughter about "Mommy's operation and coming home." The book they wrote was delightful, detailing the seven days until her return, feeling better and better and awaiting balloons and kisses., and the two of them Skyped and read it during her hospital stay. The extra benefit, of course, was that as she reassured her daughter, she was reassuring herself that all would be well.

*I Know a Guy Who...*

Stories of other people who have gone through a particular procedure help to remind us that the surgery is not unusual, and that others who have gone through it are now out and about, living their lives, free of the condition that had clouded their lives before surgery. Stories give us hope without preaching and present possibilities without proselytizing. Stories are often an ideal format for delivering suggestions precisely because they are so subtle and non-judgmental.

*Future Pacing/Implied Healing*

Most people have operations to free themselves to live more fully than they had been prior to the surgery. While it may not always seem like an improvement in their lives, as in the case of a mastectomy, the hoped-for result is that the person will be cancer-free and able to go on living many more years. Sometimes, as in a heart or liver transplant, it actually means a new lease on life. In any way that you can, help people about to undergo an operation to picture the outcome as a chance to be better off than they are at present. Help them imagine doing things they love, free of the problem and returning more fully to life. That, after all, is the goal of the surgery.

*Guided imagery*

For a pilot program at Cedars-Sinai Medical Center's Cardio-Thoracic Surgery Unit, Judith Simon Prager developed a series of CDs that patients could listen to before, during, and after surgery to relieve anxieties and discomforts and to promote healing. Many patients reported such good results from the CDs that they used them in lieu of pain medication and sleeping medication. "When we compared these patients to routine patients, we found there was a dramatic reduction in pain medicine and sleeping pills that they requested," Dr. Gregory Fontana, Director of Integrative Therapies for Cardiac Surgery, told us. Nurses anecdotally reported earlier discharges and fewer side effects from the anesthesia. For us it is one more gratifying example of how effective the protocols in this book can be.

**Verbal First Aid for Surgery**

*Pre-operative*
Even before your operation, you can send messages to prepare your mind and your body to get into a healing state." It has been shown that those people who are "ready" for surgery, but not too deeply relaxed, actually fare best. The body needs some readiness to activate some of its defenses. Too much relaxation and we are left too vulnerable. Too little relaxation and we are anxious and tense. Often, the individual

can be best helped with a toned-down progressive relaxation and a suggestion to "relax just as much as your body needs to be prepared and ready for the best possible outcome."

Then, a *metaphor:* "perhaps you can remember that story Richard told you about the boat that was taken to dock after it had sprung a small leak. So just to be safe, they fixed it 'good as new' so it could go back out to sea comfortably and quickly...."

Then, *leaving the scene:* "During the procedure, you might want to imagine yourself dreaming of someplace else, some place you love to be..."

Then, *future pacing:* "Allow your mind to drift to a week after the operation when you will be home and the operation will be behind you. Imagine yourself telling others about how smoothly it went. Imagine the surprise of your doctors when you heal more quickly than anyone expected..."

## Intra-operative

Because you cannot be there with the person, you might want to offer some of these suggestions as close to the time as the person is being sedated as possible.

First, *relaxation,* "Relaxing now, in ways your body already knows... you can become aware that every touch of your surgeon's hands is a caring, loving touch, carrying you closer and closer to the moment when you are feeling better and better..."

Then, *metaphors:* "In your body, as in a garden, you know that a gardener sometime uproots a plant to help the health and well being of the whole garden. This way the garden can then blossom in all its beauty as nature intended it, growing healthier and better every day..."

*Truisms:* "Everyone knows that [Dr. Smith] is the best surgeon around. Everything will be happening exactly as it should to move you smoothly into a healthier future. Your body can cooperate with ease, knowing that you are in good hands, caring hands..."

*Leaving the Scene*: "As the procedure begins, your body feels numb and calm and you can simply relax and allow yourself to drift and dream, perhaps even taking your mind to a place you love to be..."

*Future Pacing*: "Always remember that your body has its own intelligence and knows when to cooperate and when to begin the healing..."

### Post-operative

If possible, you can give these suggestions as the person wakes up from the surgery.

*As you/you can*: Remind the person that: "The more relaxed you are, the faster the healing will occur." Or, "As you lie back on the pillow, you can let the healing truly begin and continue even as you sleep..."

*Truisms*: "Everyone has an immune system in place to guard the body against any infection. Your arteries and veins, skin and bones are skilled at smoothly closing up and knitting together again..."

*Because*: "Because you have an immune system, you can let it do the work it was made to do, like the way it healed that paper cut in no time at all and how the skin had knit itself whole again..."

*Future Pacing*: "You will be surprised and pleased to see how short the hospital stay will seem to you as you get more and more active every day."

**Words to Help During the Hospital Stay**

Hospital stays have their own mesmerizing effect on otherwise grown-up, independent human beings. Having someone regulate when you eat, drink, go to the bathroom, wake up to have a sleeping pill (!), visit with family, and get probed and prodded, takes away your sense of independence, your sense of yourself. We all become *infantilized*. The process can seem like a scene out of a Kafka novel: they take your clothes away and put you in humiliating wraps that don't even close properly enough to hide your naked bottom. You shuffle around in paper slippers. You are wired up, monitored, stuck with tubes and drips, injected with needles, plied with capsules and pills. The doctor appears on occasion with an air of visiting royalty and answers your questions by reviewing your chart and telling you the odds. No wonder you slip quietly into another zone.

If you are visiting someone in the hospital and they are clearly unhappy and uncomfortable, you might begin by remembering all of the above from a hospital stay you might have experienced, or shared with someone you love. This establishes empathy and rapport. Then utilize the intrinsically altered state to maximize your adapted suggestion techniques.

To help a person through a hospital stay, you can:

- remind them of their body's own healing capacity (*imagery*)
- remind them of who they are—their *strengths* and *resources*
- talk to them about others who *survived* this procedure *(I know a guy who...)*
- suggest a pain relief technique from this book if they need it
- help them to imagine being somewhere else *(guided imagery)*, somewhere they love, so their body can make healing chemicals and they can be more relaxed and comfortable - help them to see or remember that the reason they're going through all this is so that they can move into the future more comfortably *(future pace)*
- *listen to them*—there may be nothing more therapeutic than allowing someone to ventilate their frustration or fear and truly understanding them.

**A Script for Chemotherapy and Radiation**

We have been invited on occasion to sit with people as they go through the process of chemotherapy, and to use our words to help them make the most of this intervention. The words we use are very like those you find in this book.

The use of *metaphor* and *imagery* have been shown to be very successful in cancer cases. Before you begin, you might first ask the person undergoing chemotherapy or radiation whether they have an image of how the process is going to help them. Some people imagine sharks gobbling up the cancer. Others are offended by the idea of *killing* the cancer and have gentler pictures in their mind. One person we know saw her body as a tree, and the cancer as brown leaves; for her the treatment was blowing the old, brown leaves off her tree so that healthy, new green leaves could grow. Another patient saw the radiation directed at her brain tumor as a host of angels with feather dusters.

**Scenario**

Arlene is undergoing chemotherapy for breast cancer. As she sits there with the I.V. in her arm, you help her to relax (perhaps with the river relaxation visualization) and then say,

"As the medicine goes through your body you can begin to imagine [whatever she told you she wanted to imagine, e.g., the wind blowing the brown leaves...] or [if she offers no picture, you might say something more literal], imagine it seeking out and destroying all of the cancer cells while leaving the rest of your body safe, well, and healthy. The medicine goes right to the site of the cancer, exactly where it is needed, does its work and then is easily and comfortably expelled from your body, carrying away all the dead cancer cells with it. Your body feels comfortable and relieved as this process works. Your body, your cells, can remember their original programming to reproduce in a normal way. The more you picture this process the more comfortable and healthy you become. As you imagine the cancer cells dying and leaving, you can imagine your body growing stronger and healthier, and your spirit growing happier. You can see your doctor's face as he [or she] tells you that all is well. You can see your friends' faces as you tell them how you got through this experience. And then you begin to move ahead with your life, doing the things you love to do, feeling blessed and relieved; you can feel those feelings even now, even as things are changing and moving you toward that future.

"Any sensations you feel tell you that the process is working, and you can begin to imagine how it *feels* when you are well again.

In this way, any *side effects* of the chemotherapy are processed as part of the healing and are welcomed rather than resisted, which would give them greater power and cause greater discomfort in the patient.

Feel free to modify this script in any way that works for you and the person you are helping, based on the principles you have already learned.

## Utilizing the Healing Zone in Illness and Chronic Conditions

People who have been shocked by a devastating diagnosis, have endured a prolonged illness, or who have been through debilitating surgery, may move in and out of altered states through the course of their illness. People in a hospital, or in a doctor's office for that matter, are in an altered state by virtue of the fact that they are fearful, uneasy, or uncomfortable. In that state, they are already unusually open to an authority figure who ideally could use words to transform their fear and discomfort into hope and relief. In Chapter 3 we discussed how to help facilitate that state so that your therapeutic suggestions will be accepted.

Because every thought and every mental image stimulates a physiological response, the pictures in our mind can directly affect how and whether we heal. When the *movie* running in the subconscious shows us declining and suffering, it generates chemical processes that create an environment in which the disease can flourish. Helping someone to perceive the situation differently, to run a different movie that sees hope or comfort as a an outcome, allows the body to create the chemicals that provide a *carpet of calm*, a bath of natural chemicals from the parasympathetic nervous system that gives the body a better environment for healing. One woman who was a survivor of the attack on the

World Trade Centers said the most important words spoken to her were, "Your feelings are normal." She explained, "I felt so insane, so out of control, that just to hear someone say I wasn't losing my mind, that these were normal reactions to an abnormal situation made all the difference in the world. I could start to relax just a bit and allow myself to start to heal."

We asked one chronic care nurse in Los Angeles, "What is the one thing caretakers can say to patients with serious or life-threatening illnesses that can make the most difference?" He replied, "I always use five words and they always have the desired effect." The words? "Can I take your hand?" Why would that make such a difference? For one thing, people with diseases are frequently not touched in a loving way. Many have lost interest in sexuality, or are too fatigued for prolonged physical contact. Then, too, in the course of their disease, overwhelmed by the medical experience, they may have forgotten the small moments that lift us all above the chaotic morass. A simple touch can reconnect them to the world. Asking their permission gains a contract in much the same way as *soliciting their help* does. They become a partner in making this connection.

**The Caretaker**

Sadly, we have all had the experience of watching someone we love suffer from a chronic or life-threatening illness, of being unable to do anything more than watch. This is even harder for the person who lives with the chronically ill patient and has to manage the day-to-day indignities and struggles associated with it. Not only is it depressing, it is debilitating mentally and physically, partly because of everything we have to do, and partly because there seems to be nothing we *can* do to make it better.

Chronic disease is by definition a lengthy process and, as such, has qualities that distinguish it from acute disease. With acute disease, there is an end-point in sight: things will either take a turn for the better or resolve in death. While it is undeniably painful, acute disease takes a different toll on the caretaker. Chronic diseases, especially wasting diseases, are relentless. They wear away at us like wind and water carving a stone.

## The Importance of Attitude

Dr. Margaret Kemeny studies at UCLA focused on the effect of thought and emotions on life expectancy. Her research led her to investigate both the general population and more specific patient communities, such as those living with AIDS. Despite all the discussion about stress, her research suggests that what really affects our health is attitude, our view of other people, and our connection with them. She contends that, "The level of *hostility* we experience can be a predictor of a shortened life span and immune system changes. *Cynical mistrust,* by itself, is the most important factor predicting "non-causal mortality," i.e., heart attacks, strokes, etc, she says, adding that it is as important a determiner of early death as smoking.

Our beliefs about the future are as important as the future itself. In a 1988 study by Jeffrey Reed at UCLA, men with AIDS were questioned about their expectations for survival. (Remember that in 1988 the prognosis for men with AIDS was almost uniformly dire.) What was interesting was that those who had *realistic* or fatalistic expectations, those who "prepared for the worst," had in fact a significantly accelerated death rate compared to those who were optimistic, hopeful and *unrealistic,* imagining that a cure would come along "any day now." Those who had the shortest survival time of all were those "realists" who had also lost someone to the AIDS virus.

Kemeny, when discussing this study, suggested that this might have had something to do with imagery. Losing someone is hard enough, but to a person witnessing the death of someone with the same disease they suffer from, the picture in their mind of a dying friend becomes their own. By the same token, a positive state can induce images that contribute to health and healing. Norman Cousins, the renowned writer and commentator, commissioned a study exploring the effect of positive mental states. Method-trained actors had their immune systems tested to create a baseline, and then were asked to evoke emotions of happiness and joy. When they were retested, it was clear that positive immune changes had occurred. In other studies, similar results emerged. Relaxation training proved to increase the activity of natural killer cells; support groups for women with breast cancer increased their survival rates; journaling (or writing about traumatic events and feelings) produced verifiable physiological changes in patients with asthma and rheumatoid arthritis.

Martin Seligman, Ph.D., researcher and director of clinical training at the University of Pennsylvania in Philadelphia and author of *Learned Optimism*, ranks individuals on an optimism-pessimism scale. In longitudinal studies he conducted, he found that optimists were more resistant to infections and less likely to suffer from chronic diseases of middle age.

Experientially, we have both seen the effect of *gratitude* on a person's sense of well being, and on their life expectancy, regardless of their diagnosis.

One such woman, Irene, lives in a nursing home in New Jersey. She has had several strokes, is now blind, has had shingles, lost her husband of sixty years, lost her savings to Medicaid, and no longer has the ability to even go to the bathroom for herself. But she has never lost her hope, her smile, or her spirit. She says, "I'm so lucky. I have the most wonderful family. I have the most wonderful nursing staff. This is the most marvelous nursing home." With that attitude, how could the nurses be anything but wonderful to her? For Irene, every day is a miracle and a joy. She has been in that home for fifteen years and, despite all predictions to the contrary, seems poised to be there for another fifteen.

Often, people with chronic disease or life-threatening illness undergo radical shifts in their thinking, a crisis of faith. The lenses through which they see the world blur and distort, their focus becoming narrow and dim. What they can see in their future is more of the same, or death, which can sometimes seem like the only way out. Time slows, and their inner world is filled with negative imagery and negative thinking (or self-talk).

They can also lose hope. One study organized by Stephen L. Stern, M.D., of the department of psychiatry at the University of Texas Health Science Center at San Antonio, asked the important question: "Why do some people die while others, who may be no less ill, continue to live?" He found that one answer to this question might lie in the presence or absence of hope. During a three to seven year period, elderly Mexican Americans were assessed for hopefulness and their cases followed. Researchers found that 29 percent of the hopeless participants died, compared with 11 percent of the hopeful participants. That's a difference of 18 percent!

Dr. Norman Cousins tells us a wonderful story in his foreword to *The Inner Healer.* Dr. Cousins had been participating in an organization known as The Wellness Community in Santa Monica, California. Organized by Harold Benjamin, it catered to the emotional and social needs of cancer patients. According to Dr. Cousins, the members of the Wellness Community all shared one extraordinary attribute, which attracted the tentative but curious interest of the medical community: they had all lived longer than their physicians had predicted.

In one group he attended, Dr. Cousins wondered aloud why that was so. One member, Mrs. A., a graceful, older and "uncommonly beautiful" woman, stood up. She remembered quite vividly, when her "moment of grace" had come. She was in her physician's office and he had just explained to her that she had cancer, it was terminal, and she had four to six months to live. Mrs. A. said she met the physician's gaze head on and said, "Go f— yourself!" At which point, Dr. Cousins recalls that everyone in the room cheered. He says, "They did not deny the diagnosis. What they denied was the verdict that went with it." At the time the story was told, Mrs. A. had lived more than six years past her "due date," and she was doing just fine.

One woman, Connie, who has been a diabetic for 32 years, told us about her experience with a *medical hex*.

"When I was ten years old and diagnosed with diabetes at Children's Hospital, a nurse came into my room and yelled at me about all the bad things that would happen if I didn't 'take care of myself.' She scolded me by saying, 'One day you will wake up and just be blind. And it will happen just like that." And she snapped her fingers.

"I was only ten years old, lying in bed in my yellow jammies and pig tails. The 'hex' did incredible damage. I lived in terror of blindness throughout childhood, and well into my 20's. Whenever my vision was blurry on waking in the morning, I would panic. I was an artist, but I was afraid to choose that as a career, because I thought I would be blind. Anyway, screw her. I'm forty-one years old and I still wonder who that woman was and why she said those things to me.

"I didn't work through the fear until I worked up the courage at about age twenty-five to *ask* the doctor to tell me if it was possible to become instantly blind. It is not. Retinopathy is a slow, progressive, and very treatable disease.

"The *hex* was very powerful for an impressionable child, because as a child you don't understand 'taking care of yourself.' You only understand that you are not *ever* doing what they think you're supposed to be doing. And children have no one to talk to except the authority figures who instill the hexes, so we can quickly become convinced not only that the authorities are right, but that we are bad people."

The consensus, then, regarding whether you have to listen to a hex or not seems to be what Norman Cousins has said all along: Accept the diagnosis and defy the verdict. But can we accept a diagnosis without accepting the *hex*? Yes, according to Gary Zukav, author of *The Seat of the Soul*. Accepting the reality of your situation is a *prerequisite* to change. The more we resist something, the more it persists. When we do not accept where we are, we become stuck. When we accept where we are, the question becomes, "What next?" And asking that question opens the door to a myriad of healing possibilities.

## Using Imagery

Many hypnotherapists using guided imagery with their clients help them discover their own images. Some use inner guides, which may be another way of eliciting one's own inner wisdom. The guide is asked for help as it accompanies the client, both of them becoming small enough to slip inside the body to the area that needs attention. In this process, the therapist *never* tells people what to expect or what to do, but simply asks them to stay a while with that area of the body, listening, touching, feeling, and asking questions. The person is given encouragement to follow the feelings that emerge, to stay with the images, and to watch and see what the images do. (Psychologist Carl Jung would tell people to watch the image until it changed by itself.) The interesting reward is that, when invited to, that area of the body may tell the patient exactly what it needs.

The parents of a 13 year-old boy, Jake, dying of a metastasized brain tumor, called in psychologist Steve Klein, FMT, a therapist in Encino, California, to help with grief work and to make preparations for their son's death. When he interviewed Jake, who had been given two months to live, Klein noticed that he had "the spirit of life in him. He wanted to live." At that time, Klein recalled some work that he had read on visualization, although he did not yet practice it himself. He broached it to the parents, who agreed that they had nothing to lose by trying.

Mr. Klein walked Jake through numerous visualizations that involved Jake's becoming very small, wandering through his body to his brain and noticing the difference between healthy and cancerous tissues. In their first session, Jake stopped the process and said, "Wait! I forgot my shit-kicking boots." As Jake went through the process, he saw the healthy tissue as *red* and the unhealthy tissue as *gray matter*. Wisely, Mr. Klein did not correct him, but allowed the process to reveal itself, trusting in Jake's intuitive body wisdom. For two months Jake "kicked the crap out of the tumor," seeing it dry up and fly away, with healthy tissue taking over. He practiced this with Mr. Klein personally and with tapes of their sessions for two months. Jake went back to UCLA Hospital for follow-up radiography, and much to the amazement of his doctors, the tumor had disappeared. They scratched their heads and called it a *remission*.

Timothy Trujillo uses the image of the cocoon for transformational healing. Ill people are invited to imagine themselves wrapped with the spun silk of the cocoon, which protects and enables them to breathe through it, while the image of the metamorphosis of the caterpillar evolving into a butterfly is being richly described. Throughout, Trujillo talks to the cells themselves about this experience, and about the feeling of impending freedom. How this metaphor is interpreted and visualized varies from individual to individual, but in every case the theme of change, healing, and transformation are reiterated and reinforced.

As you can see, guided imagery doesn't have to be literal, or even make any sense, for there to be the most profound and healing connection.

One clinician we know works with young adolescents suffering from cancer. Many of these children felt that their lives were *broken* by the effects of the disease. So, he asked them to "imagine a picture, broken into a thousand pieces. Now, begin to pick up the pieces and put them back together again." He also refers them back to times when they had successfully worked puzzles in the past, reminding them of their ability "to find some strengths you didn't know you had." While metaphors do not have to be consciously understood to be effective, they *do* have to be meaningful. The children did not have to analyze, interpret, or *think through* the broken picture for the act of reconstruction to be healing on a profound level.

Since the 1980s what Herbert Benson, M.D. of Harvard, calls the *relaxation response*, has become very popular. Deep relaxation is most often achieved by a combined use of guided imagery and alternate tensing and loosening of large muscle groups. An easy approach when working with a loved one who is feeling weak and ill and may not be able to voluntarily contract their muscles is to simply talk them through a progressive relaxation, imagining each part of the body, beginning with the head or feet, and letting each part relax in turn.

*Special Future Pacing: Time Distortion*

Let us first make the assertion that time is not what we think it is. We may live in a world of linear time and atomic clocks, but the universe does not. You know this intuitively. When you're miserable, time drags. When you're joyful, time speeds by far more quickly than you'd like. "Put your hand on a hot stove for a minute, and it seems like an hour. Sit with a pretty girl for an hour, and it seems like a minute. *That's* relativity," is the way Einstein put it.

There are two main reasons for utilizing time distortion techniques with a patient: to elicit forgotten resources and strengths, and to infuse the present with hope for the future.

In a class many years ago, Dr. Sidney Rosen shared with us a stunning example of how this works. He was treating a 40-year-old woman who had had both breasts removed due to cancer. He had her look at herself in a mirror and see herself at different phases of her life; first older, then much younger, then older again, stretching and elasticizing her imagination, preparing herself for his suggestion. After having her move back and forth through her life, Dr. Rosen finally took her forward 40 years...to 80 years old. He stopped, waited a moment and then said, "And you can look back 40 years, seeing yourself at age 40, realizing now that the period around age 40 was really a very important time in your life: the time when you really began to understand your value, your mission, when things all became so crystal clear and so meaningful."

What makes this technique so beautiful and useful is that it does numerous things at once. It subtly but strongly implies survival and long life as well as suggesting that the patient will have found meaning in her struggle. It gives her a distance from the moment that allows her a proper and potentially healing perspective. It leaves her with a sense of mastery and hope.

Time distortion is particularly valuable when working with people in pain. Although we have an entire section devoted to this enormous topic, it bears mentioning again here. Simple phrases such as, "You may remember a time when..." or "You can see yourself ... tomorrow or the next day..." allow the patient to transport themselves, imagining a time when things were better or a time when they will be.

The future creates the present as much as the past does. A confluence of events from all sides feed this moment, like hidden tributaries to an eternal sea. How we imagine our fate is critical to our current state. The opposite of Dr. Rosen's example is this: "I have no hope and my future is bleak, therefore, I feel miserable today, therefore I can't get well and have a good future." By envisioning a bleak landscape before us, we create chemicals that perpetuate that very condition.

Questions can use time distortion by playing with syntax or tense, so that the future seems present. For instance, you might ask a loved one, "And when you're better, what's different?" "When the miracle has happened, what are you doing now?"

Questions can also focus on fantasy, particularly with children. You might wonder aloud, "Can you imagine the look on that doctor's face when you tell her the cancer's all gone?! Or better, when she finds out and you haven't told her a word?" Imagining the future and telling people what you did to get there accomplishes several objectives, but most importantly it makes the outcome concrete in the person's mind, making it more possible. In fact, research with hypnosis and performance suggests that it is the visualization of the particulars in the process that lead a person to his goal, whether it be health or a gold medal.

*The Importance of Pacing in the Present*

At the risk of being redundant, we would like to remind you to begin with the ill person's current perception of reality, which may be painful, miserable, powerless, angry, frightened. Unless you meet the person there, you will not be able to take them anywhere else. Future pacing begins with a foot firmly rooted in the present Someone handed us this note after one of our talks.

*"Singing cheerful songs to a heavy heart is as*
*bad as stealing someone's clothes in the winter*
*or pouring salt on a wound."*
(Proverbs 25:20)

Although we may always wish to "cheer them up," it is pacing and not cheering that is called for here.

*Lending an Ear*

Too often overlooked is the simple act of listening: not a passive presence or an indifferent "I hear you," but a real, active listening. What that simple engagement can mean is incalculable, particularly for people who have been ill for a long time and are likely see themselves as a burden to others, not to mention to themselves. Asking how another person feels and communicating your genuine interest in that person's response can be healing in and of itself. Chronically ill people are too often ignored. Listening with compassion can help them to become part of life again, and to realize that they are real and valued.

*Past Experience/Truisms*

If you know of some major obstacle the chronically ill person has overcome in the past, remind them of that *miracle.* They did it once, so they can do it again. Remind them of the obvious truism that when a certain percentage of people have a negative outcome, that means that the other percentage have a positive one. Why should they not be in that positive-outcome percent, especially if they have beaten the odds before? Or perhaps there is a way in which they have felt *lucky* before, so they can count on that again.

*Imagery/Dialogue with the Disease Entity*

The creative process of imagining a dreaded disease leaving the body is available to anyone who wishes to explore that possibility. Edie, the woman with the benign brain tumor, pictured her two faithful, deceased Scottish Terriers licking at the tumor "as if it were a Popsicle melting on the floor, making it smaller and smaller until it's gone." Others see a vacuum cleaner sucking the cancerous tissue up, or a sorcerer's apprentice army of dancing brooms, or angels with feather dusters, all sorts of devices to clear the way to better health.

Still others communicate directly with the disease entity and ask what they could do to make it possible for it to leave. One therapist friend of ours, David Le'Chastaignier, CHT, worked with a client who had AIDS, and together they *interviewed* the disease entity. The disease, which looked like a yuppie in an Armani suit and sunglasses, very arrogantly said it wasn't leaving and it was in charge. After a more gentle approach, the therapist reminded it that, if the host died, it would die as well. The disease bowed its head when it realized that its power would also be its own undoing. "Here's the deal," David and his client proposed, "You may stay in this body just like other foreign elements that humans acquire, but you cannot take over this body's right to make its own decisions. You may remind [this person] to make more prudent choices in his behavior, but the client decides your fate. Treat him kindly and both of you can enjoy a long life. Do you understand?"

They demanded a more forceful *yes* than the first mumbled reply and then created a *legally binding document* to that effect, committing the disease to end its fight with the immune system and requiring it to live peaceably within the person. The humbled virus signed the document. Since that dramatic session Le'Chastaignier reports that his client's T-Cell count has risen steadily.

One of our patients, when asked to visualize her cancer, saw it as a red Superman suit. It surprised her by asking her to dance. "What should I do?" she said. "Are you willing?" we asked. "I am," she tentatively agreed. As they slowly danced, it gave her a bill of particulars, listing what she needed to do in order for it to leave.

*Reframing/Meaning/Acceptance and Learning from Illness*

According to some people, accepting the diagnosis and owning the disease is a prerequisite to healing. They claim that you cannot have power over anything you do not own. There are others, however, who disagree with this idea, citing the experience of all the people whose *unrealistic* denials of disease kept them alive and working for many years past their predicted death. There are numerous cases in point for both sides, and in the end the more meaningful variable may be the individual, or what we call the *innate wisdom of each individual's unconscious mind.* If we are in rapport, lovingly attuned to the other, we are able to intuit the specific requirements of each situation. For some people, *fighting the good fight* works, both emotionally and physically. With others, their higher path is the one of spiritual submission. We do not judge. We prefer to pace and utilize.

Sometimes people can see the *good* in what happens to them, and those who can have an easier time accepting and even growing from their experiences. One of the reasons that we might want to be in *direct contact* with a disease, or take ownership of it, is that it may have lessons or insights to offer us. Trujillo talks about AIDS patients who, in a support group, have exclaimed, "Becoming HIV positive saved my life!" They had been floundering, lost, and self-destructive before the disease challenged them to awaken and discover their meaning, their purpose, and their strengths. We have heard cancer patients thanking their cancers for *shaking them up.* If you can see serious illness as a wake-up call and profit from the lessons implicit in it, then it has been a gift and, by owning it, you can take your life back.

One man we know had a small stroke that was very frightening to him. He temporarily lost the use of his vocal chords, and his right side lost sensation, although it continued to function. When he learned he had suffered a stroke, and that because the blood vessels in his brain stem were quite narrow he would have to take blood thinners, he was discouraged. While in the hospital, his heart was tested and it was then that they discovered that he had a 70% blockage in one of his major coronary arteries. He was a walking time bomb and didn't know it! Suddenly, everything appeared different to him. Now he saw the stroke as his body's way of trying to get his attention so that he could have the angioplasty that could save his life.

## Scenario

Your friend, Marsha, has bladder cancer. You and she are spending a nice, easy-going afternoon together, in which you have talked of many things. She seems contemplative, and you think this might be a good time to open this conversation up to the meaning of the illness.

"So," you say, leaning back, "someone on TV was talking about 'organ language' the other day."

"Organ language?"

"Yeah, like someone's heart is broken and then they actually get a heart attack."

"Yeah, I think a person could die of a broken heart."

"Me, too."

"Mmmm."

"What do you think bladder problems means?"

"I don't know." She thinks about it. "Pissed off, I guess!" she laughs. Then she becomes quiet. "Yeah. Pissed off. And trying to hold it in."

"Hold what in, what would that be?" you might ask, going along, and then suddenly you might be there, inside her bladder where a scene is playing itself out and she has a chance to ask it what it wants of her and what it's doing there. Without playing therapist, you might simply wonder aloud what, if anything, the disease would have to say for itself if it could speak. This can become the trigger for a guided visualization, if you are comfortable with that, and whatever direction this takes clearly needs to be paced to the attitude of the sick person. Also, words are just one way to develop this communication. We've found that drawings work very well with children and with visually imaginative adults.

If this process opens up something that needs to be resolved with a therapist, you should most definitely suggest that.

Martin, a 50 year-old architect, discovered he had a large tumor in his chest. Before his illness, he had lived life within narrow parameters, dictated by work and by the expectations of his domineering father. In contrast to his father, who was withholding and judgmental, Martin's mother embraced life. Martin's own relationships, particularly with his wife and children, were stiff and estranged. His heart was closed. The advent of this illness provided a great awakening for Martin. He realized that he had modeled himself after the wrong parent and proceeded to make dramatic changes in his life. In fact Martin became so grateful to his illness that he was hesitant to give it up. He wondered, "If the cancer went away, would the joy leave me, too?"

Knowing that some people may feel this way, it might helpful to ask the question, "Now that the illness has brought you to this state of awareness, are you willing to let it go and remain joyful?" If the answer is "no," to that question, you might also ask that person, "Would it be okay to keep the cancer and stay symptom-free?" Most people will agree to stay asymptomatic. As we've seen, the unconscious mind may also agree and make the appropriate adjustments.

Sometimes there is a *secondary gain*, another reason to hold on to the illness. Often, that motivation is not accessible to our conscious minds. For instance, that 'flu you get when you're just *too busy* to go to bed but should really slow down can be a way of giving your body what it really needs. If it had been up to your conscious mind you would have chosen a week on a beach in Hawaii for R&R rather than a week in bed, but this might have been the only way your unconscious mind could enforce the rest. So, although these decisions may not be made on a conscious level, when that motivation is brought to light, we might also find a willingness to change.

*Fighting the Good Fight*

For some people, the language of challenge, battle, victory or *going on a mission*, reflects a modality from which they generally operate when they are well. A fighter pilot, a sportsman/woman, a chess master, someone who enjoys competition, might benefit from seeing an illness as the ultimate challenge. We have a friend, Toni, who is an energy healer in San Francisco. When she developed bladder cancer, we worked with guided imagery to reduce the tumor's size by half. After an operation, she found that the cancer had metastasized. Cancerous cells could now be identified in her lungs, brain and lymph system. Because she had experienced the healing power of attitude with her former clients, and because it was her nature, she decided that she could *outwit* this disease, figure out how to heal herself and bring back the answers to all those in need.

Toni's attitude and outlook has done more than give her a number good years. It has given her the strength and curiosity to investigate alternative treatment modalities, each of which she has found "interesting," regardless of their discomfort level. It has reinforced an extraordinary hopefulness and a competitive spirit that says, "I will find the answer—for myself and for other people." She is indomitable in the truest sense of the word: she has lived many years longer than anyone predicted and she has done it with vitality, love, and laughter.

The Verbal First Aid techniques you use, then, can vary dramatically depending on the person they are intended to help. With a *fighter* who is naturally enthusiastic, assertive, and risk-taking, the appeal is made to action. The Verbal First Aid words used here should be verbs that imply self-direction and give the young man something to do about the situation: "Beat this thing…" "call in the troops…" "emerge victorious…" "win…" "take charge," etc.

## The Emotional Course of Chronic or Life-Threatening Disease

Even a fighter will have moments of anger, fear, sadness, and resentment—as do almost all people suffering from chronic or life-threatening diseases. There are moments when the kindest thing we can do is nothing, allowing the other person to simply be with their feelings. We need to remember that when people resist their pain, it persists. The acknowledgment of a feeling allows it to be processed and to eventually run its course.

There is a five-stage process that was first codified by Elizabeth Kubler-Ross in her work with the dying, which was then re-presented in terms of chronic pain by Rita Cowan, Ph.D. in her book *Chronic Pain Solutions.* Most people experiencing grief may go through these stages at some point (denial, anger, bargaining, depression, and acceptance), though not necessarily all of them, in exactly the same order or at the same pace. We grieve in many different situations: over the loss of a loved one or over the change in our own level of function or due to falling short of our dreams. Serious illness changes a person's life and grief may be necessary for healing to take place. What is important in terms of Verbal First Aid is to remember there is no *right* way to move through illness. Pacing people—being there with them as they ride through the ups and downs is a gentle, yet powerful gift.

Simple phrases, "I know", "I hear you," "I'm with you," "That's really hard," "That's scary," "I'm sorry," echo deep and wide. Nods, hand-holding, a gentle touch of the hand can let a person know that you understand. Sometimes it makes sense to say, "You're so brave," and at other times, "You don't have to be brave." It's all in the pacing.

*Giving Up To Grace*

What if someone, even a fighter, has had enough? What if there is no recourse and nothing further to do? If that is the case, there are still things you can say, even at this point, to facilitate a healing that only death can bring. What Verbal First Aid offers in this area is compatible with most religions and belief systems, and we explore this issue in detail in Chapter 12.

Ultimately, however we die, who we are is defined by the grace with which we live. Debilitating, chronic and life-threatening illnesses ask much of us in the way of patience, stamina, and heart. If our words can help light the way for relief and solace, we are all, in that small but profound way, richer.

# CHAPTER TEN

# CREATING CALM: VERBAL FIRST AID FOR EMOTIONAL CONDITIONS

*"The mind is its own place,*
*and in itself can make a heaven of hell, a hell of heaven."*
*–John Milton*

In the movie *Whose Life Is It, Anyway?* the protagonist has become a paraplegic due to an accident, and in his misery wants to die. When the doctors refuse to comply, he goes to court and appeals to the judge: "You can't damn me to a life of torment [just] because you cannot see the pain. There's no blood, there's no screaming, so you can't see it." That does not mean, he goes on to suggest, that it isn't just as real.

To many people, though not all, emotional pain—fear, anger, anxiety, grief, confusion—is invisible and therefore not *real*. Broken bones, bloody noses, blisters and burns, diseases: these we understand because we can see them. Broken hearts, broken wills: these are not so obvious and, as a result, not so easy to understand. With no bandages that can staunch the flow from the wound, and—unless the situation reaches a critical point, generally no use in calling 9-1-1—when someone is suffering in the throes of emotional illness, it seems that there is very little that we can do to make it better. The only things that seem to even *touch* emotional conditions are certain pharmaceuticals…and words.

The techniques discussed in this chapter illustrate the therapeutic use of words to deal with specific situations: anxiety, panic attacks, post-traumatic stress disorder, and depression. The examples we use will give you an overview of Verbal First Aid technique in emotional situations. Because each situation is different, you will benefit most by understanding the techniques and then applying them in your own, improvised way as the situations arise. This is not a substitute for psychotherapy or other medical treatment; it is a useful complement to that treatment, especially when things seem bleak.

We are a fix-it culture. *Just Do It!* is a Nike slogan, but it could just as well sum up the thinking that permeates our time. Unfortunately, debilitating emotions are not readily set right. They are not even readily acknowledged until they become paralyzing, or affect our abilities to work or function in the world. Emotions, however, *are* real. Thoughts are real. Fear, pain, anger, sadness—all of these are real. And, as we've seen, these emotions and thoughts are so real they manifest themselves in our physical bodies. In fact, they have physiological origins and consequences.

What do we mean by this? Well, how do you know you're feeling anger? How do you know you're sad? How do you know you're afraid of someone or something? What are the indications, specifically, which alert you to danger so that you walk down the middle of the street and avoid dark corners and alleyways? Where in your body do you feel it?

In the human experience, feelings are registered in the body. Of course, where they register depends on the individual. To experience this for yourself, you can try a little experiment. As you read this, "go inside" yourself now and imagine something frightening, a moment when time stood still and you sensed danger. It could have been a nightmare, or the moment you realized that you were standing in a dark parking lot alone and you heard footsteps behind you, or a time when you were very little and someone left the closet door open and you couldn't reach the light. You may be surprised to discover your throat tightening or your stomach knotting or your heart beating faster right now. What if you imagined a sad moment, a memory that moves you to tears, a goodbye you wish you never had to say, a hand you haven't held in a long time—where in your body do you hold that sadness and that memory?

Emotions—all of them—are not abstract intellectual constructs. They have gravity. They pull on us, a tug here, a release there. We feel their weight. They move us. Though invisible, they have more power than our conscious will. They can undo our best intentions—to stick to that diet, or to curb our tempers—and they can push us to overcome the limits set by fear or conditioning. When we do not give them adequate ventilation, or respect, they explode like a trapped gas, or leak in dangerous ways.

Emotions—like the words and thoughts that inspire them—can lead to health or harm. "Type A" or driven and aggressive personalities have been linked to circulatory and heart disease. "Type C" or repressed personalities have been associated with some types of cancers. What we say, then, in emotional crises, can make a difference by changing the nature, the shape, the size and the impact of those emotions. When an emotion shifts, the body follows.

### Verbal First Aid for Emotional Conditions

In the following sections we provide tools—strategies and scripts–for understanding and speaking to people in emotional distress. Emotional distress can put people into the same altered states or healing zones they experience when they are in medical crisis. In the healing zone, their autonomic nervous systems are accessible and responsive to suggestion. Verbal First Aid techniques are not a *quick fix*, and can never substitute for a doctor's attentions. They are, however, a way to provide a calm center and begin the movement toward healing. At the very least, they are a powerful reminder of the things we ought *not* to say and the responsibility to *do no harm*.

Because emotional conditions are so individual, Verbal First Aid is most useful when you internalize its intention and its process. Once you have established rapport, you will not need the scripts. Born of empathy and desire to help, the right words will emerge at precisely the right moment.

## ANXIETY

*"I've developed a new philosophy...*
*I only dread one day at a time."*
Charlie Brown (Charles Schulz)

*"Anxiety is a thin stream of fear trickling through the mind.*
*If encouraged, it cuts a channel into which all other thoughts are drained."*
Arthur Somers Roche

According to the National Institute of Mental Health, more than nineteen million Americans suffer from anxiety disorders. Worldwide statistics may not be available, but it is clear that modern life invites anxiety, both through the frustrations it creates and through toxic substances in the environment that contribute to malfunctions in our nervous systems. Anxiety disorders can involve irrational thoughts and fears, compulsive behaviors, nightmares, and physical symptoms that can be debilitating, and can rob life of its joy.

We begin with nightmares and childhood fears because we have all been there, small and seemingly powerless to control events around us. Everything had the potential to surprise and frighten us then, and we were at the mercy of adults in our lives who might or might not protect us. Children live in a world in which the separation between imagination and reality is not clearly delineated. For this reason they are especially receptive to suggestion and guided imagery—much more so than adults.

### Nightmares

At seven years old, Joey is a little small for his age and he has had a few run-ins with bullies in the playground at school. One night in the early morning hours, the "monster under the bed" growls. There is no mistaking it; it rattles the mattress and shakes him awake. He thinks of running to his mother and father, but his legs won't carry him. He cannot catch his breath, his feet and hands are sweating, and his mouth is dry. He is paralyzed with fear. Finally, he lets out a shriek that brings his mother and father running into the room. They turn on the light. His father says, "What's the matter?" His mother runs over to him. Joey whispers "Monster…," and his father realizes that Joey has had a nightmare. He approaches Joey and sits down on the bed. He takes Joey's hand and says, "Tell me about the Monster."

*Pacing and Soliciting Their Help*

Instead of dismissing Joey's concerns as childish or "only a dream," his Dad paces the fear. "That's really scary," he nods as Joey relates the shakes and groans. Then Dad explains, "I know all about Monsters because I had them under my bed when I was a boy your age." (A form of "I know a guy who…") "You did?" "Yes, and I'm going to get rid of this one the same way my daddy showed me. Someday you'll be able to show your children how to do it. But for now I need your help. I'll get the broom, if you'll hold the flashlight."

Pacing can take the simplest form: "I know you're afraid," or, "That is scary." Other examples might be: "You're breathing seems to be calming down, now," you say, as you breathe in rhythm with the child. (For details, please refer to Chapter 6, Therapeutic Suggestion.)

*Soliciting Their Help* is a technique most mothers know by instinct— the best way to help children is to *engage* them. "While I'm getting the monsters out of the closet, you can hold the flashlight." "You hold on to Max the Bear, and make sure he isn't too scared, while I put on the light." Soliciting the help of the person in the anxious state structures their emotional experience and gives them a sense of control so that their fears are more manageable.

One of the most useful ways to deal with monsters under the bed (or in the closet or the shadows or the attic) is for the adult and the child to simply ask it to leave. This can take the form of a verbal request, a *shooing away* with a broom, or a banishment *ceremony*. Any number of spiritual traditions have found great value in ceremonies not so different from these. Fantasy and ceremony are an integral and delightful part of a child's inner life and growth; therefore a ceremony to *banish* the *monster* can be imaginative, loving, and effective.

Alternatively, you can provide children with a magic object that is "guaranteed to repel monsters:" a teddy bear that guards the bed, a stone that keeps away evil, a crucifix, a Star of David, or whatever gives them a sense of security and supports a feeling of their own power. No longer at the mercy of monsters, they can begin to develop feelings of independence and competence that can spill over into other aspects of their lives.

Joey's discussion with his father about the monster can also provide valuable access to Joey's inner life and the fears that gave birth to the monster in the first place. If the nightmares come often, or if the fears that underlie them begin to affect Joey's daily life, then his parent will want to seek the services of a therapist specializing in children.

### Future Pacing

Fears emerge from feelings of helplessness. If Joey thinks he is at the mercy of monsters under the bed, he will have to live in fear of them. When Dad says, "My daddy showed me what to do the same way I'm going to show you now. And someday you'll be able to show your children how to do it," he is moving Joey out of powerlessness in the present to a time when he will be competent to deal with monsters. To reinforce that point he could add: "And now that you know the secret, you'll be able to get rid of monsters wherever they might be."

## Other Childhood Fears

As most children do, Joey has given his fear a face, which Dad can manipulate in Joey's best interest. It has been noted that, at least until the age of seven, children's brain waves register in the alpha and theta range, rather than in beta (the conscious state in which everyday, adult conversation is held). Children are often in altered states, which makes them very receptive to suggestion, for better or for worse. Their creativity and susceptibility give rise to bogeymen in the first place. It can also make those monsters *disappear.*

### Establishing an Alliance and Getting a Contract

All helping relationships require both an alliance and a contract—whether they are articulated or not. When Joey's father comes into Joey's room and says, "Daddy's here. I've got you and you're safe," he's automatically establishing an alliance. Any statement that conveys, "I'm capable and I'm here to help" begins the Verbal First Aid process. Getting a contract, as you may recall from Chapter 4, simply refers to securing the person's agreement: "Will you do as I say?" To the small child trembling with fear because of imagined monsters, you can simply say, "Mommy's here, baby, and I'll protect you. I'll take care of the monsters and you can lie back down and feel safe. Will you do that?" If the child does not agree, this just means that the question needs to be rephrased or that another contract needs to be made. Some children are helped to feel safe when they actively participate in the monster's departure. When you solicit their help, you are, in effect, getting a contract.

### Pacing

Perhaps what is most often forgotten–and most often needed–when dealing with a child is the importance of validation, which can be most effectively expressed as *pacing.* When we acknowledge a child's point of view, even if it seems *illogical* or absurd to us, we earn their trust. This validation does not promote or increase the fear. You are not *buying into* their anxiety. You are just meeting them where they are, and walking together to a safer place, hand in hand.

**Scenario**

You are strolling down the street with your four-year-old son when a large dog bounds up to the fence and startles him with a loud bark. Your son jumps, grabs your pants, holds onto your legs for dear life and starts to scream at the top of his lungs. This gets the dog more excited, so it barks even louder.

What to do? The obvious. Pick up your child and move away from the dog. Even though your son's reaction is dramatic, it is not foolish to be afraid of a large, unfamiliar dog. As an adult, you know the fence will keep you safe. You know what you need to fear and what you can dismiss with a shrug; your son, not having the advantage of your life's experience, does not. His startle response has unleashed a cascade of adrenal chemicals. Now, he's caught up in the torrent of emotions they trigger, which loom even larger than the scary moment itself. He does not yet have the reality testing necessary to put on the emotional brakes. He can't say the things he needs to say to himself, yet.

What to say to him, then? First things first: affirm his experience. He is frightened and yes, indeed, that was scary. Your agreement with his emotional state is the beginning of its resolution. You are being reasonable and compassionate. You are therefore to be trusted, and what you say next will carry more weight.

MOM
Boy, that was some loud bark. I jumped, too.

SON
(Wailing)

MOM
I'm right here, baby. And I've got you. And
you're safe with me. Feel how I've got my
arms around you? Feel how high you are off

262

the ground? How safe you are?

SON

(Sniffles and nods.)
Doggie yell. Doggie yell.

MOM

Doggie yelled loud. But you yelled louder.

SON

(Sniffling less, he looks towards the dog and
takes a deep breath.)

MOM

Oh, that was a good breath, sweetie. Go ahead and
do that again, real slow for Mommy. Good.

SON

(Sniffles less.)

MOM

Did you see that fence? Do you know why it
was there?

SON

(Shakes his head "no.")

MOM

To keep you safe outside and the doggie safe
inside

SON

Doggie yelled loud.

263

MOM
Yes, and the strong fence kept you safe.

Mom moves a step or two closer to the fence as she says this, slowly desensitizing her son and teaching him how to assess danger. Notice, too, her use of "yes, and." Instead of denying his observation by saying, "Yes, but," Mom said, "yes, and," which means "you are right, and now you know one more thing that will help you interpret the world more fully," maintaining the rapport and moving the child toward greater understanding.

If your son or daughter demonstrates symptoms of panic or has a strong phobic response, or has repeated episodes of anxiety even after you've used these techniques to calm them down, please be sure to consult with a professional for treatment.

**Verbal First Aid Key**
**Nightmares and Other Childhood Fears**

Establish alliance/authority
Get a contract
Solicit help
Join in
Yes, and
Future Pacing

**Panic Attacks**

When we grow up we become pretty certain we understand the world and how it works. But underneath we remain vulnerable. Perhaps you identified with Joey in the last section. We've all been there, and sometimes we go there still. So what do you do for an adult when the "monster" is a panic attack, an overwhelming fear that hits in the middle of the afternoon, that no broom will drive away?

Jane, a 39 year-old woman, a young partner in a prestigious law firm and the very image of New York success, came into our office with a problem that puzzled her. "Last Friday," she said, with only the faintest tremor in her upper lip, "I was standing behind my desk, going over some last minute notes on a brief...and I don't know what happened. One minute I was breathing and the next minute I couldn't catch my breath, I started sweating; my heart was pounding like it was going to burst out of my chest. I thought I was going to die and I didn't know what to do. I was going to call 9-1-1, but I didn't. I forced myself to wait until I calmed down. I went to see my doctor and he ran all these tests, but there was nothing wrong with me. At least that's what he said. I have never been so scared in my entire life. And this week it happened again. Out of nowhere. I feel like I'm losing my mind."

People suffering from panic attacks are overwhelmed by what they experience and, often the experience is as puzzling and inexplicable to them as it seems to an observer. They suffer sudden, overwhelming fears, rapid pulse, palpitations, nausea, tremors, perspiration or some combination of these symptoms. They can't catch their breath. It is not uncommon to hear, "This is ridiculous. There's no reason for me to be feeling this way!" from the very person who's having the panic attack. However, when they hear someone else say those words, even when it echoes what they themselves are thinking, it can aggravate the situation and make it worse.

*Establish Empathy*

In emotional situations there may be no way you can *fix* the problem, and even the act of trying can frustrate both you and the person who is hurting. However, the words you use can help the person gain some equanimity, perhaps long enough to seek help. Verbal First Aid provides you with tools to promote calm and offer temporary relief in the moment.

You must be careful not to be condescending, not to play therapist, and not to change the relationship you already have with this person. Be yourself. It gives you instant credibility. Good Verbal First Aid goes beyond any technique, beyond any script. It is a compassionate and personal response to another human being in need.

A person who suffers from anxiety also suffers from a sense of help-lessness and alienation. This is a very common posture for those who suffer from post-traumatic stress, which is an anxiety-based disorder. This is why "cheer up!" or "get over it!" are not only ineffective, but serve as further proof that no one could possibly understand.

Often, of course, these extreme emotions are not simply mental processes. They are part of the mind/body continuum. Biochemical processes, such as fluctuations of blood sugar due to hypoglycemia or the imbalance of oxygen and carbon dioxide in the blood stream, can cause emotional responses such as panic or severe anxiety. Neurological episodes and physiological brain anomalies can be responsible for erratic, dangerous, even self-destructive behaviors. We strongly recommend that all avenues—both medical and psychological—be investigated for the relief not only of those who suffer, but also of those who love them.

*Presence*

What can you say to people in the throes of panic? Whether their fear has been generated by an overproduction of $CO_2$ in their blood stream or a drop in serotonin levels, or whether they've had an awful nightmare and can't get back to sleep, there are several ways to approach a person, gain rapport, and give them a suggestion that calms them down.

Since one of the most debilitating aspects of a panic or anxiety condition is the feeling that one is alone and misunderstood, the most important thing we can do is be fully present and caring. These qualities, as you may remember, are the essential elements of gaining rapport. Almost all our patients suffering from panic attacks have expressed one version or another of the notion; "At least it helps just to have someone with me." Your presence can be an enormous help.

Several people we know who witnessed the horrifying events of September 11th out their windows and couldn't tear the eyes from the terrifying sight were frustrated as phone connections failed, leaving them alone with their fears. We know one young woman in New York during the catastrophe who exchanged e-mails with a friend in another state every half hour throughout the terrifying day, providing some sense of communion when destruction seemed to be tearing her world apart.

Before you say it with words, you say it with your presence. In the 1995 movie, "Restoration," set in the court of Charles II in London, Robert Downey, Jr. plays the young physician Robert Merivel, overwhelmed by the suffering and death in the wake of the Bubonic Plague. Many people are driven nearly mad by the conditions, and Merivel helps some of them recover, saying "I can offer no cure but my presence among them. I can offer them hope."

In panic, a person is in a hypersensitive, hyper-aware state and can sense with uncanny precision exactly what you're thinking, feeling, and assuming about them. If you can allow yourself to call up your empathy, to put aside your critical judgment and join the person wherever they are in the moment, you may discover that your level of understanding has amplified. At the very least, you'll be gaining rapport by moving towards the technique of *pacing and joining* the person in his or her current state of mind.

*Pacing*

What if you had been with Jane in her office when she had her first panic attack? Unless you knew for certain that she had a history of panic attacks, or you had a very a good reason to suspect one, you would call 9-1-1, because, with the symptoms she described, she might be having a heart attack. Assuming then that you and Jane are friends, and that she has told you about her last panic attack and the doctor giving her a clean bill of health, what do you say now?

You might approach Jane with an openness that allows for whatever she is feeling. Imagine that you can feel it, as well. If she says, "I can't breathe," take her hand and breathe with her, just as if she were suffering an asthma attack. Help her to sit, if she's standing, and sit with her. If she says, "I don't know what's happening, it just suddenly came over me," a simple nod of understanding can let her know she's not alone in this. She might say, "I feel like I'm dying," in which case, you may respond, "Tell me what you're feeling," or "Tell me what's happening." As she tells you, you can listen, nod, make sympathetic sounds of agreement and understanding. You can also repeat what she has said to you to confirm that you understand. Remember that people in this state may not recall what they've said, so when you repeat their words back to them, they may feel that you have read their minds and are especially in tune with them in their time of need.

Examples of pacing are:
- "I can see it's hard for you to get comfortable."
- "It's shocking to get blindsided like that."
- "I know you're scared."

An example of repeating/mirroring would be:

JANE

I feel like I'm drowning. It's so frightening.

YOU
(Nodding)
It's very frightening.

Sometimes we can pace a person by being *on the same page,* that is, by sharing ideas or beliefs in common, we create a bond that can make the acceptance of therapeutic suggestion that much easier. We remember an incident with a young man we knew who was about to leave for China to fulfill his life's dream of studying the martial arts with his master. A few days before this momentous departure, he had reached under a house to rescue a cat. Not wishing to be caught, the cat had bared its claws and scratched the young man, injuring his elbow, which became danger-ously, painfully swollen. It seemed quite infected, and, at the very least, the young man would have to be hospitalized in order to have the elbow drained. He was taken to the emergency room of a local hospital where he sat for hours waiting to be seen.

The combination of waiting, the bad timing in regard to his trip, the inflammation, pain, and concern, along with his lifelong, morbid phobia around injections had caused him to work himself up into a frantic state. People around him tried to encourage him to relax by saying, "Everything will be all right," and "Don't worry," but those words did not even come close to defusing his intense response and allowing his body to participate in the healing process.

His mother called us to help, and when we arrived, we took him out-side to our car where we could be alone. Seeing that he was already in an altered state, we talked with him a little about his interest in Asian lore and then recited to him the words from the *Book of the Tao*. "When we know who we really are, we naturally become tolerant, disinterested, *amused*." His face calmed and we took him through a relaxation visualization.

The next day, when we called him to see how he was doing, he said that the surgery had gone very well. In fact, he said, oddly enough, he had been *amused* by the whole process. The staff, he said, had thought his reac-tion was "inappropriate," but it worked for him.

It is likely that he did not even remember hearing our words, but, because he was in an altered state and trusted us because we shared his interest in the Asian culture, our suggestions had a profound effect. As a result, the procedure went smoothly, and he recovered in time to leave for China that week.

*Paying Attention to Details, Non-Verbal Techniques*

Some of the best pacing we have ever seen with anxiety sufferers has been non-verbal. If they are walking back and forth between the kitchen and the couch, walk with them, making sure to give them their space.

Watch their body language for cues. If they move away from you you're standing too close. As in the script for asthma attacks, you can pace a person's breathing, gently leading them to slower, smoother breathing, knowing that if you can help them change one aspect of the anxiety attack, you've given them an important sense of control. You can pace their language and their actions at the same time so long as they are safe, tapping your fingers on the table in time with theirs, shaking your feet nervously as you speak, just as they do.

Keep in mind that the purpose of pacing is to gain rapport and pave the way for therapeutic suggestion. The key to its success is understanding, not mimicry. However, an observant eye is very helpful. By noticing details—the color of the cheeks and forehead, the skin's moisture, breathing rate—you can feed them back to the person as *markers* of improvement. It also lets them know that you are really with them and paying them close attention.

For instance:
- "Your breathing is smoother and slower than it was just a few seconds ago."
- "The color in your face is coming back now."

When you pay attention to details, you may also know when to offer a tissue, a cup of water, or a walk outside in the fresh air.

- "It looks like you may feel a bit warm in here [noticing her perspiring] and it's a cool, dry day outside. Why don't we go for a walk?"

*Truism/Imagery/Future Pacing*

What makes anxiety or panic attacks so disruptive is their unpredictability and their overwhelming intensity. A person will often not know when, how, why, or where a panic attack will strike. As a result, they become generally more fearful and vigilant.

Knowing that the unknown was one of the primary factors his patients had to deal with, one doctor used the *truism* technique combined with *imagery* and *future pacing* for talking down anxiety attacks. A patient called at 11:30 P.M., gasping for breath, terrified. After he re-established rapport and ruled out other potential problems (he knew the patient well), he engaged her in the following dialogue.

### DOCTOR
Tell me what's happening, now.

### PATIENT
I still can't breathe. Oh, God. Oh, God. What am I going to do?

### DOCTOR
Tell me when this started.

### PATIENT
I was sleeping. My nose is all stuffed and I couldn't breath right, I guess. I don't know. I just can't...I can't get it together. I'm sweating. I feel like I have to go to the bathroom. My stomach is cramping.

### DOCTOR
Panic attacks can do that.

### PATIENT
I don't know. I don't know. Oh, God...I just want this to stop.

### DOCTOR
Panic attacks have a natural life span, you know; they can only last a specific amount of time...and not beyond that. Usually 15-20 minutes or so.

## PATIENT

What do you mean?

## DOCTOR

As soon as a panic attack has begun, it is starting to end....So you can start counting down now. You'll notice that it's starting to wind down as you breathe, and each breath is becoming just a little easier. Notice that you are breathing easier now than when it began. You may even begin to notice the end in sight, how much easier and softer you're beginning to feel already, as the oxygen in your blood returns to normal levels...

What the doctor did in this example was to offer his patient a piece of information that she could cling to, and used it to direct her to a future state of calm that had an impact now. When she was in the pit of panic, she could see no relief. It seemed to her that the awful state of cramping and terror would either go on forever or kill her. By presenting her with an alternative outcome, a promise of relief based on fact, she could begin to move in that direction. Notice that the information he gave her was rich with imagery, all aimed at reminding the body what it needed to do to regain balance.

Truisms often combine with other suggestion styles for additional impact. Here are two examples:

- "There is always a turning point in a panic attack, a moment, a sign that says things will be all right. It could be a subtle change in breathing, a slowing down or a softening of chest and throat muscles, or even a tickle in your nose that signals a sneeze...as I sit with you here, you can let me know as soon as you notice that sign, that turning point that says things are now about to get better..."

- "Letting me know what you know so I can know how to help you is the first step...What's the first thing I can notice that lets me know you're starting to feel better?"

*Soliciting Their Help/Getting A Contract, Distraction*

When you come upon someone in an emotional crisis, the same techniques you learned for medical emergencies apply.

| | |
|---|---|
| *Getting a Contract:* | "I'm here to help you...will you do as I say?" |
| *Soliciting Their Help* | "As I get you some water, will you count your breaths for me, watching them slowing down?" |
| | "Tell me everything you think I should know so I can help you feel safe now." |
| *Distraction* | "Come, walk with me over here, so I can help you better...that's right...and, as you do, keep holding my hand just like that, tight, keeping all your attention on my hand and your hand..." |

## Phobias and General Anxiety Disorder

Phobias are anxiety disorders with very specific triggers, such as snakes, bridges, heights, confinement, or its opposite, leaving the house. They are marked by an urgent need to flee, to find safety, to escape the sense of impending death should escape prove unsuccessful. For example, when people with agoraphobia step outside, they can experience palpitations, shortness of breath, tightness in the throat, sweating, cramping, and a sense of being immobilized by fear. While phobics know that their fears may be irrational, the fears themselves feel very real, very physical, and very overwhelming. Almost universally, therapy involves desensitization, which is the gradual exposure of a person to the feared stimulus until it no longer has a negative charge, and it can also sometimes involve pharmaceuticals.

General Anxiety Disorder occurs when worry gets out of hand and becomes debilitating. It is similar to, but much more prolonged than, panic attacks. Victims of general anxiety disorder can become emotionally paralyzed, find they cannot make decisions or even act wisely in their own interest. Although bouts with generalized anxiety disorder are not as dramatic as panic attacks, therapeutic help and medication are often required and advised.

Although these topics are too large for us to cover exhaustively in this chapter, using some of the Verbal First Aid techniques described below can often calm the situation.

### Pacing/Paying Attention to Details

When someone is breathing too rapidly, we can subtly breathe with them and, as we slow ourselves down, we can bring their breathing rate down too. If they are huddled in a corner, we can sit right there with them. We can pace and support this process verbally, as well, by reflecting what is happening in a reassuring way. "In the last two minutes since we left the party, you've been swallowing more easily and your breathing has been smoother." Alternatively you might say, "I know you're scared of thunderstorms and I'm right here with you, right by your side."

Remember that when you pace, you can lead: "Even in traumatic situations, there can be moments of calm…even if those are small moments like when the *in* breath turns into the *out* breath."

### Imagery/Distraction

When people are frightened, it helps to be able to provide them with images that contribute to a sense of safety; and the richer the information and images used to convey those facts, the better. By providing the mind with clear visual images, we are also distracting the individual from the object or situation that is generating the fear.

For example:

- "Some people can imagine being wrapped in a magical cloak that keeps them safe, and for some people it's blue, a blue cloak that feels silky and soft and yet it is strong enough to make them feel protected, but it might also be another color that you would know, the color that feels safest to you...."

- "Every time you breathe, it can get just a tiny bit softer inside your chest, as more oxygen gets to your lungs and to your brain and heart. You'll notice that it's getting quieter inside, like a gentle quiet, like falling rain or water over pebbles in a babbling brook...."

- "As I hold your hand just like this, you can let your mind stay with my voice and only with my voice as I tell you a story about when I was a little girl and the same thing happened to me..."

*As I/You Can*

If the person is afraid of an object and you can remove it from the immediate environment, please do so, even if you think the fear is *silly*. While you do so you can use the contingency *As I/you can* strategy.

For example, you could say, "As I take care of this (snake, picture, etc...), you can move to that table and tell me how your breathing improves."

Other examples are:

- "Alan, I see the snake and I'm getting rid of it. Will you move ten feet to my left where I can see you as I move this out?"

THE WORST IS OVER

- "Emma, I know you don't like being in this crowd. As I take your hand and keep talking to you, you can come with me now and we'll go on home."

**Verbal First Aid Key**
**Panic Attacks, Phobias and General Anxiety Disorders:**
   Getting a contract
   Paying Attention to Details
   Joining in/Feedback/Pacing
   Truisms/Imagery/Future pacing
   Non-verbal techniques
   As I/You can

Notice here that we are not trying to cure these conditions. We are only using Verbal First Aid to calm, center, and strengthen people so that they can continue functioning and eventually get the professional help they need.

Panic attacks/phobic reactions and asthma attacks are very similar in style and substance, with breathlessness and the fear it generates being some of the major elements. For other, more physiological approaches, such as breath pacing, please turn to Chapter 7 on Asthma.

**Acute Stress and Post-Traumatic Stress Disorder**

Generally, these diagnostic categories are included under the rubric *Anxiety Disorders*. However, we felt that they deserved special mention because of their current relevance.

*Trauma*, in ordinary terms, can often be a matter of perspective. To a grown man on a military base, a deep cut may be painful and inconvenient, but it is hardly traumatic. To a child, who is then rushed to the doctor for sutures, such a cut is as traumatic as it gets. Clearly, while ordinary annoyances such as traffic jams, stubbed toes, and cranky employees are stressful, the word takes on another level of magnitude for the thousands of survivors of sexual abuse and rape, and in situations as horrifying as the Oklahoma City bombing or the attack on the World Trade Center.

Our response to trauma has a great deal to do with what we bring to the critical event—whether it is a motor vehicle accident, the loss of a loved one, or a frightening fall. The old adage, "You're only as sick as your secrets" is a truism that is made increasingly clear to us in our work. The old skeletons in the closet that you hold on to not only don't go away, but tend to reappear when we feel most vulnerable. Traumatic events tend to impact most heavily upon those who have had unhealed traumas in the past. Whenever a police officer comes in for treatment due to trauma, we not only want to know what the precipitating trigger was, we also want to find out whether there's been a history of unresolved trauma and hidden pain.

A trauma's impact is also contingent on the level of personal violence experienced: when an event involves a personal attack, it is harder to avoid, often because the anxiety is increased and that old baggage opened. When traumatic stress is ignored or denied, it may go underground where it picks up steam and builds up pressure. We may be able avoid it for a period of time, but eventually it *leaks* out in our dreams, our relationships, our behavior, which may become more self-destructive, more risky. We may become more irritable, more withdrawn. We may find ourselves getting colds more often. Protracted or intense stress is responsible for much of the disease and death in this country. Stress inhibits the immune system, increases the production of epinephrine, norepinephrine and cortisol, and is linked with heart disease and other chronic diseases, as well as infertility.

Rahul Sachdev, MD, a specialist in reproductive endocrinology at the Robert Wood Johnson Medical School has found that the stress levels of a woman struggling with infertility are similar to those of someone who's just been told they have HIV. While adrenaline helps us to prepare for emergency action, the chemical cascade it initiates inhibits our ability to repair ourselves, to digest food properly, or to reproduce. Epinephrine (one of the secretions of the adrenal glands) has been shown to constrict blood vessels. When this occurs in the uterus, it interferes with conception. When the sympathetic system is in overdrive and the stress response doesn't stop (due to a poor cortisol response), essentially what happens is Post-Traumatic Stress Disorder.

Although more than 90% of all Americans will have experienced a trauma in their life times, we continue to see our emotional responses as *weaknesses*. This denial of our own vulnerability makes the fall that much harder when it does come.

**What Can We Do? What Can We Say?**
**Verbal First Aid for Trauma**

If you come upon someone who has just been assaulted or injured in an attack, as you know your first course of action is to call 9-1-1 or the police, particularly if a crime or severe injury is involved. Depending on the injuries involved, apply first aid according to established medical protocol.

As you tend to the injuries, it is vitally important you understand that trauma is an assault not only on our bodies, but on our minds. It makes us feel vulnerable. Once sure-footed and clear-sighted, we may feel unstable, suddenly unsure of ourselves. This is particularly true when the trauma is an act of war or terror, or a natural disaster, which inherently implies continued attacks and an uncertain future. Experiments with rats whose routines are made chaotic eventuate in their developing ulcers and heart disease. For that reason, Verbal First Aid for critical situations needs to focus primarily, though not exclusively, on two techniques: Pacing and Truisms.

*Pacing*

Pacing a trauma does not always have to be verbal. Within the first few days after the attack on the World Trade Center, we were walking with a group of police officers through Ground Zero to let rescue workers know where our offices were and that we were available to talk twenty four hours a day, seven days a week. We decided to go to the most traumatic sites, such as the makeshift morgues, where we knew we would find rescue workers in greater distress. Our mission was simply to assess what their needs were and to talk. One firefighter, a seasoned and battered middle-aged man, stood facing us, blocking the door leading to what used to be a bright and busy office lobby. His eyes were piercingly blue, his expression grim and tight. "What the hell do you think you're going to be able to do here?" he waved his arm back and over a scene out of Dante's Inferno. Sheets hung over ropes tied between elegant columns of glossy marble, plastic body bags on the floor, zipped up. We held his gaze in that way that says, "I know and I'm still here." When he saw we were not budging, his face relaxed and he started talking.

Pacing can be as simple as standing still, as loving as taking a cold and trembling hand into both of your warm and steady ones, or as instinctive as a hug. The key to pacing, remember, is to take your cues from the person you are trying to help and to avoid using the situation to meet your own needs at the moment. One of the most wonderful things about pacing in trauma is its ability to ground someone in the moment. Because traumatized persons frequently dissociate and feel as if they were "not really here," pacing can serve as the rope back to a shared reality. When we are present enough to be able to reflect back and acknowledge emotions and behaviors in real time, we can stabilize someone in a moment that would be otherwise surreal and disconnected.

When we work with critical incidents, we have found it to be enormously helpful to remind people that they are having normal feelings in an abnormal situation. It is a standard, prescribed statement recommended by the International Foundation on Critical Incident Stress Management and it works. Almost everyone we encountered was surprised and frightened by the intensity of their own response to the events at Ground Zero. This is very similar to the response we see in survivors of rape and sexual assault. The questions inevitably tumble out: "What's the matter with me? Why can't I stop shaking? Why can't I sleep? Why am I so irritable? Why can't I sleep with the lights off anymore?" Pacing victims of trauma often begins with normalizing their reactions and reestablishing the event itself as *abnormal*.

Some examples of verbal pacing include:
- "It was awful…"
- "I know…"
- "I'm right here…"
- "You don't have to do anything right now except exactly what you're doing…"

Dr. Leo Shea, Clinical Neuropsychologist NYU-Rusk Institute of Rehabilitation Medicine feels that when pacing people in uniform, the police, firefighters, the military, for example, we must take into account their stance of being the "protectors." Since they are the ones responsible for guarding others, they therefore perceive themselves as prohibited from relaxing their guard and exploring their feelings. Although some of the firefighters told us they felt some relief from talking about the September 11th attack, most uniformed officers remain stiff upper-lipped. Dr. Shea suggested an oblique approach to inviting them to express their feelings. "Address the issue of how it's going for their family," he told us. "'How's your wife handling it? How are your children doing?' Then you can slide obliquely into 'that must be tough on you,' and then the feelings start flowing out."

We had occasion shortly thereafter to spend some heartfelt time with one of the firefighters whose company had lost many in their company. "How is your wife handling this?" we heard ourselves say, and his face became very open and soft. "I'm only married a year," he said, "and it's so good to have her to talk to. Even to be with me when I drift off into the fog I seem to find myself in a lot. It's so much better than curling up with another beer." And that was just the beginning of a small, healing moment.

*Truisms*

People in trauma are *wobbly* and reaching out for a line, a wall, a pillar to stabilize them. Truisms are a source of stability because they present us with information that offers hope and reassurance.

- "Every trauma has a life span—a beginning, a middle and an end—and you've already been through the beginning and *the worst is over*...and even in the middle, where you are right now, there's something that lets you know the end is in sight..."
- "Everyone knows the value of a good night's sleep..."
- "Feeling crazy is normal in a crazy situation..."
- "It's such a common experience to forget a bad dream in the morning..."
- "You already know how to breathe slowly and easily..."
- "It is hard for any person to be afraid of his own thoughts...

*Objects of Safety: Anchors*

People in trauma feel unsafe. Because they feel unsafe, adrenaline continues to be produced, creating the negative feedback loop that eventually leads to acute stress disorder or PTSD. It can be tremendously calming when we help them identify a physical location or object or an emotional cue that brings them a sense of security. It can be a smooth stone, a St. Christopher's medal, a bible, a bowl of chicken soup, a ribbon, even a point on one of their fingers that they can touch to recall a moment in which they felt safe and calm. While you can offer a safety anchor, such as a teddy bear or blanket to a child, it may be even more useful to let people choose their own anchor so that it has more meaning.

## DEPRESSION

*"And the day came when the risk it took to remain*
*tight inside the bud was more painful*
*than the risk it took to blossom."*
*– Anais Nin*

Depression is one of the most pervasive and profoundly life-altering emotional or psychiatric problems in this country. Nearly everyone knows of someone—a friend, colleague, or family member—who has been diagnosed with some form of depression. And nearly everyone at some time has been *blue*, which conveys some sense of depression, although depression is a full order of magnitude greater than the blues.

Those who suffer from depression can feel paralyzed and unable to track things the way they once could. It is as if a blanket has been laid on top of them and they can't throw it off. While their pain is intense, their sense of the world around them is muffled and distant.

No two people experience depression the same way. Some present symptoms of anxiety and agitation, insomnia, loss of concentration or memory impairment. Others are lethargic, hopeless, deeply sad, unable to get out of bed, hyper-somnolent. Still others complain of a loss of appetite, a diminishing of their sex drive and a general fatigue. Some suffer hair loss.

Depression can be acute or chronic. However it manifests, it is serious business; up to 15 percent of people with severe Major Depressive Disorder die by their own hands. Depression is epidemic in geriatric populations, particularly among those living in nursing homes. It is associated with numerous other diseases, such as strokes, diabetes, and carcinomas, and may even be a by-product of modern medical treatment, such as dialysis. Many patients with chronic disease (such as ALS or MS) suffer from depression, as well.

Depression may also be a factor in making a person more susceptible to disease. Whatever depression's etiology, psychodynamic or biological, when a person is depressed, certain chemical processes occur. It is common knowledge that naturally manufactured substances called *endorphins* are in short supply in the body when people are depressed. One of the preferred treatments for depression is medication that increases the endorphin (particularly serotonin) levels of the brain, thereby alleviating both the depressive symptoms and any anxiety associated with it. Of course, this course of treatment is not always as successful as we might hope and there are potential side effects. However, when medication is combined with therapy, there is cause for optimism.

Before we discuss Verbal First Aid techniques, we want to underscore the potential seriousness of depression and the importance of not flippantly dismissing it. If you or someone you know is depressed, get professional help. There is a great deal of help available. Considerable research has been done on this issue and there are new treatments emerging every day.

**Verbal First Aid for Depression**

Words have a very different effect when directed at someone who is isolated by a sense of hopelessness, as opposed to someone whose inner world has been opened up by an emergency. Directly communicating to the autonomic nervous system of a depressed person is not as easy, and we do not advise it.

This section is different from others in this book, because here we do not focus on inducing physiological change or healing. In most cases of depression, change is best achieved by a professional therapist in a safe and therapeutic environment where medication and alternative modalities for management have been properly considered. The Verbal First Aid proposed here is intended to facilitate ordinary communication that can lead to short-term comfort and offer realistic hope.

There are many varieties of depression. Some depressed people crave the company of others and long to speak about what hurts them. Others may be aggravated by an attempt to console them. Some sufferers become lethargic. Others function with a frenzy that belies the sadness in their hearts; the only clues to how they really feel might be grumpiness, digestive problems, addictions, and dangerous behaviors. Suicidal feelings can be the most critical situation for the depressed person, and require professional help immediately. In the next chapter we discuss suicide attempts in greater detail, but there are signs to look for that indicate a person is progressing in that desperate direction and that it is truly time to intervene. Even the sudden disappearance of depression in someone who has suffered with other symptoms of the malady can indicate that the person has made the suicide decision and is now feeling calmer about it. Call a suicide hotline (they are often listed in the front of the phone book), find a psychologist or psychiatrist who excels in this field, and educate yourself by browsing the websites listed at the end of the next chapter. And never ignore a threat. Contrary to popular wisdom, seventy-five percent of suicide threats are acted upon.

Verbal First Aid has no scripts to offer that cover all the individual expressions of depression. Following are some general approaches that may be useful in many cases.

### First, What Not to Say

Having a depressed person in your life can be challenging, frustrating, infuriating. You want them to *come back* from wherever they've gone, especially if this is a new and acute episode. It is frightening and maddening at the same time. And when the depression is chronic, patience can run very thin. However, invalidating, belittling, blaming, or dismissing only makes things worse. Even though we may feel like saying, "Come on already, get over it!" or "Cheer up!" it's important to remember that this doesn't work. Setting limits, on the other hand, is important, but should be part of a larger therapeutic program, developed with an expert.

In addition, avoid statements that might be perceived as a challenge. "I don't think you really want to commit suicide" can invite an "Oh, yeah? I'll show you" reaction, with devastating consequences. There is considerable anger buried in even the most passive depression. If we do or say things that encourage that anger to be expressed, we are inviting trouble.

Here are a few approaches that might ameliorate the situation in the short-run while professional, long-term help is being sought.

### Empathy

Sometimes there is nothing to be said, or perhaps the words just aren't getting through. Yet small acts of kindness can still have an

284

effect. Barney owned a small grocery store and found himself in the grip of such a depression that he would stand like a statue before the store window, unable to enter or leave for hours on end. A friend of ours used to try to engage him in conversation, but to no avail. Our friend had occasion to drive by the store every day and never failed to give Barney the *thumbs up* sign, although Barney seemed not to see him. One day, Barney signaled back, and this little interaction continued for months longer. Years later, when Barney was himself again, he visited our friend. Out from under the cloud of depression, he told our friend that that simple gesture, the *thumbs up* sign, had kept him going when all else seemed lost. His eyes filled with tears when he explained how much that signal, like a glimpse of light at the end of a tunnel, had meant to him.

*Resources*

In most cases, depression has not been life-long, and the sufferer can be encouraged to look back to a time *before* this, a time when things felt all right. Memories from that time can be resources on which family members and friends can draw. Reminding the person of those times—sharing photos, encouraging laughter—can summon them up, if only for a moment.

In a gentle, conversational tone, one might say, "I just came upon this old picture of the dog when you dressed him up for your sixth birthday, remember that?" We can recall the *resources* he had, strengths he showed, and challenges he met. "Do you remember how you helped Uncle John find that old dog when he sneaked out from under the fence? You were so resourceful..." It is always useful and productive to be reminded of your strengths, even if they seem remote at the moment.

In his moving portrait of depression, *Darkness Visible*, William Styron talked about how a patient with a serious illness, who "felt similar devastation," would be allowed to lie about, would be bolstered with life support tubes and wires, his suffering would appear "honorable." "However, the sufferer from depression has no such option and therefore finds himself, like a walking casualty of war, thrust into the most intolerable social and family situations."

How important to understand that sense of hopelessness and isolation and, at the same time, remain persistent in our faith and knowledge that there are other resources and that restoration *is* possible. It is a difficult line we have to walk when we want to help—balancing between pacing the suffering and leading them to wellness, between sorrow and hope, between hell and heaven.

*Future Pacing*

We can remind those who say, "It'll never get better," of the truism that everything changes. Even when we want to hold onto a particular feeling state, it slips through our fingers. "Almost everyone can remember a time," you may say, "when we wanted the moment to last forever." Of course, it never does. Another moment comes along and, with it, different feelings. It's very useful to find ways to remind depressed people how things change all the time, and that the future is not a fixed entity.

For most people, depressive episodes have a beginning, a middle, and an end. When her daughter got depressed, Mollie used to say to her, "Mark my words!" to which her daughter would smile and roll her eyes, knowing what she would hear next. "You're depressed now, but I know you and you always come through these times okay. In a few weeks you'll come home and say 'You told me so!'" Simply conveying to a depressed person that "There will come a time, maybe sooner than you think, when you can feel the way you would like to feel, can help dispel their sense of being trapped in endless sadness.

Dr. Leo Shea told us that, even in this post-World Trade Towers time when he sees so many people suffering depression, he finds it useful to remind people that whatever they're going through now is a temporary process. "They have gone through many other experiences in their life that seemed horrible at the moment—a bad mark in school, not getting into the college of their choice, a miscarriage—and have continued to live a life that is productive." He wonders aloud with them about what resources they called upon to get them through those times, what coping skills and support systems they used that they might turn to at this time.

This approach is, of course, never dismissive of the seriousness of the moment, never resorts to cheap cheerleading that could break rapport. It is, rather, an expression of faith that this person has what it takes to reach backward and forward in time and bring into the present a sense of perspective that softens the blows and makes "now" an all right place to be and tomorrow possibly even better.

Ann used future pacing in a very concrete, practical way when her mother was suffering with lung cancer and a severe bout of depression. They planted bulbs together—tulips were her mother's favorites—so that she would have them to look forward to with the coming of spring. "We always would plant them together and she would say, 'Won't they be beautiful to see!'" She lived to see five more springs than was predicted.

*Pacing Solutions, Wondering, Love*

When we pace solutions, we are focusing on what is possible, on what works, no matter how small or minor a detail, and on moments of relief and joy wherever and whenever they are found. Focusing on solutions is very helpful in many areas, including working with depressed people. When we speak about solutions, however, we always want to remember to honor people's individual perceptions and avoid trivializing or dismissing their feelings and fears by trying to *solve* their problems. When people complain that their days are horrible, that *they* are horrible, and that life is horrible, staying focused on solutions and possibilities helps us to avoid falling into the same abyss that traps them. We can hardly help them if we're feeling as hopeless and helpless as they are. While we can and should pace their pain ("I know you're feeling just awful..."), we do not have to stay there. We might want to observe carefully and catch the one *good* thing that we may be sure they are doing or experiencing. And everyone, except for the most severely ill people, has at the very least a good moment or a good day or two. For this reason, in our practices, we strongly encourage clients to keep daily journals or charts, indicating moods and activities, making special notes of anything that was positive. What people are often surprised to find is that there are more good moments than they had imagined.

*Wondering* is sometimes an effective technique. It is not a directed question or a judgment or a criticism. It's an expression of sincere curiosity. "I wonder what's different on a good day, you know?" can be a thought-provoking opening, yet it's phrased in such a casual manner that depressed people can let it pass by if they wish. If used interrogatively ("What's different when you're having a good day?") it can set a different tone that might best be left for a therapist's office, where there is a clear agreement to do that kind of work. Wondering is an invitation to muse, not a challenge or an implied criticism. Wondering opens possibilities to the unconscious mind, and allows for a movement beyond old patterns that directed commentary does not.

*Yes Sets*

Agreement is also a critical component in Verbal First Aid for depression. Finding a series of statements with which the person can agree (a "yes set") can induce a move closer to temporary comfort.

"Hi. I see you're hangin' out on the sofa."

Nod.

"You're watching that movie I rented."

"Yup."

"Good. So, as I sit over here and read my magazine, you just go ahead and continue enjoying it, okay?"

Notice that prior to the last statement there was no mention of enjoyment one way or the other. "Continue enjoying it" is actually an embedded statement that suggests the possibility that she actually has been enjoying it and can continue to do so. Getting agreement for the important things is always easier once agreements have been secured for the more obvious truths.

*The Observing Self*

Depressed people are often angry with themselves for being depressed in the first place. Their lack of control over their own feelings, thoughts and behaviors leaves them feeling isolated and humiliated. That part of the self that observes the lack of control may also be highly self-critical, blaming the sufferer in an insidious inner dialogue. As a result, the depressed person may see other people as judgmental and critical, even when they are not.

Laurel talks about her own ten-year-long depression. "I hated my own neediness, I hated the way I felt. I'd be standing there, talking to someone and all they'd do was glance somewhere else or act as if, for a second, they had something else on their minds or something else to do, and I'd perceive that as a statement about my own worth. I was too needy; therefore, they didn't want to be around me. It was a vicious cycle, because then I'd isolate myself and get even more needy and depressed."

All of us walk around with different *voices* operating in our heads. We hear our mothers, our fathers, our teachers—their gentle and not-so-gentle reminders to close the door behind us, do our part, wait our turn. Sometimes these *voices* are benevolent and remind us that we are loved and lovable. Sometimes they are not so soothing. When people are depressed, the critical voice in their head can be deafening, making it very hard to truly hear what others have to offer. This is why, if you are living with a depressed person, you may hear yourself grind your teeth, saying, not very usefully, "How many times do I have to tell you?" or "Why can't you just get it through your head?"

*Speaking to the Observer Self*

It may be a tremendous relief to both you and the depressed person to acknowledge that there is this self-blaming observer at work, and to speak directly to that observer. This involves three steps, each of which builds on the next, in order to be truly effective.
- Speak with quiet strength.
- Speak with conviction, faith and facts.
- Speak to the Observer Self.

*Speak with Quiet Strength*

Having quiet strength is a sure-footed gift that allows you to stand still while others spin. There is a Sufi story about a young man walking down an olive tree-lined dirt road when he meets an old man sitting cross-legged against a tree, meditating in absolute peace—a still, calm, blissful smile on his face. Suddenly the young man sees a cloud of dust draw near. The peaceful moment is shattered by the clamor of singing and chanting, punctuated by occasional ear-splitting screams. As the whirling dervish, spinning in religious ecstasy, moves off into the distance, the young man returns his gaze to the old sage, still sitting peacefully, undisturbed. Waiting for what seems a long time, he finally approaches the old man. "How did you do it? How did you stay so calm while he was making that racket?" The old man gets up slowly, brushes off his robes, looks at the young man, and says, "I let him spin."

Quiet strength does not need to make a fuss, or react, or take things personally. Quiet strength is not a cheerleader, nor does it need to fix, put a smile on someone's face, or make *nice*. It is as certain as the earth beneath your feet that all things should be exactly as they are, and that there a greater purpose and meaning to it all, even depression.

*Speak with Conviction, Faith & Facts*

As much as possible, you will want to speak with the tone, the posture, and the phrasing of a person who knows, believes in and has the data to prove what he or she is saying. This, of course, would be a wonderful way for all of us to go through life, all the time. But it is particularly valuable when you are dealing with a person who constantly questions himself, his behavior, his very value. To this end it may be useful to familiarize yourself with some of the research on depression; you might also log on to some of the web sites on depression, where hundreds of recovered sufferers share their successes.

There is an ample reservoir of data to support the belief that people suffering with depression can enjoy full recoveries. There are psychological supports, medications, and alternative treatments available coast to coast. When you say, "I know you can get through this," *know* it to be true!

One of the most poignant and saddening aspects of depression is that depressed people feel that there is no hope. As Lucy from the comic strip "Peanuts" once wondered, "Do you know what it's like to have to wake up every day and know you're hopeless, it's hopeless?" We can offer hope most effectively when we know our facts and present them with conviction. To say, "It'll be fine!" is not the same as saying, "This research shows that exercise boosts endorphin levels, and that just by moving we literally change our brain chemistry!" Or, "They just found that only 30 minutes a day of comedy significantly reduced symptoms of depression in 4 weeks. Shall we start laughing now or later?"

*Speak to the Observer Self*

When we have quiet strength, conviction, faith, and a handful of facts, we are ready to speak to a special part of the depressed person. One patient, a 35 year-old graphic designer, had been suffering from episodes of major depression for a number of years. She had finally found relief in a combination of homeopathy and psychotherapy. She recalled that during those plunges into the abyss, she would forget who she really was. She would begin to believe that she *was* the depression and, as a result, that she was bad, hopeless, and worthless—and would continue that way forever.

Verbal First Aid for her was useful simply to remind her who she really was. "I see you. I know who you are. I see who you are without the depression and I know it's not the same you. I see you as you really are." These simple words can have life-saving impact.

Knowing that the *Observer Self* of a depressed person is more often than not being extremely critical, what we say needs to be sensitive to that, and to counteract it. According to some experts in depression, there are other *Observers* that also speak to depressed people in ways that defend their lives, their goodness, their dreams. Unfortunately they speak so quietly that the negative voices nearly drown them out. Some experts suggest that depressed people write out all their thoughts. There, among the shards of misery will be glimmers of hope and belief in one's self: "I am a good person." "If only I tried, I know I could do it." "There are people who love me."

One of the things the *Critical Observer* says is, "You'll never get through this!" Gentle reminders, such as, "You got through this before and you can do it again," can be reassuring and hopeful. One woman's father used to tell her, "Hang in there, baby. Things keep changing." Although the idea seemed impossibly unrealistic to her at the time, he himself was so credible to her, was such a fount of quiet strength and conviction, that she could not dismiss what he said. Nearly 20 years after the depression lifted, what she remembers most of that struggle is hearing her father's words through the tunnel of her despair. The power of words is such that even when they don't effect immediate change, they sow seeds in our consciousness that take root, sometimes without our awareness, and flower with blessings at the moment that we need them in ways that surprise and delight us.

Obviously, we have not nearly covered the gamut of emotional conditions that plague modern life. However, we have addressed the most common problems you are likely to encounter. We hope the ideas and techniques in this chapter will provide you with material you can tailor to develop your own variation of Verbal First Aid which can help your friends and loved ones attain some measure of peace in times of emotional turmoil.

**Verbal First Aid Keys – Chapter 10**
**Emotional Conditions**

Utilize early learnings/memories
Future pace
Wonder
Love
Yes Sets
Resources
The Observing Self
Quiet Strength
Non-verbal techniques
Getting a contract
Paying Attention to Details
Joining in/Feedback/Pacing
Truisms/Imagery/Future pacing
Non-verbal techniques
As I/You can

# CHAPTER ELEVEN

# VERBAL FIRST AID FOR SUICIDE ATTEMPTS

*"To be or not to be: that is the question."*
*William Shakespeare*

*"Suicide is a permanent solution to a temporary problem."*
*Phil Donahue*

Suicide is terrifying. And it is among the top ten causes of death in our country today. It is the ultimate weapon we all have in our own hands. With it, people can choose to declare war on themselves and on all who are in the fallout area of their self-destructiveness.

Words are no guarantee against it. Any words could be the *wrong* words, depending on the mind of the perpetrator. Even "I love you" could feel like a knife in the heart to someone in the psychic pain that drives a person to self-destruction. So first of all, try to avoid the panic and self-blame that swirls around the threat of suicide. Sometimes it is too late for words. Sometimes the best words cannot be heard. Sometimes the kindest intentions are thwarted.

Needless to say, the threat of suicide is an emergency—one that requires the skills and steadiness of those who literally defuse bombs. Unfortunately there is no universal protocol for suicide threats because each situation brings its own combination of volatile elements. Every word is a step in a dance whose outcome is unknown and unknowable. However, sometimes the right words can make a difference.

Suicide attempts begin long before someone stands on a ledge or holds a gun to a temple. There are warning signs and ways to respond to them. We will point you to resources for that purpose at the end of this chapter. Here we will focus on that most difficult moment, when you are faced with an active suicide attempt.

Obviously, if you can, before anything else, call 9-1-1 or, even better, your local Suicide Response/Emergency Rescue (or Crisis) Team immediately if one is available. They are usually associated with large, teaching hospitals and listed in the front pages of the phone book. In the meantime, if the individual is brandishing a weapon of ANY kind give him a wide berth, keeping yourself out of harm's way if at all possible. Wait for professional help to arrive.

For the most part, those who contemplate suicide believe they have come to the end of their options. They are desperate and just see no other way out, no other answers. While they want hope, they may be too frightened to feel hopeful. Perhaps they've been betrayed by hope before. In their minds, the course for suicide might already be set—they have planned for it and here they are, at the end of the line. Sometimes, though, the right rope thrown at the right moment can have a tremendous impact.

The basic Verbal First Aid techniques to use in an immediately impending suicide, beyond calling for help, are the following:

1. You'll want to gain *rapport* of a special kind, even beyond pacing and mirroring. You'll want to try to *get inside* the mind of the person, to understand as best you can the feelings roiling around, about to explode in an irrevocable act.

2. At the same time, you'll want the kind of *detachment* that protects you, should you not be able to turn the situation around. And you'll want to cultivate the kind of detachment that takes your ego out of the picture. This is not about you. Even if the

other person is trying to hurt you, *for now, this is about them.*
Take the focus off yourself. Remain detached but loving.

3. *Center yourself* as you would in an emergency. Repeat a mantra
such as this one (or any that works for you): "Part of me is entering the mind of this person trying to see the world through
his or her eyes. Another part of me is stepping outside myself
so that I can separate from my feelings and just be useful. Both
parts of me pray for guidance."

As we said earlier, there is no way to even guess what the right
words would be in this potentially catastrophic situation. However,
here are a number of approaches that you might consider using while
you wait for the emergency rescue team to arrive.

First, what *not* to say. This is so important that it bears repeating:
*when speaking with people who threaten suicide, never challenge them.* Never
say, "All right, then, go ahead." Never even say, "Don't you dare even
try!" That's a challenge, too.

"I'll show them," is a powerful motivation to kill oneself. Suicides
are often acts of anger, not only against the self, but against the world.

Whatever their reasons for wanting to commit suicide, no matter
how small or even absurd they may seem to you, they loom large to them.
Honor that and do not dismiss their concerns. It is not the size of the
problems, but the lack of ability to cope with them that makes one desperate. Remember, too, if nothing seems to be working, it is sometimes
better to *say nothing* than to aggravate the situation with the wrong words.

*Questions to Keep Them Talking*

Listening is *key.* As is true with all of us, talking about one's problems and being heard can defuse a troubling situation. By letting
someone vent, by being sympathetic without being judgmental, you

may be offering a potential suicide the one thing that has been missing in their lives—the feeling of being understood.

Whether you know the person or not, it is often a good idea to begin establishing rapport by asking questions. Get the person talking. If it is a person you do not know, avoid stating anything as truth unless it clearly is, e.g., "It's the middle of the afternoon." Ask questions. *Keep them talking.* Ask as many "what" questions as you can reasonably come up with. Or "when" questions, or "where" questions, or "who" questions.

Just remember that sometimes people find it difficult, and frustrating, to respond to "why" questions, especially when they're upset.

Sometimes distraction can be a valuable tool for defusing potentially violent situations, even if it is a temporary stopgap. In *Saving Private Ryan,* one of the soldiers is fed up with the mission and threatens to go AWOL. Another soldier, frustrated and exhausted beyond endurance, points his gun at the young man as he begins to stalk away, cocks the trigger. The fury and tension reach an impossible pitch. The other young men rush to the captain, played by Tom Hanks, pleading that he *do something.* The captain, who had kept his private life to himself up until this point but knew that everyone was taking bets on what he did as a civilian, chose this moment to tell them all who he was: "I'm a school teacher...I teach English." As the captain tells his story, the spell is broken and the gun is holstered.

To choose the right words, the rope that might bring them back off that ledge, you need information. You need to observe carefully and ask as many questions as you can. If they are talking, they are not killing themselves. If they are talking, they are still just thinking about it—at least for that moment.

If you see that your questions and comments are becoming annoying, or if they seem to make the person more agitated, switch tactics. Do not stay with or force an issue or line of reasoning that is not working. Back off gracefully. Apologize if you think it's needed or helpful. Remember that there are no foolproof words, no words that might not provoke a person in despair or desperation. Again, *saying nothing and being lovingly present is still doing something,* and it may be the only viable thing.

A few of the kinds of questions that might keep them talking:

- *What would have to be different for you to agree to go on living?*
- *What people would have to help you with that?*
- *What would you like help with?*
- *What do you want people to understand about you?*
- *And the most simple: What hurts?*

Many experts believe that by being willing to discuss the suicide option, you are defusing it rather than fueling it. Depending upon how this line of inquiry is going, you might consider some of the following questions.

- What people should be notified that you are about to do this?
- When should I tell them?
- Should they come now?
- What should I say to each of them?
- What made you think about ending your life?
- When did you first consider it?
- What do you think will be better about not being here?
- Who is going to miss you? If they say, *nobody,* follow with, *Are you 100 percent sure about that?* If the answer to that is *yes,* then you could follow with: *Was there a time in your life when there were people who would miss you when you were gone?* [Yes] *Who were they?* and *What went wrong?* Then follow with: *What would have to happen for you to have people in your life who would miss you when you were gone?*

Illustrating how this line of conversation can sometimes work, a 9-1-1 telecommunicator told us this story. A young man called 9-1-1 to say that he was lying at the edge of a cliff and he was about to roll off and commit suicide. The operator talked calmly to him but was getting nowhere when she said, "Of course, we'll have to notify your mother." Suddenly the young man became very quiet. He hadn't thought about that. He gasped and said in a panic, "No, that would kill her!" "Well, she'll have to find out..." she said. And, she told us, fortunately there *was* someone who would miss him terribly and realizing that, he changed his mind on the spot.

### Suggested Topics

Beyond keeping them talking with questions, we offer for your consideration a few approaches that might turn the tide. As always, but especially at this critical juncture, your tone should be loving, receptive, and caring; never superior, preaching or judgmental.

1.  *You've made your point. Now we understand.*
    As in the story of the jumper in the Introduction, sometimes just asking, "What hurts?" can give people the realization that someone is listening, and that may be all that they wanted in the first place—a fair hearing, a sense of someone there on the other end. Using empathy, you may begin to see the world through that person's eyes. Kind, deeply sincere, nodding agreement that life is difficult can be a balm to a person who thinks no one could possibly understand.

2.  *What a dismal world it would have been if you had never lived* (theme of the movie: *It's a Wonderful Life*)
    If you think they might be open to an infusion of hope, and if you know enough about their lives to do it, it can help to overlay the *It's a Wonderful Life* scenario onto their experience. In as firm a voice as possible, with as much strength and conviction as you can muster, tell them all the things that are good and positive that wouldn't be that way if they hadn't been born. "And there never

would have been little Jennifer, and the school board would have fired Mrs. Coburn, and maybe those kids across the street would have been killed if you hadn't yelled, 'Look out!' when the fire truck sped by."

In offering hope, take care to avoid being a *cheerleader*. There are few things as irritating or easy to dismiss as feigned cheerfulness in the face of tragic feelings.

3.  *Consequences—You matter to other people.*

You may also be able to remind them of the implications of the action they are considering: that there are people who love them and who would be grievously hurt by their suicide, if that is indeed the truth. Don't make up what you don't know. Specify for them what would be missing in everyone's life without them, using what you have learned about their lives. You could remind them what they have to live for. There might be unfinished business that, upon recalling, stakes a claim in their future and requires them to stay a while longer to see it through.

A woman we know postponed suicide (as it turned out, indefinitely) because she realized that if she killed herself, the terrible husband who was driving her mad would be the one who would raise her beloved two-year-old daughter.

Use anything you know that is meaningful to them—all's fair in life-and-death issues, as long as it is kind and caring. "And what about Rover? Do you think anyone else would mean to him what you do? How could we explain it to him? He'd be lying at your grave, waiting for you to come home. You know how he gets if you even go out of town for the weekend! Do you want him to end up with your *parents?*"

4.  *Always time for suicide.*

You might say, in a pinch, when no other argument seems to hold sway: "There's always time for suicide. It's always an option.

You don't have to do it this moment, because you can always do it tomorrow." That is a truism. And there might be a better time, or a better way to live, down the road.

5.  *A Terrible Way to Die*

Speaking of a better way, George Thompson, Ph.D., author of the brilliant *Verbal Judo: The Gentle Art of Persuasion*, spoke to us about a bizarre suicide attempt during his tenure as a police officer in Emporia, Kansas. The potential suicide was sitting in a tub of water, with a cord wrapped around his toe, poised to pull an electric heater into the water to electrocute himself.

Who among us would not feel the pressure of that situation? The police around him had tried every conceivable angle: "Come on, buddy. You don't want to do that," "You'll feel different in the morning," "Just come on out, dry off, and we'll talk about it." But nothing was working. The fellow stayed in the tub and wouldn't get out.

The simple fact—that he was still in the tub *and he was alive*—gave Thompson hope.

And it gave him an idea. To Thompson, it became clear that if the man had really wanted to kill himself, he would already have done it. Thompson astutely surmised that the man wanted to die less than he wanted a way out of his pain, out of his predicament, whatever that was.

Thompson changed strategies. Instead of fighting with him to live, he would discuss ways to die.

He got down on his knees, shook his head and said it was too bad that of all the hundreds of ways there were to die, this man choose the most painful. Thompson backed it up with research, claiming there were studies that showed that dying by electric current in water can take minutes, even up to ten minutes of excruciating pain, so that he would smell his hair burning, see and feel his skin turning red and boiling back from his arms, his chest split open. If he thought his life was tough before, he was in for an unimaginable ride.

Then Thompson added that there were lots of other, painless ways to die and if the fellow was interested, and he would step out of the tub for a moment, he'd be happy to talk about it.

In an instant with a splash, before anyone could take the next breath, the man sprang out of the tub.

We asked Dr. Thompson about the research he cited and he admitted that he'd made it up. But at that moment, kneeling next to a tub with a live wire poised over it, he was the world's foremost authority on the subject. His authority was so great he was able to turn an invention into a truism. And the reason it was able to work was because Thompson had developed a substantial rapport by pacing the man from the very beginning—moving with him and leading him out to safety.

6. *There's No Going Back/Karma*

Go to the ends of the earth and beyond, if you think it will work. Some people respond to the notion of past lives and *karma*. We have had patients who have been deterred from ending this life with the suggestion that, when people do not complete things properly here this time around, they have to come back and repeat those lessons until they are learned. Since they do not want to find themselves in this situation again, and, in fact would do anything to avoid it, by this logic suicide has to be ruled out.

*When You Have Advance Warning*

Sometimes there are signals, a warning before the suicide attempt is made. There might have been a previous attempt. There might be veiled threats or talk of suicide. Be alert to these, and take them seriously. Contact suicide hotline resources or mental health personnel for advice and resources. Several are listed at the end of this chapter.

While you should take every suicide threat seriously, it is possible that not all people who threaten to kill themselves are truly intent on suicide. Some people may be choosing to hurt themselves as a way of getting attention, or as a way of hurting other people. Some people are only *thinking* of suicide. They don't really want to die, they just cannot think of anything else to do. Sometimes pointing out their aberrant logic can help ahead of time, or even while the ambulance is on the way.

In the 1990 Tom Hanks/Meg Ryan movie *Joe Versus the Volcano* written by John Patrick Shanley, one of the three characters Meg Ryan plays asks the Tom Hanks character if he's ever thought about suicide. He is shocked, but she persists. He says, "If you have a choice between killing yourself and doing something you're scared of doing, why not take the leap and do the things your scared of?"

We once knew a woman who was very overweight, who felt unloved by the world and claimed she "only lived at 50 percent," whatever that meant to her. We asked what would happen if she lived at 100 percent. Her eyes clouded over and she said, "Oh, I would die!" "So what?" we said, much too cavalierly. We don't advise this, but it did have an interesting effect. "What would be lost by living at 100 percent? You're not happy with the way things are now. You might as well take the chance and see what happens." Even though we felt very odd having said that, not wanting to sound as if we did not take the threat of death seriously, she told us later that that was the most important thing anyone had ever said to her. We were suggesting that, if it isn't working by being less than you can be, why not try giving it your all? Why not live at 100 percent— what did she have to lose? She couldn't go on the way she was. The point here is not that dying would be acceptable, but that she should try *living* differently. And when she turned on the wattage, she said, people around her were amazed. It was quite powerful and wonderful.

Ultimately, it is not your decision whether a person threatening suicide lives or dies. It's theirs. You do your best; you pray; you are present and supportive. It is impossible to know what, if anything, will turn the tide. We knew a woman who attempted suicide eleven times and succeeded once, although she was brought back to life by technology and extreme measures. She was on a variety of anti-depressants, but still she courted death constantly. Life was too hard, she said, and all the people she loved had already passed on. It was clear that she was not trying to get attention or to change anything. She just wanted to die.

However, once, when she was in an altered state, we asked her what she thought the meaning of her life might be. She said, "To love." "How can you do that?" we asked. (She was an agoraphobic who never left her apartment.) "It will be hard," she said. "Are you willing to accept that assignment, that challenge?" we asked her. "Yes." Later, we asked her about her death wish. "Death would be kind. It would be nice," she said. We recognized that she felt that way and did not deny it. But then we said: "Do you think that death would be better than love?" She thought about it for a while then said softly, "No." "Could you put all the energy you put into seeking death into seeking love?" we asked. She wondered. And she's still wondering. Amen.

Ultimately, as we said, it is *their* decision. The gun pointed at their head is in their own hands. And you have to forgive yourself if you fail to rescue someone who chooses death. We once knew a police officer who was at the scene of the arrest of a schoolteacher who had killed her boyfriend. She had shot him, gone back to the classroom and graded all the papers for the day, leaving them in a neat pile, and then gone to the bank to get money to get out of town. When the police surrounded her, they told her to gently drop her purse and suitcase, that she had to surrender herself. She surreptitiously reached into her purse, pulled out her gun, and before anyone could move to stop her, shot herself in the head. It was years later that we met him, this hardened officer who sees plenty of trouble, and he was still simmering with "if only's." What could he have done differently? What could he have said? It reminded us of the last scene of the movie *Thelma and Louise.* Might there have been words that could have made the difference?

Ultimately, Verbal First Aid for potential suicides or those actively seeking their own deaths (on a ledge or with a weapon) is practiced very simply: *Call 9-1-1 or a suicide hot line, say as little as you can, try asking questions to keep them talking (as long as they're talking, they're breathing), be as loving and gently hopeful as possible, and pray a lot.* Keep the basics in mind: Gain rapport, get a contract if you can, and give positive suggestion, using the same techniques you would for any other emergency.

We offer this chapter as food for thought. Every move and every word in a situation as volatile and unpredictable as a potential suicide is highly risky. There are no guarantees, especially since the person you are dealing with may be insane, temporarily or otherwise, in which case that person is functioning in a world where your words may have little or no meaning. In those situations, prayer and loving intention may be the best you can offer.

For immediate help:

Look in the front of your phone book for a crisis line or Call 1-800-SUI-CIDE in the U.S.

**(800)442-4673** .....1-800-442-HOPE – same routing as 1-800-SUICIDE

**(877)838-2838** .....1-877-Vet2Vet Veterans peer support line

**(800)784-2432** .....1-800-SUICIDA Spanish speaking suicide hotline

**(877)968-8454** .....1-877-YOUTHLINE teen to teen peer counseling hotline

**(800)472-3457** .....1-800-GRADHLP Grad student hotline

**(800)773-6667** .....1-800-PPD-MOMS Post partum depression hotline

These numbers and much more information and help can also be found at:

www.preventsuicide.us/hopeline-new/
and click GET HELP NOW (on the left)
For hotlines outside the US, here's a link
www.befrienders.org

For teens, call Covenant House Nine Line, **1-800-999-9999.**

Call a psychotherapist, a good, wise friend, a religious or spiritual advisor.

# CHAPTER TWELVE

# DYING: VERBAL LAST AID

> *There is no death, only a change of planes.*
> *—Chief Seattle*

Goodbye. That is the one word most of us do not want to hear or have to say. And this is the chapter in books — as in life — that everyone wants to skip over. Death, dying: these are subjects fraught with sadness, fear, and loss. On this plane, from this vantage point, the loss is irrevocable. The loneliness, and its accompanying pain, can be profound, even devastating.

The Verbal First Aid techniques we have presented throughout this book all derive from an affirmation of life. First aid is the front line of survival, the beginning of the restoration of health. First aid makes it possible for life to go on. But the need for first aid often arises when the prospects for survival are placed in doubt or jeopardy. Life is challenged by death, and although we instinctively struggle for life, there at times when death wins.

What can you say, what approach can you use, when the end of life looms, despite all you may have said and done to prevent it? This is the chapter on *last aid,* not first aid. And for this most difficult of transitions, we will provide you not only with words to use, but also with a method for determining when the shift from life-affirmation to acceptance of death is taking place.

What remains constant in any situation in which you desire to help is the need to *center yourself* and to *establish or build rapport and empathy.*

In fact, these tools may be even more essential as you face the ultimate mystery that we call death.

**Centering in Cases of Dying**

The need to center ourselves when dealing with issues of dying is fundamental. The ghost of our own mortality can loom large at such a time, causing us to lose our own equanimity. It is precisely because the breath is about to leave a fellow being that we must focus on our own breath, and gain the courage to be calm and wise. There is, if you are open to it, something in the universe—think of it as "nature," or "consciousness" if you can't name it God—upon which you can call at this turning point. Take the time to breathe. Take the time to go "inside" and *feel* the presence of whatever Spirit calms your own, and quiets your fears and sadness.

**Empathy and Rapport in the Face of Death**

Once you have centered yourself, connect with the spirit of the person who is dying. Death seems to be a journey everyone has to take alone. But, as we will explain shortly, there are cultures that recognize we can make the transition a shared experience. When we connect deeply with someone about to make that mysterious journey that awaits us, too, we recognize that we are all part of an interwoven tapestry with threads and patterns beyond what we can see. Listen deeply. Become aware of the dying person's vision and experience of this process. Be there. Be present in a peaceful way and share that peace with someone who truly needs it. Saying the right thing is a function of being of the right mind. Knowing, sensing, and believing in the connectedness of the world and of all God's creatures, makes the dying person's journey a voyage *Home*.

*Keep the dialog open*—don't be afraid of what you may stumble across. Sometimes the most painful, awkward, difficult subjects lead to the most treasured moments and profound insights. Let yourself be led by a holy spirit and by the person who is dying. Be sure to keep the door open and let them know you're not put off by *touchy* topics. Listen. There is much to learn from the dying, especially the children.

Dr. Elisabeth Kubler-Ross, author of *On Death and Dying*, was struck by paintings she saw on the walls of a concentration camp in Maidanek. She knew that the children there had lost their families to the gas chambers and were aware that they themselves would shortly follow. "The walls in the camp were filled with pictures of butterflies, drawn by these children," she said. "It was incomprehensible to me. Thousands of children going into the gas chamber, and this is the message they leave behind—a butterfly." And she explained that her interest in the field of death and dying began there.

*Treat the dying as a person*, not a disease. Joanne Lynn, M.D., Professor of medicine at Dartmouth-Hitchcock Medical Center, tells the story of Alice, an elderly, bedridden woman, who was in the care of her overly solicitous sister. Alice was dying and the family tried very hard to make her comfortable, asking her frequently what she wanted—sherbet, tea, and juice. To Alice, all of these offers missed the point. Finally she turned to address her sister, who had asked her once again if she could get her something, and said, "What I really need is a tender morsel of juicy gossip." Until the very end, keep involving the person in life as long as they are willing and interested. Please remember not to speak in front of them as if they were no longer there.

*Remember the many ways we can connect.* Engaging in a conversation that is true and open, that faces fears, that honestly confronts the prospect of death frees you as well as them. But words are not the only tool in such a situation. Don't forget your soothing presence, your touch, the sound of your voice as you hum a favorite song. Verbal First Aid is not just about the judicious use of words—it's also about the judicious use of silence. When someone is ready to let go of life as we know it, perhaps one of the most loving things to say is nothing, to let that person be reassured of your love with your presence and your touch. If all you say is, "I'm right here," you've said a great deal. In their book, *Speech and Man*, Brown and Van Riper recall a student who witnessed a terrible and fatal accident. The student ran up to the car and lifted glass away from the driver's face. Without opening his eyes, the driver mumbled, "Give me your hand." The student took the man's hand and held it as the man died.

## Death in Contemporary Culture

Some people say that death is the last taboo. In the twenty-first century, much that has previously been off-limits can now be found on television or on the internet. We are willing to be shocked or scandalized in the name of free speech or voyeurism or cheap thrills. Taboos have fallen by the wayside and almost any subject has its ardent, vocal proponents. But rarely do we deal with death, at least, in a thoughtful, personal way. In America death is hushed up, like a dirty secret whose name we dare not speak.

When Bill Moyers proposed the television series *On Our Own Terms: Moyers on Dying* to PBS, there was considerable concern about whether people would watch a program about a topic they would rather keep at arm's length. The fact that life includes a death sentence for each one of us is something we prefer to deny. A cartoon in *The New Yorker* by Barbara Smaller depicts a bleak and deserted cemetery. Prominent among the other, ordinary headstones is a large, stolid gravestone. The words carved into it read: "Why me?" This denial of our own inevitable demise can only be maintained by practicing a rigorous avoidance of the ultimate reality.

In some ways, we have made death a fictional companion since childhood. On average, an American child will have watched 100,000 acts of televised violence, including 8,000 depictions of murder, by the time he or she finishes sixth grade. But those anonymous, distanced, often bloodless deaths serve only to inure us to sympathy, and to help us keep meaningful death at arm's length. Father Richard John Neuhaus, Editor in Chief of *First Things*, says we have *problematized* death, reduced and depersonalized it with medical technology, demystified it with repetitious "sob shots" on the evening news ("So, how do you feel now that he's dead?") and de-ritualized it, when in fact, there is nothing more personal, more mysterious, more deserving of intimacy and wonder, and more in need of ritual than death.

We know a young boy who, while riding in a car, rode past the scene of a fatal accident. It was not until a full day later that he began to cry, realizing that the people he saw lying in the street were real people who had actually died. Even more poignant is the death of a person we know or care about, observed close up, which serves as an unavoidable reminder of our own mortality. What is more, because we have been so oddly sheltered from death, those we love often die out of sight in institutions. When they do, we are often at a loss for what to say, or think, or feel.

In the early part of the last century, when physicians still made house visits, and put their ears on their patients' chests to hear their hearts beat, people passed away at home, and those who loved them exchanged final words, held their hands, and sometimes actually saw the curtain at the window flutter as the spirit made its graceful exit. As active participants in the community, and as part of the family's support of the dying person, children, too, saw and knew death.

But as life has become more transient, less deeply rooted, and more material, in our desperate need to cling to the tangible world we know we have become terrified of death. And anything we fear becomes in equal measure more powerful. Like the ominous image from Ingmar Bergman's *Seventh Seal*, the idea of the cloaked, spectral *grim reaper* coming for us keeps us running the other way—awash in pills and plastic surgery and fear, until our adrenal glands are exhausted and we get sick. And if death is the great enemy—partly because of its own inherent mystery, partly because we shun it and lock it away from view—dying is to be avoided at all costs.

In some cultures, death is not so much feared as seen as part of the natural course of life. In the acclaimed book and movie about his passing, *Tuesdays with Morrie*, Professor Morrie Schwartz says, "Death is as natural as life. It's part of the deal we made." But our contemporary Western medical establishment has its own way of looking at the situation and it is almost entirely biological/chemical/mechanical/physical. It has nothing to do with spirit, the "will to live" or spontaneous remissions. Medical textbooks see death as *the Enemy*. In a study for the Project on Death in America (PDIA), 50 medical textbooks were reviewed. Betty Farrell, RN, PhD reports that in all of those thousands of pages only 2 percent had content about the end of life. There was almost nothing about pain at the end of life or its emotional content. Joanne Lynn, physician and teacher, writes, "Throughout the textbooks, frankness about death was strikingly absent. Sometimes dead persons were termed 'non-survivors.'" Doctors consider death their failure.

We knew of one woman in her 90s who was quite overweight and had lived a very full and rich life. In an examination, it was determined that she had lung cancer. The doctors, in their enthusiasm to save her, decided that they would break open her rib cage, operate on her lungs and, when she was recovered enough, begin a course of chemotherapy for her. She looked at them in horror. "Are you mad?" she said, reasonably. "Thank you. Rather than live out my last days in pain like an invalid, I think I'll retire to my garden." And so she did.

**When and Why**

Most of the Verbal First Aid techniques you have learned to this point are geared to those who wish to continue living. They are based on the benefits of life affirmation and the dangers of the death sentence. As actor Bill Bixby said, "I'm not dying of cancer. I'm living with cancer." Here are two brief stories that illustrate this point.

One woman we know, Tanya, was diagnosed with skin and breast cancer more than twenty years ago. Her cancerous lumps were removed and she had a course of medical treatment, although she received no chemotherapy. The doctors were not overly optimistic, but she said to her family, "Who cares what they think! I have too much to do to waste my time being sick." Some two decades later, she is still working and traveling the subways. She walks slowly and she stops some times to catch her breath. But at 94, she's got right to take it a little easy.

Another woman, Tillie, was diagnosed with liver cancer. The family requested at the time of diagnosis that she not be informed, "because it would just kill her right away." Five years later on a routine follow-up exam, a new doctor in the clinic casually mentioned the liver cancer to her. She was dead within six weeks.

Contrary to everything we have told you thus far, there is a downside to rejecting the possibility that one is dying, the way Tanya did. When death's time actually comes, the *life prescription* may become a liability. There comes a time when the effort to continue living becomes simply too much. The struggle, life itself, becomes an indignity, threatening to rob life of its final sweetness. There comes a time for death.

The first step, therefore, if you desire to be of help to people who may be declared "terminal," or who clearly may be approaching what could be the end of life is to *take their spiritual temperature*. Ascertain whether they are *living* with their condition or *dying* from it. You can do that by observation: are they listless, passive, or resentful, or are they getting up every day, ready to participate in life to whatever extent they can? You can readily make this evaluation with an ordinary conversation, using attentive, empathetic listening skills.

People who are dying may understand all the ramifications of having a terminal illness, and may simply be preparing in their minds for the ultimate journey or fighting to live. Neither response is right or wrong. It is just the person's unique approach to an insoluble situation. However, understanding which position you are dealing with can help you to choose your words and pace people more skillfully.

Dying might have as its marker the point at which medical science says, "There's nothing more we can do but make them more comfortable." Of course, there are as many responses to that notion as there are people who have to hear it, but below are some thoughts on how to speak to people reacting in various ways to the idea that they are *dying*.

## Acceptance of Dying

Some people refuse to accept the suggestion that they are dying. They get energized by the challenge and dismiss the assertion. These people are not *dying* no matter what the outcome. They are living their life in this moment fully and with the conviction that there are answers beyond the realms of medical science. Or that medical science will find the answers they need. Others, though, choose not to fight on for any number of reasons. Professor Morris Schwartz, of *Tuesdays With Morrie* fame, became a kind of guru of thanatopsis by viewing his dying as a great journey, his last, in which he was pioneering the way and in the process telling people "what to pack."

Sometimes people are tired, or they feel they have fought enough and are ready to move on. In the days of black and white movies, when milk was still delivered in glass bottles, the family doctor who made house calls would exit the room of a sick parent or wife, holding his little black bag, put his hand on the shoulder of a husband or grown child and say steadily, "She lost the will to live."

Rachel Naomi Remen, physician and author, tells the poignant story of a child with leukemia who suffered long and futilely in the hospital in a battle for his life. Toward the end, worn and exhausted, he told a nurse that he was "going home tomorrow." That threw the staff into an uproar as they tried to learn who had been so cruel as to tell this child that he would be discharged when in fact he wasn't strong enough to leave, and might never be. Whoever had said that would have to be the one to go in and straighten him out.

But no one confessed to having given the child that idea. After a while, Dr. Remen went into the child's room and learned from his own mouth where he got the idea that he was going home. He told her that he knew he wasn't leaving the hospital, but he was going "home."

Tomorrow. She left his room in tears, explaining to the staff the meaning of his pronouncement. The next day he was gone. It was time. He wasn't afraid.

Once the decision seems to have been made, once it is clear that the time for farewells is at hand, there are a number of Verbal Last Aid techniques that can ease the way.

## A Life Perspective

Somewhere between "Is this all there is?" and "What was it all about?" there are answers. The "brief candle" that is life offers us a chance to express who we are. Impending death invites us to sum it up. What was the meaning of it all? Why was I born? What is my legacy? One study of the terminally ill asked them to relate the stories of their illnesses. It turned out that some people had a *life theme* that, when expressed, affected how they approached their disease. For example, when people characterized themselves as *warriors*, they identified with the behavior of telling the truth and standing up against pressure. This sense of a core identity helped them to keep their lives integrated, and gave them a sense of meaning. Perhaps understanding patients' life themes through their eyes can give caregivers a useful frame of reference for reflecting back to people the meaning of their lives on the brink of their deaths.

1) You can do dying people a great service by simply listening as they re-live special moments in their lives, as they look back on the highlights of a lifetime. This kind of review can be very helpful to orient people as they prepare to make their final transition.

2) You could, if you know the person's history, add to that life review. Listen to the stories and then share your own. Imagine the medicinal effect of hearing someone say, "I always thought of you as my role model. I watched your courage as you…" Or even, "I'll never forget how you…" You can use photo albums, news clippings, diaries—whatever is

appropriate and available. You can write a journal together or put together a scrapbook. Remember that it is *their* life's meaning, not yours. Let them come to their own conclusions. You have a separate opportunity to say what their life has meant to you.

Words you might use to elicit life themes might be, "I am so moved by your courage." Or, "I appreciate how brave you are." Generally, the person will protest, not feeling like a hero, but perhaps basking for a moment in that role. They may say, "Oh, I'm not really brave, I'm just feeling…" Whatever they say, do not let your own fears about the subject of dying detract from that sacred moment. Witness it. Touch the dying person's hand.

3) Bring in people who can participate in this ritual of remembering and affirming. Remember that show, "This is Your Life," in which everyone from a third grade teacher to a current employer tells a story about the subject? Any way that you can reinforce a global view of this life as something that has been worth living is well worth doing.

## The Aspen Effect: We are Not Separate and Apart

Perhaps the reason we run from death so fearfully is that, in our culture, it is such a lonely experience. Perhaps this feeling of solitude causes death to seem so overwhelming—the sense that, no matter what we shared in life, now we die alone, cutting lifelines that connect us to everything we know and love. Perhaps we would experience death differently if we sent our loved ones off as the Native Americans do.

Mala Spotted Eagle, a Western Shoshone and Cherokee Native, talks about the Native America view of death.

*The People gather about the dying person so that he is not alone. There is a song. It's an intertribal song that can be used for crossing over, to help the spirit on its journey to find its path in a good way for wherever it needs to go. If the person has enough strength, he joins in and if not, everybody around sings it for him. It's a song that a lot of people know. Some tribes use their own tribal song—but the one I am*

*thinking of is used by many. It is a prayer to the Creator and the ances-*
*tors asking that the journey to the spirit world be a good journey, that*
*the person's needs be taken care of, that they connect with the ancestors*
*in a good way, and go where they need to go.*

*It asks for the ancestors to come help guide you, to walk with you*
*on your journey. When people hear the song, they are usually aware*
*that it's time. And they are happy for it. It feels like then they have the*
*People there lending them the strength so that that journey can be made,*
*helping to call the ancestors. You're not doing it alone. You have lots*
*of help.*

*[In my culture] it's like you don't really die, there's no death, just go-*
*ing from one form of life to another form of life in our journey. We don't*
*fear death. We believe that our thoughts, our words, what we feel in our*
*hearts have a lot of power and energy to them. If you really believe in a*
*certain way with a lot of others, you create that way. There is not just one*
*spirit world or path, there are many creations that people have believed.*
*There is Heaven and Hell if you believe it. We believe in a spirit world.*
*When you are totally completed, then you go on to the spirit world, living*
*in harmony with animals, the buffalo, and we all work together again.*
*To the People, the greatest gift is to go back and live that way. If your*
*lessons weren't completed, you cross over and your spirit would look for*
*where you needed to be reborn into for the lessons you needed to complete,*
*and you are guided back to that spot. So that is one of the reasons [our]*
*people don't have fear of death—there is nothing to fear there.*

Even though it seems that we die alone, it does not have to be that
way. We are in this together, together with each other and with Nature,
or God, or the Spirit World, or the Universe. When we are able to accept death, face it, embrace it, we can be there for the dying person in
a way that is intensely intimate and supportive. As Bill Moyers puts it,
"While America is founded on, and driven by, a myth of rugged individualism, when we get to the end of life, rugged individualism doesn't
do the trick. We need witnesses to our death…."

Colorado is filled with endless fields of Aspen trees, glorious, graceful, bending in the breezes, gold leaves flashing. To the casual eye, they seem to stand separate and apart. Remarkably, the Aspen tree is one of the largest organisms in the world. For beyond our sight, deep underground, it is a network of shared roots, all interconnected. Those trees that appear single and divided are aboveground expressions of one being.

What if, beyond our sight, we too are all connected? By being "sung" into the next world by those you love, you never walk alone.

## Finding the Death Story

Because death is a mystery, we each enter it with myths of our own making, depending upon our upbringing, our culture, our beliefs. With the possible exception of nihilism, whatever a person believes can provide some comfort at the end of life.

1) Religious beliefs. When people hold traditional religious beliefs, it gives them a framework and a blueprint for dying. Final rites, forgiveness, blessings may all play a role and it is a good idea to respect these beliefs and ceremonies, even if they are not yours. Facilitate them and accept that there is magic in them simply because they are deeply held and comforting.

Richard John Neuhaus relates his own terrifying dance with death and the words that changed his perspective. He had been operated on for a colon tumor that had ruptured his intestine. He awoke with a surgical scar stretching from the rib cage down to his pubic bone and shortly afterwards began to hemorrhage. He was wheeled into surgery once more and spent days in intensive care where he had what he called his "near life experience."

He had been wired up with all sorts of life-saving bleeping machines when it suddenly seemed to him that he had sat up, although he knew that his body was prone on the bed. He felt himself "jerked into an utterly lucid state of awareness." He saw "two presences" and somehow heard a message that "Everything is ready now."

The presences disappeared and left Neuhaus in bed alone to contemplate the message and what he discerned was this: "They were ready to get me ready to see God...The decision was mine as to when or whether I would take them up on the offer." This reminder of an eternal truth brought Fr. Neuhaus great peace.

> 2) Spiritual beliefs. In contemporary society, many people may be spiritual without being religious. They may hold beliefs in a higher power or an inter-connectedness, or believe that their spirit is eternal, and take comfort in ceremonies that affirm this view. Prayer circles and support groups are resources for those who are dying.

One spiritual approach that has found adherents around the world comes from the Buddhist tradition; it is *The Bardo Thodol*, also known as *The Tibetan Book of the Dead*. It provides, perhaps, the original and ultimate Verbal Last Aid—what to say to those who are dying and dead to affect the ultimate outcome. It is a guide that is meant to be studied before death, and to be read to the deceased at the time of death and again 49 days after death. Ram Dass, project leader of the Living/Dying Project in San Francisco, says it is hoped that reading the *Tibetan Book of the Dead* to terminally ill patients there will provide them with a "new metaphor" for death, so lacking in our Western, clinical approach.

The philosophy behind the *Tibetan Book of the Dead* holds that life is an illusion, an on-going cycle of birth and death from which we can be freed only by enlightenment. Enlightenment is the recognition of our true purpose and connection with the *Clear Light*. There are words and images that can guide us through the Bardo—the planes of the intermediate state between death and rebirth—helping to train the mind to experience the *Clear Light* that is both empty and radiantly blissful. In that way, the mind, which cannot die, can be awakened and liberated from the wheel of eternal reincarnation or, second best, can find a "good human birth."

When the person has died, the desired end is to move toward the light. Some people take wrong turns out of fear. Some do not accept that they have died. It is important for the person to recognize that life has ended, that now is the moment of death, in which the mind is in total transparency, empty, without color or substance, but sparkling vibrant and pure, encountering no obstacle that can stop it, without beginning or end. The words we read from *The Tibetan Book of the Dead* remind the dead person that there is nothing to fear because death has already happened. (The worst is over!) The person is told to go toward the light, to merge with it.

Because this book can be read before death, it offers, to those who accept it, a roadmap for crossing successfully to the other side.

Ekhardt Tolle has put it another way: "Life is not the opposite of death. Life has no opposite. Birth is the opposite of death. Life is eternal."

3) *The Inspired Connection with the Infinite.* Some people recognize that the life they have lived is, as Plato suggested, a shadow of something much richer. They experience proof of the eternal in song, nature, love, those things that elevate the spirit and make us seem larger than our names, our jobs, our bodies–the labels we agree to, just to get by. Poets more artful than we have expressed this in ways that can inspire hope for eternity in those leaving this plane. One of our favorite writings on this subject is the famous poem, "Death Be Not Proud," by the metaphysical poet John Donne.

*Death be not proud, though some have called thee*
*Mighty and dreadful, for thou art not so;*
*For those whom thou think'st thou dost overthrow,*
*Die not, poor Death, nor yet canst thou kill me.*

*From rest and sleep, which but thy pictures be,*
*Much pleasure; then from thee much more must flow,*
*And soonest our best men with thee do go,*
*Rest of their bones, and soul's delivery.*

*Thou art slave to fate, chance, kings, and desperate men,*
*And dost with poison, war, and sickness dwell;*
*And poppy or charms can make us sleep as well*
*And better than thy stroke; why swell'st thou then?*

*One short sleep past, we wake eternally,*
*And death shall be no more; Death, thou shalt die.*

4) *Answers from Science.* Some people require a scientific approach, including studies and proof, before they accept a belief. They may want to believe that death is not the end, but are looking for assurance in a clinical way. Until very recently, death was a one-way ticket into the ultimate unknown. Today, however, we live in a time in which people can die and come back to life again. Their brains, their hearts, their entire systems can shut down completely, and through the awesome power of technology, those people can be resuscitated and revived. Interestingly, because science has made it possible to revive people who have technically been dead, it has become possible to examine what happens after life is medically declared over.

The stories of near-death experiences (NDE) are often dramatic. Generally, people see a white light, a tunnel, and loved ones or spiritual beings greeting them. Often, a change of heart or a vast respect for all of life seems to be the result. There are many stories of children reporting the help of angels while they were dead, stories that are particularly convincing because they involve concepts the children had not yet learned in this life.

One of the most beautiful and well known is the *Birdies* story. This story has circulated on the Web, was written up in a book, *Beyond the Final Frontier*, by Dr. Richard Kent and David Waite, and is generally believed to be true. It was presented by Lloyd Glen to a church congregation in California in June of 1994. His three-year-old son, Brian, had been crushed under a garage door and was clinically dead, although a neighbor had performed CPR on him and had rushed the boy to the hospital. His sternum was crushed right over his heart. The damage to his brain and body could have been devastating. Miraculously, young Brian regained consciousness. Even more miraculously, tests showed he had suffered no lasting neurological damage from his trauma. Brian's homecoming, on his release from the hospital, was a joyous occasion.

One day, a month after the incident, Brian spoke in full sentences beyond his three-year-old vocabulary, to tell his mother what had happened to him when he was stuck under the garage door. He told of the awful pain and then explained that he heard a "whoosh" and then the *birdies* came and took care of him. They wore white and green clothing he said (although he had not yet learned his colors). One *birdie* even rushed to get her, while they stayed with him and told him that "the baby" would be all right. When the mother asked, what baby, he answered that it was the baby under the garage door. The mother, upon hearing this, realized that Brian had been out of body through the pain and suffering, and had watched the scene under the protection of his angels. Brian told his mother that he had heard her speak to the baby, telling him to stay and not leave. The mother was shocked. She had indeed told him not to go, had asked him to stay if he could.

Glen told the congregation that Brian's experience taught us that if we look with our hearts, not our eyes, we can see that the *birdies* (that is, our angels) are always with us. Brian had told him that if we listen, we can hear them whispering to us. What he was saying was, essentially, that we are guided beings, we are not alone. He added that the *birdies* have a plan for us, because "they love us so much."

Children's reports of NDEs have a guilelessness that makes them quite stunning, even to a cynic. We remember once hearing a story reported on the evening news of a car crash involving an entire family. The mother and son were killed, the daughter died and then came back to life, and the father survived. Upon being resuscitated, the girl was not told that her mother and brother had passed away, but she reported being in a place with a beautiful light and "Mommy and Johnny were there, too."

Scientists and physicians in Great Britain who are studying NDEs methodically have made the claim that *consciousness seems to exist outside the body*. A study presented to scientists in June of 2001 at the California Institute of Technology by a British scientist studying heart attack patients offers evidence that consciousness may continue after the brain has stopped functioning and a patient is clinically dead.

Sam Parnia, M.D., is one of two physicians from Southampton General Hospital in England who have been studying NDEs. The results of a yearlong study published in the journal *Resuscitation*, tracked 63 "clinically dead" heart attack patients. The patients were revived and interviewed within a week of their experiences. Four *reported lucid memories of thinking, reasoning, moving about and communicating with others after doctors determined that their brains were not functioning.* The physicians explained in an interview that these "studies are very significant in that we have a group of people...who have well-structured, lucid thought processes with reasoning and memory formation at a time when their brains are shown not to function." This seems to indicate an on-going source of consciousness beyond the realm of the physical body, independent of the brain.

If studies such as this one help us to eliminate our fear of death, there could be many good consequences. First of all, when we're in fear, as we have explained earlier, our bodies make harmful chemicals. By reducing the fear of death, we may also be reducing chemicals that have been impeding healing. If we are not in fear but calm, we may even heal. Secondly, there are many traditions that believe that dying consciously has important implications for the transition. Certainly, if one died peacefully, the implications for those left behind would be very beneficial.

The Second Law of Thermodynamics states that energy and matter can neither be created nor destroyed. We are, essentially, as human beings, made of recycled stardust and information encoded in our DNA. The calcium in our bones could be older than the White Cliffs of Dover; the iron in our blood is definitely older than the sun, since it has been shown that it would have taken a heat greater than the sun to forge it. Our bodies will be recycled again, forever. And so will our energy. According to the Bhagavad Gita, one of the sacred ancient texts of India, "Just as you throw out used clothes and put on other clothes, new ones, the Self discards its used bodies and puts on others that are new." Whatever you call that thing that animates our skin and bones—call it Self or Spirit or Soul—according to many belief systems it cannot be destroyed.

All of this *documentation* is meant to help those inclined to believe that our consciousness goes on after death, who are still looking for substantiation. In this case, these studies and reports and laws of thermodynamics constitute *truisms* that can help put a frightened mind to rest.

**Reconciling and Unfinished Business**

"Don't go to sleep angry," some people admonish, with the implication that, if one "should die before I wake," there will be no chance to make up and forgive. Forgiveness is golden. It soothes psychic pain and opens the heart. "Don't go to death angry," might also be a wise admonition.

For those who have a belief system, if they see their approaching death as God's will, you can help them by suggesting that the universe is a safe place, that God is good, that their life has been meaningful.

You might also help them by wondering, without judgment, "What do you think God would want you to do about your relationship with your son/daughter/husband/wife/mother/father?" This simple question could provide opportunities for healing, for bringing old family business to closure. Surely God would not want them to "go away" mad, and they may at some level recognize that. Reconciling is in everyone's interest while it still can be accomplished on this plane.

Dr. Donald Trent Jacobs, psychologist, paramedic and author of *Patient Communication For First Responders and EMS Personnel, Teaching Virtues: Building Character Across Curriculum,* was called to a dying man's bedside in a room crowded with family members who stiffly and formally lined the walls. There was little conversation and less intimate contact. There had been lots of bitterness in the family, especially between the dying man and his son. The man seemed unconscious, and Don wasn't certain what he was expected to do or accomplish. Three relatives sat on a small wooden bench. Behind them was an old upright piano, covered by an old, dusty cloth. Jacobs felt the irresistible urge to play the piano. Much to their surprise, the relatives were shooed off the bench, and he sat down and started playing a song from the 1920's called "Whispering." This was not a tune Jacobs was given to whistle. He had no idea where the thought came to him to play it, but he did. And when he did it was as if a bolt of lightning struck the dying man: his eyes opened and he sat up and asked for a glass of orange juice. Somehow, at some level, he had recognized that he had unfinished business, and he lived for 11 months longer so that he and his son could repair their wounded relationship.

**Giving the Dying Person Permission to Leave**

Occasionally, people are ready to leave, but hesitate, unwilling to disappoint a loved one, or out of a feeling of obligation to stay for someone else's sake. If you recognize that the "fight for life" is over, hard as it might be to let loved ones go, it is an act of love to *give them permission to leave* if they must. When a friend's father was dying of lung disease, his devoted wife and his three daughters hovered over him. "We were so reluctant to let him go. We all adored him so. He must have felt that, even though he was in a coma. Finally we recognized that he was lingering for our sake and that as long as we were there, he would not desert us. In a house full of women, he had always been our protector. Now, he was suffering, hanging on, to keep *us* from the pain his loss would cause. How I wish I had known what to say then. I would have said to him, 'Dad, we love you. You are always alive inside of us, for as long as we live. And we understand if you have to go. Nothing will diminish our connection. We know you'll do whatever you must.' Within an hour of our leaving the hospital, we received the call that he had passed away."

If you recognize a situation like this one, you might want to give the dying person permission to pass on, with loving words such as, "I love you and want you to know that I understand if it's time for you to move on now. If you must go, it is all right with me, I'll be all right, and you will always live in my heart."

Remember, too, that death is their choice. Have no agenda but their highest good at heart. It is not up to you to resist or insist, only to witness and allow.

### Words for Other States of Consciousness: Alzheimer's' Syndrome and Comas

What follows is a magical story that happens to be true about two well-known people and a revelation about Alzheimer's disease.

Dr. Elmer Green began his career as a physicist at the Naval Weapons Center, received a PhD in biopsychology, founded the Voluntary Controls Program at the highly respected Menninger Foundation, co-founded the International Society for the Study of Subtle Energies and Energy Medicine, and with his wife, Alyce, wrote the best-selling book, *Beyond Biofeedback.* Prior to the Greens' studies, it was believed that the body's autonomic functions (e.g., heart rate, digestion, blood pressure, brain waves, etc,) could not be voluntarily controlled. However, by studying Indian yogi masters, the Greens proved that the nervous system and metabolic rate could be consciously regulated and began using biofeedback to alleviate a wide range of ailments.

Several years older than Elmer, as Alyce moved into her 80s she experienced Alzheimer's disease. When, in her confusion, she demanded of Elmer, "Who are you?" and he answered, "Your husband," she would dismiss him with a haughty, "That's what they all say!" Still very much in love with her, Elmer tended to her needs and one day, as she lay in a coma, he decided to read to her from the *Tibetan Book of the Dead*. Suddenly, she opened her eyes and spoke lucidly for the first time in a long while. "Thank you Elmer, for reading that to me. Now I know exactly where I am." She told him that Alzheimer's occurs when the spirit leaves, but the mind and body must stay to complete something. She also said, conversely, that autism occurs when the mind and body enter this world, but the spirit does not. And for some time thereafter, she spoke to him from "the Bardo state," the after-life or intermediate state described by the Tibetans as a place between life and death.

All this, and much more, fills a 900-page book written by Elmer, called, *The Ozawkie Book of the Dead: Alzheimer's Isn't What You Think It Is*. The point of this story is that even people suffering with Alzheimer's might be reached with the right words.

When someone we love dies, we can become so immersed in our own grief that we can forget the love we have for others, and that others have for us. If there's even a slight possibility that the dead can still see and hear what we are doing and saying, shouldn't we be paying just a bit more attention to how we behave in this life? Doesn't it make fights over wills and family disputes all the more painful to think that our departed have to witness it? Recognize that kindness and love are the elixirs that heal, even when all else seems lost.

**Seize the Day**

Sometimes the loss is sudden, unexpected, and you never get the chance to say the things that flood your thoughts and heart now that the loved one is gone. The most essential Verbal First Aid principle to remember *is always say what's in your heart if it is loving.* It doesn't cost a thing, it makes you and your recipient feel wonderful, and you'll never have to regret *not* having said it. Whenever you feel it is a good time to say it. Looking at someone, being flooded with love and then saying, "You are so beautiful." or "I just have to stop everything and tell you I love you," is like sun kissing flowers, like music wafting across a field, like the footloose laughter of an innocent child. We must always say what is truly in our hearts while we can, even if the person to whom we address the words is in a coma and we think they cannot hear us. But if you have missed that chance, you might want to remember what *Tuesday With Morrie's* Professor Morrie Schwartz had to say about that: "Death ends a life, not a relationship."

PART FOUR

# About You,
# The Caregiver

# CHAPTER THIRTEEN

# THE AFTERMATH: HOW TO COPE AFTER A MEDICAL EMERGENCY

*"... that best portion of a good man's life:*
*his little, nameless, unremembered acts*
*of kindness and love."*
*–William Wordsworth*

Anyone in a traumatic situation can feel helpless and hopeless. We have written this book in the belief that when you help others with Verbal First Aid you also help yourself to get through the situation by taking control and by having something positive and concrete to do. When you suggest healing to others, your unconscious mind is listening in at the same time. That's another way in which this information can be so important and so vital.

Inevitably, though, that time comes when the paramedics are gone. The person you helped is now in the hospital, but you may still have adrenaline running through you. However courageous you have been, however effective in applying Verbal First Aid, you now sit by yourself and face your own feelings.

People in the rescue business—firefighters, police, paramedics, SWAT teams, nurses, doctors, and so on—know what dealing with trauma costs them emotionally and mentally, as well as physically. At its most debilitating, this can become a clinical disorder: Post-Traumatic Stress Disorder (PTSD).

In many circles, the standard protocol for dealing with post-emergency traumatic stress is called Critical Incident Stress Management (CISM). Jeffrey Mitchell, Ph.D., developed this program in 1983 based on his experiences as a firefighter-paramedic and regional coordinator of emergency medical services for the Maryland Institute for Emergency Medical Services. It is the single most widely used and successful tool in dealing with critical incident stress reactions, whether we're talking about emergency personnel or victims of a terrorist incident.

There are seven distinct steps to the debriefing process, which usually takes place in groups and with the combined help of a CISM-trained peer officer (EMS, police, or firefighter) and a mental health professional. The essential purpose of CISM and critical incident debriefings is to identify those group members who seem to be having strong reactions to the incident and may need further psychological support. In the process of sorting out thoughts and feelings, the majority of participating rescuers leave the debriefing better able to continue their work and manage their own lives. If you have used Verbal First Aid in an emergency, you've been in the same position as those rescuers. And the feelings you are left to deal with are the same.

**The Feelings**

Blessedly, during the trauma or emergency itself something happens to most of us that allows us to set aside our feelings in order to deal with the urgent needs of the moment. We may experience a lot of different feelings: fear, confusion, impotence, anguish, anxiety, frustration, anger, sadness; we also feel things you might not expect, like relief, closeness, silliness, pride in having helped, indifference, or numbness. The range of emotions is as varied as we are. None is right or wrong. Yet somehow we manage to hold these feelings in check until we're done. That's what allows us to use the Verbal First Aid techniques…to be clear enough, calm enough, and in control enough to help.

Afterwards, however, once the emergency has passed and your adrenalin has begun to retreat, those feelings may re-emerge. It's not at all uncommon.

Feelings of helplessness or a lack of control on the scene of a medical emergency or a critical incident have been shown to increase the pressure on rescue personnel. It was entirely too common to hear comments such as, "I couldn't do anything," "I was powerless," "It just all came down and I couldn't stop it," over and over again at New York's Ground Zero in the aftermath of September 11. While this agony is familiar to anyone who wants to help, people who are trained to save lives find it doubly difficult to tolerate that frustration.

Robyn Robinson, Ph.D. & Jeffrey Mitchell, Ph.D., both on the Board of Editors of the International Journal of Emergency Mental Health, evaluated 172 emergency, welfare and hospital personnel and concluded that the death of a child and multiple fatalities, line-of-duty deaths, and incidents that put them or their colleagues in danger were far more likely to cause aggravated acute stress symptoms. It would be hard to imagine anyone not being deeply affected by witnessing those events.

Helplessness brings with it a slew of other feelings, depending on your life experience and nature. Most people, especially those who are trained to help, abhor the feeling. Its residue is often anger, frustration, self-blame, or blame of others. In more serious reactions, a person can become obsessed by the experience and isolated.

Sometimes people respond in surprising ways when they feel frightened or threatened. A woman we know tells a story about a time when her three-year-old son stuck a bingo ball up his nose. They couldn't get it out, and he began to have some difficulties breathing. The mother rushed the child to the emergency room of a nearby hospital, chattering all the way. "This is my son," she said, in a lively, almost cheerful manner, to the receptionist upon arrival, with what she was certain was great equanimity. "He has a bingo ball up his nose. He was playing and, of course he knows better, but for some reason, he—" she continued. She watched as the receptionist picked up the phone and said, "I have a child with a foreign object up his nose, need Peds consult," and then, to her surprise, turned his head, whispering into the receiver, "and the mother is very upset."

In some situations, when the victim is a child, or a person very much like yourself, either in age, looks, or circumstance, it is easy to unconsciously identify with that person. When you see that person in trouble—whether it's being hurt, sick, or killed—a part of you fears for your own safety and well being. You begin to feel very vulnerable.

Vulnerability is truly the critical issue. After all, seeing someone get seriously hurt or seeing someone die reminds us that we, too, are mortal and our time here is limited. That is the truth of the situation. And it is hard to face. Our vulnerability also includes the pain of loss. We will, inevitably, if we live long enough, lose people we love.

If you have been using Verbal First Aid with a stranger, you may find yourself less emotionally involved, which is thoroughly reasonable. They are not part of your everyday life, nor are you part of theirs. Although you want to help them get well, it is likely that your first encounter with that person will also be your last. Much like a 9-1-1 operator or an emergency room physician, you may never know what happens to that individual after your job is done. Does that person recover? Did you help? Unless you make a concerted effort to find out, you just won't know. The result is that while you may have less vulnerability, you also have less opportunity for closure. On the other hand, if the patient is someone in your family, or someone you care about, your emotional investment increases dramatically. While you may get more closure, you will also be more vulnerable.

**When a Helper Needs Some Help**

Having all the feelings we discussed—sadness, vulnerability, anger, frustration, grief—is a normal, predictable human reaction to illness, trauma, and death. Sometimes, however, these feelings do not fade as we might expect. Sometimes they grow stronger and begin to take over our lives, changing us and our relationships in potentially destructive ways.

As we mentioned before, there's a name for this syndrome: Post-Traumatic Stress Disorder or PTSD. Not every person meets life on the same terms. Those of us who are particularly caring and sensitive may be easily hurt. Others of us play tighter hands and don't talk or show their feelings. Either way we can get overwhelmed by what we've experienced in helping others through terrible trauma. PTSD is not uncommon. If you see signs of PTSD over a period of time, in yourself or in someone else, we urge you to speak to someone with experience in its treatment.

Although you might feel as if you are going crazy or try to ignore it, or that you've failed in some way, or even figure (wrongly) that there's something shameful in your feelings, getting help is absolutely the right idea. With the right support, in short order you should find yourself back on track.

PTSD is a treatable ailment. Increasingly, and importantly in our judgment, the medical profession is coming to see emotional disorders much the same way it does physiological problems such as diabetes or pneumonia: symptoms lead to a diagnosis, which leads to treatment and a cure. PTSD is as real a problem as a broken bone, and with proper medical care, it's every bit as treatable.

Helping goes in circles. If you are experiencing any of these feelings or symptoms, call someone you trust and get the help you deserve.

### Signs & Symptoms of Acute Stress and PTSD

Acute stress and post-traumatic stress are both reactions to traumatic events involving either direct personal experience of a life-threatening event, a serious injury, a threat to one's life or physical safety, witnessing a death or disaster, or experiencing a grief reaction to a family member or close associate's death. Acute stress differs from post-traumatic stress in that it lasts approximately four weeks from the date of the critical incident. Post-traumatic stress disorder is only diagnosed when the symptoms last longer than one month.

What to look for in stress disorders:

1. Undue survivor guilt.
2. Rigorous avoidance of situations or activities that remind one (even vaguely) of the incident, which begins to interfere with normal life activities.
3. Impaired range of affect, meaning that whereas once you were able to feel a wide range of feelings, such as love and joy, now you are feeling only a dull numbness.
4. Self-destructive or impulsive behaviors.
5. Dissociation—a feeling of not being in one's own body.
6. Increased somatic complaints—headaches, stomach and GI upsets, back pains.
7. Feelings of shame, ineffectiveness, despair, or hopelessness.
8. Withdrawal and isolation from others, feelings of detachment.
9. A feeling of being "damaged," "worthless."
10. A loss of prior beliefs, a loss of faith.
11. Hostility and anger on a short fuse.
12. Hypervigilance—a feeling of being vulnerable and threatened where no such threat is ordinarily perceived and an exaggerated startle response.
13. Recurring nightmares and difficulty falling or staying asleep.
14. Flashbacks—a sense of re-experiencing the trauma.
15. Difficulty concentrating.

**Steps Towards Self-Healing**

There are some simple things you can do for yourself, beginning with your inner dialogue.

*Change Your Thoughts*

As you told the victim, it's important for you to realize and tell yourself: *The worst is over. These feelings are normal and natural. I did the best I could and now it's in the hands of the doctors.* Become aware of what you're saying to yourself, of your inner dialogue (see Self Talk, next chapter). Are you blaming yourself? Are you angry at yourself or someone else? Are you filling yourself up with negative thoughts or positive ones? Do your thoughts help or hurt you? A simple and obvious way to remind yourself of your own thought processes, and the fact that you can choose your thoughts, is to put little Post-it® notes on your refrigerator, car, or mirror. Have each note be a reminder of a thought you need to hear, whether it's "the worst is over," or "good work." When you come across an inspiring thought in a book or article, write it down and add it to your Post-it® collection.

*Remember Your Strengths*

When we are frightened or worried, we tend to become overly focused on the negative. It's a natural form of self-protection to try to prepare yourself for the worst. However, at this time it serves you better to remember who you really are and what you truly are capable of doing, and what you have, no doubt, been able to do before. Lean into your strengths, your hobbies, the things you're "known for" (Your pies? Your jump shots? Your flower garden?).

You may feel that you, too, are a victim of this emergency and while that may technically be accurate, it's not in your best interest to think that way. If a negative thought finds its way into your thinking, you do not have to allow it to become a permanent fixture. Let it go. You have that power. And, once again, if you find yourself unable to manage this on your own, a good therapist can help restore your peace of mind.

*Pray*

If you're not religious, you can read this section heading as *having hopeful thoughts*. As we mentioned in the first chapter, Larry Dossey, M.D., has reported numerous double-blind studies that validate the healing power of prayer. In the well-known Byrd study in San Francisco, a group of heart patients was divided into two groups. One, the experimental group, was the object of prayers, and the other, the control group, was not. The experimental group showed fewer side effects from treatment, as well as shorter hospital stays. Studies at Duke University and the University of New Mexico have subsequently demonstrated prayer's power in healing.

Even if you don't know what to pray for exactly, "Thy will be done," has been demonstrated in studies, as reported in *Healing Words* by Dr. Dossey, to be qualitatively even more powerful than specific requests. "Whatever is in his highest good," may prove the same.

Prayer, whether for yourself or another person, works. Even if you don't fully believe this model, the act of praying is meditative. And meditation has been shown empirically to have positive effects on all major body systems.

*Talk About It*

Studies on support groups, particularly with cancer and AIDS patients, indicate that the simple act of sharing an experience can have all sorts of beneficial effects. Talking makes us feel less alone, opens our own hearts toward others, and can give us a new way of looking at what we have been through. It can also give us models of success: if others have been through it and they seem okay, we can do it too.

Sometimes just venting works. Use a conversation to blow off steam. Sometimes people have good ideas and solutions for you. And, sometimes, just hearing yourself complain one time too many leads to change.

*Write About It*

Writing about a trauma forces us to slow down our thinking and focus. We have to collect our thoughts before we can articulate them on paper. And writing is not a just a conscious process. As you write all kinds of images, memories, feelings come up that you may not have expected. The connections made by your unconscious mind will surprise you. You have access, in this way, to parts of yourself that you may not have heard from in quite a while. Writing gives them a voice. According to Dr. Joshua Smyth, assistant professor of psychology at North Dakota State University, this "process [of writing] is very different from the intrusive and upsetting rumination that often follows traumatic events, a process that has been shown to have physiological effects, among them increases in heart rate and in the level of stress hormones."

A study reported in the *Journal of the American Medical Association* **[JAMA, April 14, 1999 - Vol. 281, No 14 1304-1309]** found that patients with bronchial asthma and rheumatoid arthritis who wrote about trauma for twenty minutes for three days had physiological changes in their blood to indicated medical improvements in their conditions. Studies on "healthy" people's immune system showed that when they wrote about trauma, there were marked improvements in the IgA in their saliva, indicated that their immune systems grew stronger.

Another way to use this process is to write a letter to the person who's been hurt or taken ill. You may never actually deliver this letter, but writing it allows you to freely express and examine your thoughts and feelings.

*Surround Yourself with Loving People*

This is pro-active self-love. If the people around you don't understand you, support you, or are consistently negative, you may want to consider associating with different people during this time, at least until you've regained some of your characteristic balance. Negativity feeds off negativity, and positive energy works the same way. If you haven't spoken to a dear friend who lives out of state in a long while, then this might be a good time to call and hear a loving voice from a happier time.

And don't forget the salutary effect of our "best friends," wonderful dogs and cats. Having a pet has been shown to have numerous healing benefits, from lowering blood pressure to increasing our immune systems efficiency. One woman undergoing a panic attack pounded on the door of a classmate in her dorm in the middle of the night. "I'm so upset," the first woman said, hardly able to catch her breath. The classmate opened her door wider to let the woman in. "Want to hold my hamster?" she said to the woman in panic. Who could have guessed that the furry critter would be the very source of all things calm and dear?

*Eat Right, Sleep Right, Breathe Right*

Don't forget the basics of healthy living, starting with a good breath. At any given moment you can change the way you feel by focusing on, and slowing down, your breathing. Similarly, if you're stressed and not eating, or are sleeping poorly, you are only further depleting your body's natural defenses. Eat realistically—don't gorge on sugar and starches. They may give you a temporary boost, but there's a price to pay afterwards when you bottom out. Sleeping is when your body repairs itself. It's absolutely essential that you get the sleep you need. Everything looks and feels different after a good night's sleep. We have found that *Bach's Rescue Remedy*™ is a gentle way to soothe the feelings brought on by shock. It a natural, herbal remedy made from the dew of flowers; four drops in an ounce of water helps bring you back into balance; eight to twelve drops helps many people sleep like a baby.

*Stress Reduction*

There are different ways to manage your stress, including exercise, meditation, hypnosis, progressive relaxation, simple visualization, yoga, tai chi, conscious breathing practices, and prayer. The method you choose is up to you. Many people use more than one. There are hundreds of excellent current books and tapes on this topic. Now would be a good time to buy one.

*Neuro-Linguistic Programming/Visualization*

Neuro-linguistic programming, or NLP, is a form of psychotherapy that manipulates images in the mind to make them easier to handle. One of the techniques that NLP therapists use is to ask their clients to visualize the traumatic or unpleasant event bothering them on a large movie screen in full color. The next step is to see it on a smaller movie screen. Next you see it on a wide screen TV. Then you transfer the image to a smaller TV. Finally, you see it on a tiny, black & white screen. Stay there a moment, then reach out, grab the knob and turn it off.

Remember that the imagination is accessible at every moment. It is courtesy of your imagination that you keep seeing upsetting mental pictures to begin with. Come up with a mental picture you can call up at will to make you laugh or evoke joy.

*A Touch of Kindness*

You tried to help. However it turned out, you've done your best. Despite our efforts to direct events, life has its own agenda. We don't call the shots. In providing Verbal First Aid to the best of your ability, you gave someone compassion, support and hope. Now, give yourself some of that same kindness.

Any second thoughts you may have, any blame or anger you may be feeling, these are not working in your best interest. To quote the Buddha, "Resentment is like a hot rock you hold in your hand in the hopes you can throw it at someone." Let go and go on living. That's the best way to help yourself and all those around you.

**Verbal First Aid Checklist for Yourself:**

When the Worst is Over, Have You...

1. Done something kind for yourself?
2. Eaten properly? Replenished yourself with lots of fresh water?
3. Called someone you care about?
4. Listened to a good piece of music?
5. Taken a walk, gone to the gym, done some yoga?
6. Prayed? Compiled a gratitude list?
7. Played with your cat, dog, or other pet?
8. Shared your thoughts and feelings?
9. Written down whatever bothers you?
10. Laughed at a good joke?

## CHAPTER FOURTEEN

# SELF TALK: HOW TO COMFORT YOURSELF AS A CAREGIVER

*"The angels fly because they take themselves lightly."*
*–G.K. Chesterton*

There is a theory among some psychologists that we are all schizo-phrenic, but those among us presenting a uniform personality to the outside world get to walk around outside the institution walls. For certain, we are bombarded by the cacophony of voices in our heads. They judge us and find us wanting. They praise us and think we're unique. They provoke us to do things we know we shouldn't and keep us from doing things we know we should. They are sometimes childish ("I'm outta here!"), and sometimes parental ("You always mess up; you can't do anything right.")

These voices, especially those that prod and pinch at our weakness-es, emerge in their fullest force when we are at our most vulnerable — when we are tired, hungry, frustrated, hurt, angry, confused—all states easily reached when we have spent a great deal of time trying to help another person in danger or in pain.

The healthiest thing you can do for yourself if you are helping others, and even if you are not, is to monitor your own thoughts. By now, if you have gotten this far in this book, you appreciate the inor-dinate power of words and thoughts on your physical body and your emotions. If you step outside your thoughts and listen, you may be surprised at what you overhear. It is said that we have tens of thousands of thoughts per day, many of which are the same thoughts we had yesterday—and most of which are negative.

Simply paying attention to your thoughts gives them less autonomy, and therefore less power. Even without making an effort to change them, through the very act of noticing them many of the useless ones seem to slither away.

There is a joke that goes: "Do you know how to make God laugh? Tell Him your plans." Clearly we are not in charge of much in our lives, but the one thing—perhaps the most important thing—that is truly ours is our attitude. Rich or poor, sick or well, when someone asks if you are happy, you get to answer for yourself. If you say and believe that you are, no one can contradict you. Abraham Lincoln, one of the most depressed men ever to sit in the White House, used to say, "Most of us are just about as happy as we make up our minds to be." We cannot change the external world, or at least we can't always control it, but our attitude, our peace of mind, can be inviolable if we so desire it, in the face of any obstacle. The Buddha said that life is not about what happens to you, but about how you react to it. And that it is your own hands.

Energy flows. If it is simply flowing **out**, you become depleted.

You are not worth anything to those you would help if you are depleted, dejected, demoralized. You cannot help a man out of a pit when you share it with him. Allow your attitude to keep you safe from harm, warm even in the cold, and kind at heart.

*Some Words You Can Say To Yourself When the Going Gets Rough*

1. You didn't cause it, and you can't cure it. The trauma is not your fault. The behavior problems are not your fault. The illness is not your fault. The difficulties in adjustment and frustrations the patient experiences are not your fault. The changes, therefore, that patients must make are theirs to make. Not yours. Learn the distinction between what you can do and what you cannot. Sometimes this is particularly

difficult when emotions of guilt (perhaps you have survived the accident intact) or love are involved, or when there is unresolved grief for someone who is alive but is forever changed. But blame costs precious energy and does more harm than good.

2. You can help them, but you can't get well for them. For some people, perhaps for you, this is a very difficult concept, especially if your heart is involved. Judith Simon Prager remembers taking her infant daughter to the pediatrician for an inoculation. The baby was so young and precious that, as she held her in her arms, she felt almost incapable of delivering her over to the doctor who was going to stick a needle into her. "You want to take the shot for her, don't you?" the doctor said, smiling. And that was true. But it doesn't work that way, and sometimes for very good reasons, we can't spare each other the pain.

If you have their best interest at heart, and we know you do, it is very important to allow the victims or patients to do whatever they can for themselves. If it means they will spend five or ten more minutes tying a shoelace or getting dressed, so be it. Even if it means they will become frustrated. When someone has had brain trauma, whether from a cerebrovascular accident (CVA) or a car crash, recovering lost skills or functions requires hard work over a long period of time on the part of the victim. That isn't your job. One of the miraculous features of the brain is called *plasticity*, which means that new pathways are formed based on new activities. Brain cells from one part of the brain can fill in for cells lost in another when these new pathways are formed. Even when the task does not build new neural pathways, in most cases of illness or emotional disability, even making an attempt builds confidence and every little victory can build morale. For all these things to happen, we need to let the patients themselves do the work.

3. Have an attitude of gratitude. It's easy in the midst of a storm of worries to forget to notice life's small blessings. Somebody says, "Nice day," and you look up, surprised. When did it stop raining? Somebody brings

you a container of homemade soup and, if you choose to, you can feel nourished. Everything, as Einstein pointed out, is relative to the observer. You may be surrounded by treasures you have overlooked. Remember that a loyal dog, a car that runs, flowers that bloom in a kaleidoscope of color, or an "aching back" that doesn't ache right now, is a blessing. Gratitude means that you notice the small gifts when and where you find them. It's a quality we can nurture by giving it our attention.

When cell biologist Dr. Bruce Lipton says that we receive 4,000,000 bits of information into our nervous system every second and can only consciously register 2,000, he is saying that on some level we must be choosing what we register as information. By changing the lenses through which we filter that information we can actually see a different world. If the bits we choose to register are the ones that make us smile, the world we see and hear and feel before us is that much richer.

4. Remember that in life there are no medals for martyrs. In fact, martyrs often make other people uncomfortable or angry just by being holier than everyone else. Even if your every gesture of help seems fully appreciated, be careful of how far you go in that effort to help. In Zen, there is the notion of Idiot's Compassion, which occurs when we give a person a fish instead of teaching him how to cast a line.

Moreover, when we give too much, to the exclusion of our own needs, we are leading ourselves down the path of bitterness, resentment, isolation, and ill health. As Edna St. Vincent Millay said, "My candle burns at both ends. It will not last the night." Becoming a martyr on the cross of care giving is not a selfless act. It does little good to help others to our own detriment. You are best equipped to help when you know how to help yourself. And from the perspective of your patients and loved ones, they need you to be well and strong.

5. In neuropsychologist Rick Hanson's new book, *Hardwiring Happiness*, he reminds us that we are built with a "negativity bias" which causes us to remember those things which might cause us harm more

concretely than the good ones. He offers techniques to develop the neural networks that support inner strength, resilience, and happiness. He uses the word HEAL to remind us to Have a positive experience, Enrich it, Absorb it, and (optional) Link it to the negative to soothe and replace it.

6. Perspective makes perfect. This time and place, these circumstances, this job of care giving, these are not all there is to you or to your life. Give yourself a broader context. When we are overwhelmingly concerned with helping a victim or ill person, we have a tendency to become excessively focused. Use a wider-angle lens. "Okay, this is awful. But what else is there? What else am I seeing? Thinking? Feeling? Hearing?" Even broadening your world by exploring new sensory perceptions in the present can be very helpful. It breaks the negative trance we all fall into from time to time.

See beyond the limited descriptions of your current life in all directions:

- Look back. Remember yourself before this time, and call up strengths from those happier, perhaps more carefree times. Who were you then? You are still that person. Look for him or her inside of you.

- Look forward in time, bringing the strengths you found in your history into your future.

- Look sideways. Is the view broader than you thought when you look beyond the narrow road on which you march?

- Look up and get a spiritual perspective. A friend of ours, exhausted by frustrations as she helped others, feeling always that whatever she did was not quite enough, asked the "heavens" why nothing was working. She shakes her head as she tells it now, because as soon as she asked the question she heard these words in her mind: "Oh, but you should see how you're shining from here!"

7. You are not alone. When Dr. Larry Dossey writes about the power of prayer and non-local thought, he describes ways that we are interconnected in this moment, but might not yet accept. Dr. Bruce Lipton believes our thoughts are not contained in our heads, and cites magneto-encephelograms that can measure our thoughts well outside our skulls; if you think your body establishes the limits of who you are, you might well be wrong.

Take a breath and imagine connecting with every soul that has ever belonged to a being who has done good work. Mother Theresa, Mahatma Gandhi, Albert Schweitzer, Elizabeth Kubler-Ross. Feel their goodness. Now, feel their exhaustion. We once saw a TV interview that Mother Theresa had granted, and at that moment she was downright cranky, with good reason. What she was trying to do was difficult, and not always rewarding. You may occasionally be saintly, and occasionally be grumpy, and on the whole, be making a wonderful contribution.

Now connect in your mind with the person you are helping. What can you know about him or her that helps you help? What can you know about yourself that can make you more effective? Allow yourself to be both imperfect and yet much more than you thought you were and you will be rewarded in ways you cannot yet imagine.

8. Have a spiritual context for your life. Adding God to the equation always tilts the odds in your favor. According to a Harris Poll in 1998, 94 percent of Americans believe in God, 90 percent believe in Heaven, and 20 percent believe in reincarnation. In the world at large, as many as 80 percent of us believe in multiple lives.

Having a faith in something greater than yourself, knowing that there is a *Plan*—as little Brian's *birdies* described it– particularly when someone you love is hurt or lost, when things look their most bleak, feeling yourself in God's hands is an enormous comfort and relief.

When things don't seem to be working out when you've tried to be the one at the helm, surrendering can be the relief you've been looking for.

And always remember, if you are or someone you know is in distress, please do not hesitate to call a professional. There are therapies that are specifically designed to aid people who have suffered traumas.

# CHAPTER FIFTEEN

# HUMOR FOR HEALING:
# THE LAST LAUGH

*"Seven days without laughter makes one weak."*
*–Joel Goodman*

A book like this, of necessity, is filled with heavy topics with hardly any relief in between. Everything from motorcycle wrecks to cancer, from nervous breakdowns to suicide attempts and dying. We have offered a variety of verbal approaches to help turn those situations around. But there is one more technique we thought we might mention, and in so doing go out on a laugh or two, while informing you of still another element of healing with words.

*A woman went to the doctor's office—one of those big practices where you see whatever doctor happens to be on rotation when you come in. She was seen by a doctor, but after just a few minutes in the examination room, she burst out, screaming as she ran down the hall. An older doctor stopped and asked her what the problem was, and she explained. He had her sit down in the waiting room and relax while he tried to get to the bottom of things.*

*Then he marched back down the hall and demanded of the new doctor, "What's the matter with you? Mrs. Terry is 63 years old, she has four grown children and seven grandchildren, and you told her she was pregnant?"*

*The new doctor smiled smugly as he continued to write on his clipboard. "Cured her hiccups though, didn't it?"*

Did this story make you laugh? "Hee-hee healing," a new form therapy now being pioneered to treat illness around the world, could save your life. No joke.

According to the American Association for Therapeutic Humor, there are currently more than 100 studies suggesting the beneficial effects of humor and laughter on the body, the mind, and the spirit. Laughter has been found to boost the immune system, increase natural disease-fighting killer cells, lower blood pressure, lower cortisol levels, and have beneficial effects on conditions as diverse as cancer, rheumatoid arthritis, and serious allergies. It can trigger the release of endorphins, the body's natural painkillers, and produce a natural sense of well being.

Taking their lead from Norman Cousins, who pioneered research in the healing power of humor thirty years ago, scientists and physicians in Japan tested the healing power of humor on allergy sufferers. Twenty-six men and women with allergic skin rashes and serious allergies were taken off their allergy medications for three days. Then, the day of the test, they were injected with allergens and shown the movie *Modern Times*, starring Charlie Chaplin. Their skin welts were measured before and after they were shown the 87-minute video. The procedure was repeated and the volunteers were shown, instead, a weather video. The weal responses triggered by dust-mite allergens, cedar pollen and cats were unchanged after watching the weather video, but were significantly reduced after Charlie Chaplin had his way with them.

When a friend of ours learned he had a 70 percent blockage in a major artery in his heart, doctors placed a stent in that artery to hold it open. The operation was a success, but it bothered him greatly to have the surgical procedure in common with then Vice President Dick Chaney, with whom he had radically differing political views. While complaining about it loudly to friends, someone started singing, "Unchain-ey my heart..." and the room exploded with laughter. One joke and our friend's attitude changed forever.

Researchers have been taking the subject of humor very seriously in an effort to learn whether humor has a direct effect on our physiological systems or whether it simply counteracts the erosion of our well being caused by stress and anxiety. Dr. Michael Joseph, a pediatrics specialist at the University of California, wonders, "Is it the physical act of laughing itself? Is it the brain pathways which are activated? We simply don't know and more research is needed." Whatever mechanism is responsible, we do know, through both personal experience and empirical studies, that humor makes us feel better.

What about people who seemed to have lost their zest for life, who are depressed and unhappy? Does humor help them? Psychologist Jason Goodson of Utah University conducted a study on depressed people to see exactly how humor would impact their emotional states. He put together a group of clinically depressed volunteers who watched tapes of stand-up comedians for thirty minutes a day for four weeks. Goodson showed a 42 percent reduction in the volunteers' scores on clinical scales measuring depression—a very significant figure.

Health can be a state of mind no matter what the state of body. Some people can suffer the most debilitating diseases, yet their hearts are clear, their eyes bright, their souls uplifted and uplifting. It is axiomatic in mind/body medicine that good health has more to do with what is going on in our heads than in our bodies. We can think of countless individuals who, despite seemingly overwhelming illness and misfortune find lots of room for joy in their lives and no room for complaint. They experience life fully whatever they are doing, wherever they are, even when they are approaching the end of their time here. "Look down at your feet," they tell us. "Remember to be where your feet are and know that is where your joy is." One moment with people like these and you know you have been changed forever because now you know that you, too, can choose joy.

## How You Can Use Humor

Although this is a very serious book about very serious subjects, we end it on this chapter about humor because humor uses words to heal outside of the medical setting in ways that still go straight to the heart.

Humor helps us connect in ways unrelated to our circumstances. Strangers bond in a instant when a floppy puppy trying to stand up or a baby playing peek-a-boo makes them burst out laughing in a moment of unselfconscious joy. Laughter can also heal relationships fractured by resentment or anger. When people are able to laugh at themselves, they get a new perspective and can begin to see that the things that stood between them were less important than the relationship itself.

Barbara has been taking care of her elderly mother, Brenda, for a long time and both of them are tired, frustrated, and restless. They both want a break. Her mother doesn't want to be sick, and Barbara wants to go out with her friends for one, long, carefree evening. Her mom asked Barbara for a glass of orange juice thirty minutes earlier, and Barbara, sidetracked by dozens of chores, has forgotten about it. Brenda yells, "What's the matter with you, I asked you for that orange juice hours ago!"

For some reason, this moment reminds Barbara of something funny that they both had a good laugh about some time before, so she starts to laugh. "What's so funny," her mother asks, still indignant, and Barbara says, "Remember when Aunt Helen poured the orange juice on Uncle Phil's head and said…" Her mother hoots with laughter. The tension evaporates in an instant, and the two women re-establish their bond.

A friend went out to the movies leaving his sick, elderly mother at home. Upon his return, she asked what he had seen. It was a comedy, and when he started telling her about it they both dissolved in laughter over the silly plot. "I didn't know you'd be interested in it," he said, feeling suddenly closer to her. Then she said something that moved him deeply. "I look old, and I am ill, but it's the same October night for me that it is for you." Fifty years later, he still tells that story, so profoundly did it change his perception.

Obviously, what we find funny is personal and often contextual. But there are some guidelines to make humor *healing* as opposed to just funny.

According to Dr. Ed Dunkleblau, a psychotherapist, those who would use humor therapeutically should avoid sarcasm and abusive humor, which means, simply put, try not to laugh at someone else's expense. Humor should be kind. It is often unexpected, and we can always recognize ourselves in it. While humor can be healing, too much humor can seem dismissive and can leave people feeling that their issues are not being taken seriously.

Nobody can tell you how to be funny; it must grow organically out of your own nature and the situation. But we can remind you to allow yourself to see humor wherever it can be found, knowing that it can refresh the soul, calm the anxious mind, lighten the heavy heart, and help heal our accumulated wounds.

We can't put humor into our scripted protocols because it is too perishable. It is based on circumstances and perceptions, which are always changing. It requires tuning in to the moment to test its waters, a spark flashing only in that particular moment in time, and it is subject to the emotional temperature, the shared experiences, and the funny bone of those involved. There will be many situations that call for Verbal First Aid in which humor will never be appropriate at all. But, in the end, humor may be what saves you. In the aftermath of tragedy, something may strike you as amusing and you will feel the weight of the event begin to dissolve. It may even be possible for you to share moments of lightness with those whose suffering you are hoping to ease.

# SOME FAMOUS LAST WORDS

And so we are almost at the end of this book. And true to our purpose of finishing a very heavy subject with a smile, we will leave you not with our last words, but with the sometimes inadvertently funny last words of famous people on their death beds, who might have wished they'd had a book like this on what to say when making a final exit.

*Die? I should say not, dear fellow.*
*No Barrymore would allow such a*
*conventional thing to happen to him.*
—John Barrymore, actor, d. May 29, 1942

*Friends applaud, the comedy is finished.*
—Ludwig van Beethoven,
composer, d. March 26, 1827

*I should never have switched from Scotch to Martinis.*
—Humphrey Bogart,
actor, d. January 14, 1957

*I am about to – or I am going to – die:*
*either expression is correct.*
—Dominque Bouhours, French grammarian, d. 1702

*Go on, get out –*
*last words are for fools*
*who haven't said enough.*
(To his housekeeper, who urged him to tell her his last words so she could write them down for posterity.)
– Karl Marx, revolutionary, d. 1883

*Get my swan costume ready.*
—Anna Pavolva, ballerina, d. 1931

*They couldn't hit an elephant at this dist…*
(Killed in battle during US Civil War)
– General John Sedgwick, Union Commander, d. 1864

*I've had eighteen straight whiskies,*
*I think that's the record…*
–Dylan Thomas, poet, d. 1953

*Don't let it end like this. Tell them I said something.*
—Pancho Villa, Mexican revolutionary, d. 1923

*Either that wallpaper goes, or I do.*
—Oscar Wilde, writer, d. November 30, 1900

# VERBAL FIRST AID WORKING IN THE WORLD: TESTIMONIALS FROM YOU

*Since The Worst Is Over was published in 2002, we have received many letters and e-mails from first responders, therapists, medical personnel, care givers, and people who, in the course of their lives, have used it to great advantage. We wanted to share some of those stories with you.*

*I. From -Gretchen Bear*

*I've been in three really big car accidents, once as a pedestrian and twice when others have run red lights, and there's always been somebody there who got my attention and got me calm. When I heard you on NPR, I put it together and understood. What they say is so vitally important. In the second one I was unconscious. Someone began talking to me in my ear. "I was a witness," she said calmly. "I'm putting my phone number in your purse and your purse is going with you in the ambulance." When I woke up, I remembered my purse, the police got her number and it was amazing.*

*Your information really rang true to me.*

*The day of this current accident I witnessed, I was driving my son to music class and I saw a woman jump out of a car that had just been hit, drag her children out, throw them on the sidewalk, curl up in a ball, and begin wailing.*

*I grabbed a blanket and threw it over her legs. I said, "You know, I'm taking a look at your kids and they're doing really well. They're in good hands. Someone's called the ambulance and in two minutes it will be like a whole hospital will be here to help you." I saw that her arm and stomach had been bruised and her other arm was bleeding. I touched her leg and asked how that felt, transferred awareness to a healthy spot.\**

*\*[The technique she used is to touch a person where they're NOT injured and ask how that feels. When you do that, three things happen. First, it takes their mind off the pain of the injury. Second, it lets them know there are parts of them that are still all right and whole. And third, because they start feeling better (from the pain relief of changed focus you're your presence, they trust you and you've gained some rapport.]*

*I was there for an hour. I was the point person for the police, fire department witnesses, I was the center point. trying to get her husband on the cell. I helped her get calm, get her head together, asked her, do you have a husband or friends I can call.*

*When they showed up it went crazy.*
*At the time of my first car accident, no one would even talk to me. I was bleeding, my head went through the windshield. People would look at me in horror. I wondered how bad it was, was I paralyzed. One man came up to me and said, "You look beautiful." He said my legs were looking good. He acknowledged me and said something positive, and I knew I'd be okay after that. I just ignored everyone else there.*

*In an accident the amount of time seems so long. You may be slipping into shock. When somebody locks into you and gives you a foundation, you can feel normal and be dealing again, not tied up by the blur that is fear, not pain because the shock handles that.*

*When I heard you on NPR, I knew it was important and I gave a copy of your book to my doctor, and one to my mom and one to my husband.*

*The woman from the accident called me a couple of days ago, to say, "I just hope someday I get to be the person who gets to help someone else out, as you helped me."*

*I'm so moved, your book just popped into my head and I knew what to do.*

*II. From* Jason B. Palmer
Chaplain (CPT) USA, 1st Infantry Division
*Sat, September 11, 2010*

*I have begun to use the verbal first aid techniques discussed in your books in my professional ministry as well as my personal life (i.e., with my three little boys). No only was I able to discuss your ideas with fellow chaplains, I distributed several of your books to the medics in 1st Battalion, 5th Field Artillery. During the entire month of July, we trained at the National Training Center at Fort Irwin, CA. I used verbal first aid during dozens of simulated mass casualty scenarios: some involving Soldiers from my unit asked to pretend as if they were injured in a particular way and others involving a combination of Soldiers assigned to Fort Irwin and Hollywood-style role players (some of whom were real life double amputees). I found verbal first aid techniques to be very well received by all. In fact, the entire group influenced by your book—myself as chaplain and our medics—received extremely high praise from outside evaluators for our overall caregiving methodology which I contribute, in part, to the impact of your work.*

*Since returning from that training experience, I was transferred to a new battalion, which is scheduled to deploy this fall in support of OPERATION NEW DAWN in Iraq. While I pray it never becomes necessary, I look forward to passing along any meaningful experiences that occur while deployed for your use in further research. I again want to thank you for your investment in the form of the books you so generously sent.*

*Very Respectfully,*
*Jason B. Palmer*
*Chaplain (CPT) USA*
*Brigade Special Troops Battalion*
*2nd Heavy Brigade Combat Team*
*1st Infantry Division*

*III. From Colette Claude, Bowen Practitioner*

*I had the best experience about a week ago when I was driving into town. An accident had JUST happened– I was two cars back. There was a big old truck barely damaged and a little regular car all crunched up with smoke fuming out. No one had stopped, so I decided I should see if there was anything I could do to help. The owner of the truck was calling the police, and so I went over to the driver of the small car. She was shaking and shivering up a storm, and sitting in a car full of noxious fumes. She couldn't speak, just staring straight ahead in a daze, her mouth hanging open, and looking shocked out of her mind.*

*I started to speak to her slowly and quietly. I told her that the worst is over and that help is on the way. Eventually, I remembered to tell her that her body knows exactly what to do, and that we could trust everything that was going on.*

*That was all I could remember of your paragraph, but it was enough. I can't believe how powerful those words were! Not only for me–giving me an anchor of something to offer, but for her. It may have been 5 minutes that I was there. She went from shaking to expressing disbelief (at her first accident) and some anger, to eventually crying while I touched her body. By the time the police arrived, she was calm, completely coherent and back in her skin.*

*It was a remarkable experience, and I am SO grateful that you were there with me!!*

*IV. Another from Colette Claude*

*Along with knowing what to say when I come across a car accident, I now also know what to say at the bedside of someone who is dying: "The worst is over. You are safe. You have support all around you, and we won't leave. There is a special place waiting for you on the other side. You can do this in your own way, but when you're ready, you will be able to go. The worst is over. Your body knows exactly what to do. Your lungs know what to do, your heart, etc. Trust your body, it knows what to do. You can let your body carry you."*

*Last night, I was sitting with a friend in Hospice, and it suddenly dawned on me how to speak to her so that this new and foreign experience might be easier. It was such a relief to realize that this was another emergency and that your paragraph—the parts I remembered—could provide a framework for speaking to her mind and her body as she was dying.*

*I began using these sorts of phrases when she was still fairly conscious, although completely preoccupied with her struggle for breath. She turned toward me with a flash, and I knew that she was listening. Because it seemed to be meaningful to her and because all of us in the room were also relieved by what I was saying, I continued for a couple of hours, every so often, until she was near her end. It was such a relief to have a sense of what to say, and to know in my bones that it was helping.*

*So thanks once again!*

*V. From Deb Devine, MFT*

*Margie [names have been changed] was a fellow student in an undergraduate psychology course (I am now a marriage and family therapist intern).*

*I noticed Margie's hands shaking in class and tears streaming down her face as most students left the room after the lecture ended. I stayed a moment to watch her asking the instructor something and he was shaking his head in a posture that indicated the flavor of "no".*

*I saw Margie later that day sitting in the university hallway with her face in her hands near the registrar's office and asked if I could sit with her. Margie shared a heartbreaking story that included the recent death of her mother, a fall in her grades that led to her financial aid tuition to be denied and the upcoming eviction from her small apartment (that she feared would include the loss of her two beloved cats Corkie and Zing.) Margie struck me as a shy and somewhat socially awkward person who was remarkably bright...she once wanted to be a research psychologist and now was in such deep sadness and overwhelm that she spoke of suicide.*

*Knowing that I was not trained to handle the situation, I tried to refer her to the counseling services on campus and just be there with her until I could get her there. She refused to go stating that her experience there was one in which she did not feel cared about and that it just added to her grief. I knew I needed to get her more experienced help, but in the meantime I remembered some material from a book I read called* **The Worst is Over: What to Say When Every Moment Counts.**

*I asked her what would have to be different to agree to go on living, who could help, and what she wanted people to understand. (found on page 246). I also was very present and connected, focusing on what strengths and solutions could be drawn out of this terrible time for her.*

*We discovered that to go on living she would need to find a way to keep her cats, and a place to live and some food. She was able to identify some friends she hadn't thought of who could help her once she calmed. We even brainstormed how to advocate for her financial aid to be restored and get the situation communicated to the appropriate people who could help see her as a good student who had falling grades due to the grief of her mother's death. We re-framed most everything that needed to be different including what Christmas would be like shortly without her mother....into a ceremony that honored her mother's presence and wishes for her only daughter. Margie not only pulled through this difficult time, she met a woman who is a psychologist that helps people who are homeless keep their pets. This is the work she decided to pursue. I learned that helping others can sometimes be as simple as caring, connecting and having the right tools to turn the trouble into solutions. Verbal First Aid offers just these sorts of solution possibilities and in a graceful and dignified way that supports those in need to help themselves. This is of course a great support to those of us who want to really make a difference when the moment counts.*

## VI. From Linda Sleeter, RN

*I visited my son and grandsons over the holidays. One day we noticed nine year old Ryan's right eye was red and swollen. That evening the infection had moved to his left eye also. His eyes looked so painful but he was very brave. The next day we took him to the doctor for the last appointment of the day. By the time we got home with the prescription, it was almost his bedtime. I told him, "I have put eye drops in many people's eyes and I know how to do it without hurting". Ryan was on the bed and I let him relax and told him to tell me when he was ready to have the eye drops. When he told me he was ready....I said, " As this drop of medicine comes in to your eye, it starts your whole immune system working to attack the germs and make you healthy again." He was very attentive and I said it again as I put the other drop in.*

*I remembered some of the things mentioned in the book so I started talking to him about the changes that were happening right then in his immune system and how much stronger it was getting. I asked if he could imagine the powerful cells of his body attacking the germ cells. Then I asked him specific questions about what they looked like. Without any hesitation he answered me as if we were having any other conversation and he described*
*the cells, their shape and color. ( I could have cried.) He described the immune cells as being white and round. They had little arrows and weapons sticking out of the round cells to attack the germs.*

*I went to get him some water and when I returned I saw a pad of paper on the floor by his bed. I picked it up and to my amazement there was a picture that looked just like what he had described to me. I asked him and he said that is what it was. He had a systemic infection that triggered his asthma so he woke during the night. Each time we repeated this same process. The next morning he woke in good spirits, no problems breathing and his eyes barely pink. When we asked him how he felt......little Ryan said, "Extraordinarily well."*

*Thank you for your interest, Judith. I know it made an impact on his healing. Thank you for all the many people you have helped.*

*VII. From F/Lt. Mike Harvitt, Michigan State Police*

*While working the midnight shift my partner and I were dispatched to a motorcycle / van personal injury crash. The motorcycle had misjudged his distance while overtaking (passing) the mini van and the back tire of the bike caught the front of the minivan. Upon arrival my partner and I began to search for the rider of the bike, as all we could see were bike parts and blood trailing off into a ditch. I located the subject and much to my surprise he was alive, however silent. I got down in the ditch to his location and found him to be responsive. With a quick glance at this body I noticed that he was missing the better part of one leg that had been torn off in the crash. The injury was very graphic and bleeding severely. The subject began talking to me and said that his leg hurt and asked me how bad it was, and at the same time began to try to move. To keep him from moving I put my hand down, directly on his chest and told him that I wanted him to lay still and that I would stay with him and that an ambulance was on the way. He again asked me about his leg and wanted to know how bad it was. As he spoke I could feel his heart pounding and his breathing increase. I looked at his leg, and looked back at him and told him that his leg was injured and bleeding and that I was going to stop the bleeding. He laid his head back and I told him that I needed him to control his breathing while I stopped the bleeding. I used my uniform belt that was under my duty belt as a tourniquet. The majority of the bleeding stopped immediately and I told him that I could use his help by telling me about how the rest of his body was doing. I placed my hand back on his chest and after acknowledging his injury and then asking how the rest of his body was doing I could feel his heart rate decrease and breathing begin to slow down. As we talked about the rest of his body and looked for any other injuries I continued to keep my hand on his chest where I could feel his heart rate and breathing. As his heart rate and breathing came down I was able to see that his focus was now off of his leg and he was focused more on our conversation. What seemed like a long time was only a few minutes until the ambulance arrived, however I continued to reassure him that help was on the way and that they would take good care of him. Shortly thereafter we placed him in the ambulance and he was assisted by more advanced medical professionals. I believe that if he had been further upset about his leg, it's likely it would have increased the bleeding and negatively affected his heart and his recovery. Although he lost a leg, fortunately that was all. As part of the Michigan State Police in service training,*

*I have taught the Verbal First Aid techniques to 1600 officers and the feedback from the field has been great.*

*VIII. And Another from F/Lt Mike Harvitt*

*Just wanted to let you know that on Tuesday night I spoke to the Holland City Police Victim Services Unit. I presented Verbal First Aid to them. This is the same unit, although now with some new members, that I presented to approximately 5 years ago. Most counties in Michigan, and 5 police departments, have victim services units. These are people that go out and assist police and firemen with a variety of calls where victims may need someone to lean on. Death notifications, fires, natural deaths, suicides, serious crashes and so on.*

*This particular group recently received an award for being the top victim services unit in Michigan!*

*IX. From Jane Nicholls, Magazine Editor*

*I've been meaning to email you and tell you the Sunday morning after we saw you, Rosie bit her tongue (took a good chunk out of it actually) as she bounced out of the pool at lessons...she was crying a bit, and Gracie said to me, "Mum, talk like Judith, say things Judith would say to help her... About how her tongue knows how to heal and all that." So I did. And hey presto!! I had to say it a few more times...and for other stuff, as Rosie is perpetually "in the wars"... but it's a good tactic...more than good...GREAT...so thank you!*

*X. From Dr. Deb Kern http://drdebkern.com/blog/ Emergency Practice From her blog*

### FEBRUARY 28TH, 2010

*In my desire to always combine business with pleasure, I recently took my family with me to Colorado on my way to a Team Northrup Retreat. The plan was to ski for a few days as a family and then I would head to Denver for the retreat.*

*On the first day, my husband and I dropped off our son, Micah, along with his friend, Sam, at Snowboarding School. My husband and I then decided to have a nice quiet day alone instead of going skiing. But about an hour after dropping off the boys we got a call from the school saying they were bringing our son down the mountain on a stretcher. NOT THE CALL ANY PARENT WISHES TO RECEIVE!*

*Instantly I knew I had a choice of thought patterns: fear or love. I made the decision to keep myself in a vibration of love as we drove to the base of the mountain by saying out loud all the things I was grateful for: the fact that they reached us immediately, that we had a car, that the roads were clear, that there was an excellent medical team on the spot, etc... Then I began to envision my son in vibrant health and envision the team of paramedics working efficiently.*

*When we arrived we were greeted by the paramedics as they loaded my son onto the ambulance truck. NOT A SIGHT ANY PARENT WISHES TO SEE!*

*Once again, I was struck with the choice to have thoughts of fear or love. I began thanking the paramedics and feeling huge waves of gratitude for their kindness and skill. Then, because gratitude allows the higher regions of the brain to function best, I remembered a book I read five years ago entitled "The*

*Worst Is Over: What to Say When Every Moment Counts–Verbal First Aid to Calm, Relieve Pain, Promote Healing, and Save Lives" by Judith Acosta and Judith Simon Prager. In it they teach phrases and imagery to use in emergency situations that help calm the patient and accelerate the body's healing process.*

*As I rode in the back of the ambulance with my son (whose left ear was pinned to his left shoulder and could not move his neck at all) I began saying things like: "The worst is over. Now your neck is beginning to relax and heal." And when he got fearful that his neck was broken, I would shift his attention by asking "How does your left knee feel? How about the thumb on your right hand."*

*As I spoke to him I also sent out prayers that there would be an Osteopath or Physical Therapist at the hospital who would know the best thing to do for my son. When we arrived, a lovely physician came in to ask Micah questions. I was so relieved to see "D.O." on her name badge and, when there was a lull in conversation, asked her where she went to Osteopathic Medical School. She looked surprised and asked me, "How did you know I was an Osteopath?" I told her I had seen the "D.O." on her badge. She then flipped her badge over and over again to show me that it doesn't say "D.O." or Osteopath anywhere on her badge. It was at this point that I felt the presence of angels and all the people who love Micah and me in that E.R. bay. The room felt warm and cozy and safe – and I knew all was well.*

*Our wonderful Osteopath spend hours coaxing Micah's neck to relax and straighten in order to get X-Rays. During this time I watched as Micah's oxygen saturation level would go way down and I would coach him to do deep yoga breathing. Each time he shifted from 'fear breath' to a deep yoga breath he could bring his O2 levels up from 84% to 92%.*

*And, serendipitously, although I forgot my coat and gloves in the rush to meet the ambulance, I DID have homeopathic Arnica and Arnica cream in my purse. So I was able to start giving him Arnica right away!*

*Finally, his neck was straight enough for x-rays:*

*Thankfully, the x-rays indicated no vertebrae damage. His only injury was whiplash. And by 11:00 a.m. the next day – with the doctor's blessing – he was skiing with his good friend Sam (with a soft neck collar underneath his bandana!)*

*I am so grateful to the medical staff at Copper Mountain.*
*I am so grateful to the ability of a body to heal.*
*I am so grateful for all the years of mind/body/spirit studies that came into*
*practice this day.*

*X1. From Dolores Kaneshina*

*Watched the interview with Barry Kibrick on PBS and it was interesting that you mentioned the reaction people have to a bloody nose. My son was subject to this problem since he was a year old. The doctor explained what caused it and that he would outgrow it. So, when it occurred, no one in the family got excited, or scared, etc.–one day at school, his older sister (in kindergarten) had a bloody nose. Well, the teacher panicked, her classmates were scared, but bless her heart, my daughter calmly told the teacher that she needed to sit quietly, took a tissue and pinched her nose until the bleeding stopped. After school, the teacher commented on how calm my daughter was throughout the incident and how she had calmed the class and the teacher herself in minutes. She asked me how I had taught her to react in that situation. I told her that the doctor had explained her brother's problem to the family and since her brother frequently had a bloody nose, it was not a life threatening or scary thing.*

*I truly believe that words have great power especially in dealing with children. I was both a teacher and administrator in education for 34 years and witnessed the results of what a parent/adult negative comments can do to children. I plan to buy your book read it and give it to my children who are now parents. They are good parents, but I know that your book will validate the manner in which they deal with their children and give them extra tips.*

*Thank you for writing a book on this topic, it is much needed!*

*XI1. From Blair4630:*

*Hi, Judith, I read your book* **The Worst is Over** *several years ago. It is still a part of my collection. It was a great read, and one of many "non-traditional" books other than my fire/EMS books that have helped me help others.*

*XIII. From Rasa Lila:*

*After I got out of the hospital, I went to a cranial sacral therapist. I settled onto the table and she made contact with her hands. She said, "Your body did a great job handling the accident. The accident is over now." With those words, my body relaxed and the healing energy flowed. My body stopped trying to protect me. I had no idea I was still holding tension. It was such a relief to let go!*

*XIV. From Barry Howard, Lt. Col., U.S. Navy, Retired:*

*I was an Air Force 1Lt many years ago. I was in the Congo with the UN forces. It was around noon when a vehicle came roaring up to the hangar where we were waiting for a mission for our C-130 providing food stuff for civilians. The vehicle's occupants had rescued an Army Warrant Officer with some serious stab wounds and he was bleeding badly.*

*No one seemed to be responding to this man so this Lt (me) went over to him and started applying pressure to his wounds with a towel I had around my neck. It was obvious he needed to get to a hospital.*

*I told him we would take care of him and that we were going to get him to a hospital as soon as we safely could. He became more calm. He was suffering because he thought that he would be left there, but I believe that telling him we were there and being as strong willed and bossy as I am calmed him down as I applied pressure to the wound. It gave him confidence in our plan. We left him at the hospital. I never got the guy's name but I learned that helps to stabilize a person by letting him know that he is being taken care of and that there is a real plan.*

*XV. From Peter McLaughlin:*

*Peter shares two wonderful stories with us:*

*I responded to a three-car MVA. I'm both a volunteer firefighter and EMT so when I arrive on a scene I can be deployed in either or both capacities. The first thing I noticed was one of the cars involved in the accident had an EMT leaning into the driver's door. He was speaking loudly telling the driver to relax. When I came upon them, he told me to take over. I saw that the woman was breathing very heavily, apparently quite agitated. She told me she was scared.*

*After identifying myself and asking her if she had any injuries, I told her to look directly into my eyes. When she did this, I said, "The worst is over. Everything gets better from here forward."*

*She told me how upset she was. I asked her what she needed to feel better. She said, "a cigarette." I asked her if she was sure this would make her feel better and she answered yes. I said, "OK, close your eyes." I had her imagine she was taking a deep breath. While she did this, I breathed deeply at the same time, loud enough for her to hear me. When she opened her eyes she was totally calm. Her breathing had returned to normal and her face was relaxed. The whole process took about 2 minutes.*

*Peter's second story is just as wonderful:*

*I responded to an early morning call about a hiker who'd fallen and possibly broken his leg. I was with a group of firefighters who hiked, climbed and scrambled up a very steep hill to reach the man who'd fallen. He was complaining of intense pain in his lower leg. As we were maneuvering him into a Stokes basket he continued to cry out in pain. I got near his head, looked into his eyes and told him that the worst was over, that we'd soon have him in the ambulance and soon after that the hospital. I said we were all here to help him.*

*I then asked him if he preferred the mountains or the beach. He said the beach. I told him to close his eyes and go there now. I told him to imagine the warm sun and lying on the beach listening to the waves. I told him he could just enjoy that place while we took care of him. He immediately calmed down. A minute later, the basked jostled as we lowered him down and I explained everything was still okay and he could go back to the beach.*

376

*XVI. From Bruce Kilburn*

*I was the Fire Chief in Lake George, NY when the Ethan Allen tour boat capsized and 20 people lost their lives that day. I can remember as if it was yesterday. It was 14:56 hours on 10/2/05 when the call came in and I was the chief that responded.*

*I was on the scene in a very short time. I was the IC that day and little did I know I would pull from every class I have taken to stay in control and try to cover all the bases...*

*One medic was at the dock and he told me he had two in cardiac arrest. At the time I thought, okay, we can handle this. But it was 30 seconds later that he called me again and we had three more in arrest. When it all stopped I had twenty senior citizens lying on the ground next to me all covered with sheets. This will do things to anyone's emotions and it did mine.*

*I felt so helpless...I almost lost control at one point and if it hadn't been for a very good friend telling me, "Bruce, you have to stay focused and do your job and you'll be fine..." Those few words brought me back.*

*Your survival guide tips are the best and it makes me feel better knowing that the emotions I feel are okay. I liked, "There is meaning to all things, even suffering." That says it all.*

*XVII. From Teresa Bevin, a crisis counselor in Santa Fe, NM*

*Gisela (name changed) had come to my office five times and I hadn't been able to help her feel better. She was only 12 years old, but had the posture and stance of an old woman. Her early childhood, back in El Salvador, had been plagued by fright and uncertainty. She had seen war, known grief, and she had been raped by a group of soldiers.*

*When she arrived at her new school in Washington, D.C., her teacher recommended she be taken to a doctor, as she complained of leg pains and sometimes she stayed in her classroom during recess so she could sit quietly, rubbing her legs. The doctors found nothing wrong with her legs. In fact, it was found that she was in remarkably good health for the ordeal she had lived through only a few months earlier.*

*During my time with her, on her sixth visit, she casually told me that her oldest brother had been tortured in front of her, and that a soldier had fractured his leg with the butt of his rifle. I immediately suspected the pain in her legs had to do with the incident. Later I asked her about the time she had been raped, but she clammed up, as usual.*

*Feeling ineffective in front of this damaged child, I let my intuition take me and I asked if she liked her biology classes. She nodded. I asked her if she knew we were made of many, many cells of different kinds. She nodded and let her chin sink into her chest. I let her stay in her silence while I spoke in a whisper.*

*"You know, Gisela, cells are continually renewing themselves. Older cells die and new cells are born to take their place. Our skin cells fall away all day long, when we shower, when we sleep and are brushed by our sheets, when we get dressed. All of our cells are rejuvenated regularly... Think of this... All of the cells that were in your body when those men took you, they have all died to let other new cells take over. You have no cells left that were touched by them. All of your cells are new and don't know what happened to the others."*

*Gisela lifted her head and looked at her arms and legs. She felt the skin on her neck. She didn't say anything. But I knew a change had taken place. That day she did not limp when she left my office. She looked back at me and smiled. The following day her teacher called me to tell me that Gisela had joined the others during recess, that she no longer complained of leg pains and that she smiled frequently.*

*To me, this was confirmation that the right words at the right time can perform miracles.*

*XVIII. From "Lindy"*

*Lindy had learned about Verbal First Aid by personal experience. We met when she had come for treatment herself. She was articulate, kind, deeply sensitive and fragile. She was also dying of liver disease. She had been placed on a transplant list, but no donors seemed to be forthcoming. She was scared and on the verge of giving up. She felt the urge to drink, to say "the hell with it." But she also dearly wanted to live.*

*We recalled one of Erickson's strategies.*

*"You want so badly to feel better," we said to her intently.*

*"Yes," she sighed.*

*"And you've stayed sober for almost one month, now, haven't you." This was not phrased as a question but as a statement.*

*"Yes," she looked up, her posture slightly more relaxed.*

*"And you have said that you would do anything to feel better, to change your life," we said seriously.*

*She held her gaze steady. "Yes."*

*"This is what you do. When you leave this room, walk down the street to your car and get into your car. Drive to the nursery down the road. Look through the greenhouse until you see a cactus. You will know the right cactus when you see it. Perhaps it will be flowering. Bring it straight home and place it just so... so that it will receive all the light it needs... and leave it there. You may have thoughts about watering it until you remember it is a cactus and must be **cared for according to its nature** and you will let it be. And in the days and weeks ahead you will watch as it grows and perhaps flowers, noticing how healthy it is when you just let it be."*

*Many months later, long after we had parted ways, a call came in. It was Lindy. She's got good news. She's leading AA meetings, getting engaged, and she's off the transplant list. "What do you mean, off the list?"*

*She explained that after our work, they had done another series of tests and had found that the damage they had seen in her liver had disappeared. They had never seen anything like it. She laughed, "They don't know what to make of it."*

*xix. From David J. Turner, NREMTP, IC*
*University of New Mexico School of Medicine*
*Emergency Medical Services Academy*

*As a paramedic in Albuquerque, NM, The Worst Is Over provided me with tools I could use every day, communicating and establishing rapport with all my patients. Little did I know, just a few short weeks after reading it, I would have the opportunity to use the techniques of Verbal First Aid.*

*I was dispatched to a residence for a female pt who had attempted suicide. Upon entering the residence, I found a very distraught patient sitting on the kitchen floor in a large pool of blood. Her wrists were wrapped in blood soaked towels that continued to drip onto the floor. The fire fighters who had arrived first were standing at an awkward distance, at the perimeter of the room, and looking-on uncomfortably. I immediately recognized a tremendous opportunity to use the techniques I had learned.*

*I took a few seconds to focus and commit, although there was no time to plan my actions. Instinctively I marched into the kitchen, directly to the patient. I lowered myself into the blood, and knelt next to her, setting my bag down next to me in the blood. I made eye contact, introduced myself, and assured her that we were here to help. I immediately opened my bag, removed several wound dressings, and confidently applied them around the continuously dripping towels.*

*In her eyes, I saw panic and desperation. Her emotions reached out to me as we looked at each other. I asked her to help me as I attempted to wrap her wounds tightly enough to control the bleeding. Our connection was strong, and seemed to allow me to read her emotions. As I questioned her about when and how she made the wounds, I could sense her regret, and her love for her family, who were watching from a distance. I felt the apology in her eyes, as she glanced over at her husband. I asked if she would let me help her stand so we could get her on the stretcher and head to the hospital, she agreed. I reassuringly held her arm and shoulder as my crew assisted her to the stretcher and then into the ambulance.*

*Once enroute to the hospital, I immediately knelt down next to her. I noticed that her wounds were still bleeding. One had slowed, but was beginning to soak through the dressing. The other had not slowed and had already soaked through the dressing and was dripping steadily onto her lap and the stretcher. I asked her to help by holding the dressing tightly on the more severe wound.*

*She held the dressing and we began to talk. I usually avoid talking about the reasons why patients have attempted suicide. Nevertheless, she was comfortable sharing with me, and I was eager to listen. The conversation quickly led to her family. I continued with sincere eye contact and heartfelt touches from the floor next to her. Struggling through tears and emotions, she revealed to me her recent troubles. Several times, she mentioned her love for her family, and particularly her connection with her daughter.*

*I asked her to talk more about her daughter, and she was very willing to. She explained that her daughter was compassionate, confident, and full of energy. She loved to help people and was interested in a career as a firefighter. I began talking about my experience in the field of EMS and firefighting. I described the excitement, the personal satisfaction, the emotional satisfaction, and the long-term benefits. We discussed the beauty of the city we live in, our lives, and our families.*

*We had a wonderful conversation, and an indescribable connection. I felt her panic and desperation start to wash away, and sensed a new feeling of hope. I told her frankly, that I could see she did not want to die. I knew she wanted to live to see her daughter graduate high school, become a firefighter, and grow to be a happy and successful adult. She agreed.*

*I then looked confidently into her eyes and told her that she could stop bleeding, right now, that it was over. The emotions, the regret, and the bleeding were no longer necessary. From this point on, things will only get better. Your energy needs to now be on healing. Get to the hospital, get the help you need, and move forward. Through her teary eyes, I could feel her agreement, her consent. Then her bleeding stopped.*

*At the hospital, we had an emotional goodbye. She thanked me for my support and care, and I thanked her for her strength and her trust. With a last touch, and a look, our short relationship came to an end. A sentimental and happy ending for us both.*

*I want to sincerely thank the authors of this book. I learned to communicate better with my patients, and have improved the care I provide. Verbal First Aid has helped, and will continue to help save many lives. Thank you.*

## The Wrong Words

*While we don't like to dwell on the how the "wrong" words can make a difference, here are two stories that illustrate that concept so well.*

*The first is a story a hypnotherapist friend told a story on herself about coming upon an accident and making a mistaken suggestion.*

### XIX. From Melissa Roth. CHT

*I was driving on the interstate when a guy on a motorbike hit something in the road in front of me. His bike flipped 3 times and fortunately landed off the interstate. I was the first to get to him. He was thrashing about and screaming that he couldn't breathe. I knew I had to get him to lie still and calm down. So, I calmly told him the worst was over, that I wanted him to be still, to stop bleeding and conserve his blood and to breathe slowly and deeply and remain calm until the paramedics got there.*

*I can't remember what all I told him but he did quit bleeding and his breath did slow and deepen somewhat—until the paramedics got there. Then, he started bleeding again and became hysterical again. At that point it wasn't my problem anymore and I left.*

*At first I couldn't figure out what happened until my own words kept shouting in my mind. The mistake I made was that I told him to stop bleeding, release the pain, breathe easily and stay calm until the paramedics got there. So, he was fine for the 15 minutes or so it took for the paramedics to arrive. But as soon as they pulled up he went right back to bleeding, writhing in pain, and all the other issues.*

*I hope I never encounter another emergency like that but I'll for sure never make that mistake again.*

*XX. From a Medic at a Convention*

*At a convention in Baltimore, a medic came up and said, "What do you think of this as the worst Verbal First Aid? I was at the doctor's for tinnitus and he looked in my ear and did whatever exams and then he said, 'Oh, you're gonna go crazy from this. We got studies.'"*

# GLOSSARY

**Alliance** – An affirmation that the helper and the person being helped are on the same path, that the helper is someone who can be counted upon to understand the sick or injured per-son's predicament and act in that person's best interest. It is necessary for good rapport in order for therapeutic suggestions to be accepted.

**Altered State** – A state of being that is more highly focused on internal processes, both mental and physical; a state that is distinct from the ordinary, waking state of consciousness; a more highly suggestible state of mind.

**Anchors** ("Cues") – Signals strategically used as a physical reminder of the relaxed state.

**Contingency/Conjunctive Statements** – A suggestion that begins with "As I…" and leads into "you can…" For instance, "As I touch your hand, you can stop the bleeding."

**Control Group** – The group of subjects in an experiment who **do not** receive the intervention being tested, so there is a neutral field against which to measure the results.

**Contra-alliances** – Counter productive statements that do not facilitate the development of rapport or trust, e.g., "I told you never to do that!" or "Now you've really hurt yourself!"

**Dissociation** – The ability to shift our awareness, narrowing it to one small aspect of ourselves or our environments, while diminishing our awareness of all other aspects.

**Distraction** – Distraction can build rapport by helping people focus on something other than their pain or injury, thereby reducing distress, increasing comfort, and building trust. For example, "I can see that your leg needs attention. Would you take a few minute right now to scan the rest of your body and see if there is anything else the rescue team should be aware of when they arrive to help you?".

**Experimental Group** – The group of subjects in an experiment who **do** receive the intervention, protocol, or medication being tested, as opposed to the control group.

**Future Pacing** – Using visualization to help people imagine a time in the future when the current situation is resolved and they are living their lives more fully. Because ill and injured people often have a negative picture of the future in mind, due to their present circumstances, this technique is very important in giving them an alterative picture toward which to move.

**Healing Zone** – A naturally occurring state (emotional, physical and mental) in which we are especially suggestible. This can happen to anyone at anytime—in a medical crisis, an emotional trauma, fear or upset, or as a result of chronic pain or discomfort.

**Iatrogenics** – Physician-induced illness; infirmities suspected to be caused by unconscious suggestions made by health care professionals, e.g., "This medication may make you nauseated."

**Ideomotor** – Using fingers to signal intention to a hypnotherapist while in trance, e.g., right index finger = "yes" and left index finger = "no."

**Implied Healing** – giving the suggestion that the healing is happening or has already happened, e.g., "You know that itching like that is a sign that the healing has begun."

**Illusion of Choice/Double Binds** – giving a person two options, both of which lead to the desired result; e.g., are you more comfortable sitting up or lying down? Whichever is chosen, the person has "agreed" to greater comfort.

**Joining In/ (see Pacing)**

**Metaphorical imagery** – the use of symbols to represent ideas and body functions, which can then be manipulated toward wellness and healing. "Your problems tumbling and floating down the street like fall leaves blowing in the wind…"

**Mind/Body Medicine** – The modern merger of Vitalism and Reductionism, the underlying essence of which is the notion that the mind and body are inextricably interconnected.

**Neurotransmitters** – Chemicals that enable information to pass from one neuron (brain cell) to the next.

**Pacing** – Reading another person's signals and moving with them in order to gain alliance and cooperation; identification with a person's point of view or certain aspects of a person's behavior along with a verbal or non-verbal communication of that identification; can include rhythmic breathing or a comment such as, "Yes, it hurts."

**Pacing and Leading** – Joining with a person by mirroring a person's thoughts, feelings and or behaviors either verbally or non-verbally with the goal of moving (leading) them toward a more healthful or comfortable position.

**Parasympathetic Nervous System** – One of the two divisions of the autonomic nervous system; its primary function is to calm the body down again after a critical (adrenal) response to a stressor.

**Personal Resources** are people's own historic strengths, the parts of their story that they forget in times of illness, but of which they are most proud. Reminding them of who they are and what they have done well sends their minds on a mission to find those strengths at a time when they are most needed.

**Placebo** – An "inert" substance given to subjects in drug trials to even the playing field between experimental and control groups. For purposes of this book, this reaction is notable in that a little sugar pill and the *suggestion* by an authority figure (usually a physician or scientist) can (in 30-75% of cases) actually cause the body to manufacture the chemical necessary for the desired end state, thereby proving the connection of mind and body, and the power of words.

**Rapport** – An understanding communicated to another person; empathy; a state in which a relationship of trust, compliance, and healthy expectation can be nurtured. Rapport is key to Verbal First Aid; it is what makes acceptance of therapeutic suggestions possible.

**Reductionism** – A philosophical school of thought; a term originally coined by Descartes; an approach to medical science in which the human being was seen as a machine of many parts, with the mind controlling only thoughts, while the body functioned as a separate entity.

**Reframing** – Restating a belief so that we can see the benefit in it, rather than seeing the problem in it, e.g., "If I hadn't gotten sick, I would have kept on going so fast my life would have slipped away, and I never would have noticed how much love and beauty there is in it."

**Soliciting Help** – Utilizing the alliance we've made, we can encourage other people's participation in their own health and/or recovery. This technique can also provide distraction and pain relief, as in the instance of asking someone to hold the bandage as it is being applied. The person from whom we solicit help changes on the spot from victim to helper.

**Sympathetic Nervous System** – One of the two divisions of the autonomic nervous system, the parasympathetic nervous system is responsible for preparing the body for action in the face of a threat, diverting blood from the gastrointestinal tract to the skeletal muscles, raising blood pressure and pulse, dilating pupils, and stimulating the adrenal glands to produce epinephrine.

**Therapeutic Suggestion** – An indirect implication ("You may notice a tingling…") or a direct statement ("Your breathing is becoming more regular") that suggests a change of awareness or a different physiological or psychological process in another person, moving that person toward healing.

**Trance** (see Altered State)

**Utilization** – Developing and encouraging the positive, healthful resources that are already present.

**Vitalism** – A philosophical school of thought, one of whose primary proponents is Samuel Hahnemann, M.D.; it holds that the human being is a complete organism. In the healthy human state, the vital force (or "life force") enlivens and governs the material body, keeping it dynamically in balance, mentally, physically, emotionally and spiritually. Without the life force, the material organism is little more than its chemical components.

**Verbal First Aid** – The art and technique of utilizing words to calm, relieve pain, facilitate healing, and save lives.

**Yes Set** – A helper generates a series of "yes" responses in another person (unconsciously or consciously), usually by referring to things that are indisputably true. The more yeses to easy statements, the more likely it is that therapeutic statements will be accepted. For example, "I'm here with you now, and the ambulance is on the way, and you can begin to relax a little and let your body start its own inner healing."

# ABOUT THE AUTHORS

**JUDITH ACOSTA, LISW, CCH**

Judith Acosta, LISW, CCH, is a licensed psychotherapist, hypnotherapist and crisis counselor, as well as a certified classical homeopath. She is the co-author of *The Worst is Over* (Jodere, 2002), hailed as the "Bible of Crisis Communications", *Verbal First Aid* (Penguin, 2010) and *The Next Osama* (2011). She has written countless articles on Verbal First Aid, culture and the media, the importance of religion and mental health, trauma, and alternative medicine. She's had a regular column with the Journal of Emergency Medical Services on Verbal First Aid and communication strategies for use in the field, is a regular contributor to Huffington Post, Ulster Publishing, Opednews, Future Health, The Sandoval Signpost, and American Thinker.

Since 1994, she has trained paramedics, fire fighters, police officers, teachers, and medical/mental health professionals in therapeutic communication and Verbal First Aid around the United States. She served for many years with POPPA, a non-profit peer support organization for the New York City Police Department. She has also given seminars on animal-assisted therapy, trauma and burnout, stress reduction, and workplace risk/crisis management to hospitals, professional organizations, corporations and private groups.

In private practice as a licensed clinical social worker and classical homeopath, she specializes in the treatment of trauma, anxiety, depression and grief, working especially closely with military, paramilitary and first response personnel. She is based in Placitas, NM with her husband and rescue dogs, although she works with people around the country. She brings nearly 25 years of successful experience to clients all over the country and may be reached at www.wordsaremedicine.com.

## JUDITH SIMON PRAGER, PHD, CHT

Judith Simon Prager, PhD, CHt is a clinical hypnotherapist with a PhD in psychology and a practice in the Los Angeles area. As a consultant to Cedars-Sinai Medical Center, she developed a "Guided Imagery for Surgery" series of pre-intra-and post-operative and ICU creative imagery CDs that have been used with significant results in a pilot program in the Cardio-thoracic Surgery Unit. She has been a consultant to Children's Hospital of Orange County and introduced Verbal First Aid to the psychiatric nurses at New York University Hospital immediately after September 11th. She has trained physicians, nurses, and first responders across the United States in hypnotic language for pain and stress relief in emergencies and magical interactions with children and provides keynotes and talks at conferences and medical centers across the country.

Internationally, she teaches Verbal First Aid biannually in England at the European School of Osteopathy, has taught at the Universiti Brunei Darussalam in the Kingdom of Brunei, and was brought to China to train crisis counselors after the 2008 Sichuan earthquake that killed 80,000 people.

Dr. Prager has been a best selling novelist, TV writer, columnist, artist, and creative director of major New York and Los Angeles advertising agencies. She is the author of *Journey to Alternity: Transformational Healing Through Stories and Metaphors*, author of *Owie-Cadabra's Verbal First Aid for Kids*, and co-author of *Verbal First Aid: Help Your Kids Heal From Fear and Pain—and Come Out Strong.*

She lives in Los Angeles with her husband, Harry Youtt. They teach together in UCLA Ext. Writers Program, where they were awarded "Outstanding Instructors" in 2004 and were recipients of the Extension's rare "Distinguished Instructor" award in 2012.

You can reach her through her website, www.judithprager.com

# BIBLIOGRAPHY/RECOMMENDED READING

Ackerman, Diane, *A Natural History of the Senses*, Random House, 1990

Borysenko, Joan, *Minding the Body, Mending the Mind*, Bantam, 1993

Blank & Blank, *Ego Psychology*, Columbia University Press, 1974

Bandler, Richard and Grinder, John, *Frogs Into Princes*, Real People Press, 1981

Benson, Herbert, M.D., *Timeless Healing; the Power and Biology of Belief*, Simon and Schuster, 1997

Brennan, Barbara, *Hands of Light*, Bantam, Doubleday, Dell, 1988

Brown, C.T., and Van Riper, C., *Speech and Man*, Prentice Hall, 1966

Chopra, Deepak, M.D., *Creating Health*, Houghton Mifflin Company, 1987; *Quantum Healing*, Bantam Books, 1990; *Unconditional Life*, 1991

Cousins, Norman, *Anatomy of an Illness*, Bantam, 1979

Dass, Ram and Gorman, Paul, *How Can I Help?* Alfred A. Knopf, 1988

Dolan, Yvonne, *Resolving Sexual Abuse*, W.W. Norton & Co., 1991

*International Journal of Emergency Mental Health, Vol. 2, No. 1, Winter 2000, and Vol. 3, #3, Summer 2001,* Chevron Publishing

Dossey, Larry, M.D., *Healing Beyond the Body*, Random House, 2001; *Be Careful What You Pray For*, Harper-Collins, 1998, *HealingWords, the Power of Prayer and the Practice of Medicine*, Harpers 1997; *Prayer is Good Medicine*, Harper-Collins, 1997; *Recovering the Soul*, Bantam Doubleday, 1989. *One Mind: How Our Individual Mind is Part of a Greater Consciousness and Why it Matters*, Hay House, *2013*

Erickson, Milton H., M.D. and Rossi, Ernest L., Ph.D., *Hypnotherapy*, Irvington Press, 1992

Frankl, Victor E., M.D., *Man's Search for Meaning*, Pocket Books, 1984

Friedman, Edwin H. *Friedman's Fables*, Guilford Press, 1990

Gilligan, Stephen & Price, Reese, *Therapeutic Conversations*, W.W. Norton & Co., 1993

Gold, Mark S., MD, *The Good News About Depression*, Villard Books, 1987

Grant, Harvey, et. al., *Action Guide For Emergency Service Personnel*, Brady Communications, 1985

Grinder, John and Bandler, Richard, *Trance Formations*, Real People Press, 1981

Grossman, Lt. Colonel Dave, *On Killling*, Little, Brown & Co., 1996

Hahnemann, Samuel, M.D., *Organon of the Medical Art*, Edited by Wenda Brewster O'Reilly, Ph.D., Birdcage Books, 1996

Hammond, D. Corydon, Ph.D., Editor, *Handbook of Hypnotic Suggestions and Metaphors*, W.W., Norton & Co., 1990

Hanson, Rick, *Hardwiring Happiness*, Random House, 2013

Harney, Corbin, *The Way It Is*, Blue Dolphin, 1995

Hay, Louise L. *You Can Heal Your Life*, Hay House, 1984
Hilfiker, David, M.D. *Healing the Wounds*, Pantheon Press, 1985

Hilgard, Ernest, M.D. & Hilgard, Josephine, Ph.D., *Hypnosis in the Relief of Pain*, Brunner/Mazel, 1975

*Hypnosis for Medical Emergencies* (Video) Westwood Publishing Company, Glendale, CA

Jacobs, Donald Trent, Ph.D., *Patient Communication for First Responders & EMS Personnel: The First Hour of Trauma*, Prentice Hall, 1991; *Primal Awareness*, 1998

Komaroff, Anthony L. M.D., Editor-in-Chief, *The Harvard Medical School Family Health Guide*, Simon & Schuster, 1999.

Kreeft, Peter, *Making Sense Out of Suffering*, Servant Books, 1986

Levine, Stephen, *Healing Into Life and Death*, Doubleday, 1987

Lipton, Bruce, video, *The Science of Innate Intelligence*, 2001; *The Biology of Belief*, 2005, *Spontaneous Evolution: Our Positive Future and the Way To Get There From Here*, Hay House.

Locke, Steven, M.D. & Douglas Colligan, *The Healer Within*, Signet, 1986.

Masterson, M.D., James F., *The Real Self,* Brunner/Mazel, 1985

Mills, Joyce, Ph.D., and Richard J. Crowley, Ph.D., *Therapeutic Metaphors for Children and the Child Within,* Brunner/Mazel, 1986

Meyers, Gail E. and Myers, M.T., *The Dynamics of Human Communication: A Laboratory Approach,* McGraw Hill, 1992 (3$^{rd}$ printing)

Moyers, Bill, *Healing and the Mind,* PBS-TV, Doubleday, 1993

Mutke, Peter, M.D., *Hypnosis: The Mind/Body Connection,* Westwood Publishing
Company, Glendale, CA First published as Selective Awareness, 1976

O'Hanlon, Willian Hudson *Taproots: Underlying Principles of Milton Erickson's Therapy and Hypnosis, W.W. Norton & Co., 1987*

Pincus, Jonathon, M.D., and Gary Tucker, MD *Behavioral Neurology,* Oxford University Press, 1985

Reyes-Guerra, Antonio, DDS, Editor, *Modern Anesthesia in Dentistry,* Franklin Institute Press, 1977

Rogers, Carl, Ph.D. *Carl Rogers on Encounter Groups,* Harper & Row, 1970

Rossi, Ernest L., Ph.D., and Cheek, David B., M.D., *Mind-Body Therapy,* 1988

Rossi, Ernest L., Ph.D., *The Psychobiology of Mind-Body Healing: New Concepts of Therapeutic Hypnosis, Revised,* W.W. Norton & Co., 1993

Rossi, Ernest L., Ph.D. Ed., *The Collected Papers of Milton H. Erickson, Vol. IV,* Irvington Press, 1980

Rush-Presbyterian-St. Luke's Medical Center, *Medical Encyclopedia,* World Book, Inc., 1991

Samuels, Michael, M.D., *Healing With The Mind's Eye,* Summit Books, 1990

Seligman, Martin E.P., Ph.D., *Learned Optimism,* Simon & Schuster, 1990

Siegel, Bernie S., M.D., *Love, Medicine & Miracles,* Harper & Row, Publishers, New York, 1986.

Shone, Ronald, M.A., *Autohypnosis,* Sterling Publishing, 1983

Smith, Bradley and Stevens, Gus, *The Emergency Book,* Simon & Schuster, 1978

Spiro, Howard, M.D., et al., Editors, *Empathy and the Practice of Medicine,* Yale University Press, 1993

Styron, William, *Darkness Visible: A Memoir of Madness,* Random House, 1990

Thompson, George, Ph.D. *Verbal Judo,* Quill/William Morrow, 1993

Wallas, Lee, *Stories That Heal,* Pantheon Press, 1985

White, Marjorie T, Ph.D., and Weiner, Marcella B., Ed.D., *The Theory and Practice of Self Psychology,* Brunner/Mazel, 1986

Wolinsky, Stephen, Ph.D., *Trances People Live,* Bramble Company Press, 1991

Woolis, Rebecca, MFCC, *When Someone You Love Has a Mental Illness,* Tarcher/Putnam, 1992

Vissel, Barry, MD and Vissel, Joyce, RN, *The Shared Heart*, Ramira Publicaitons, 1984

Yapko, Michael, Ph.D., *Trancework*, Brunner/Mazel, 1990

Zimmerman, Lucille, *Renewed: Finding Your Inner Happy in an Overwhelmed World*, Abingdon Press, 2013

Zohar, Danah, *The Quantum Self: Human Nature and Consciousness Defined by New Physics*, Quill 1990

# INDEX

Made in the USA
Monee, IL
26 September 2022